IMAGES
of America

RESERVOIR HILL

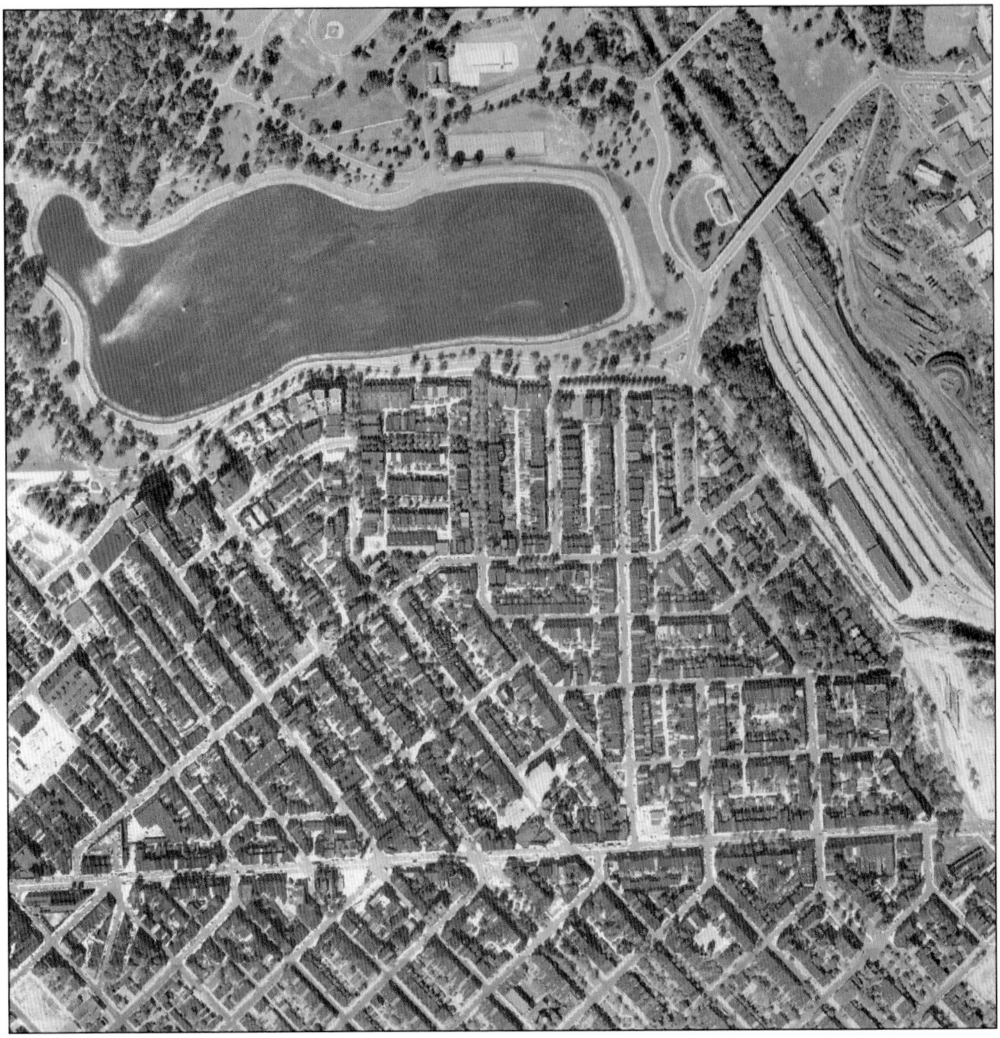

This aerial photograph was taken in 1957 and shows the entire Reservoir Hill neighborhood prior to urban renewal. The Jones Falls Expressway was still in the planning, and Mount Royal Terrace was still overlooking the main entrance to Druid Hill Park. Also, the main streets of the neighborhood connect to the streets south on North Avenue in the Bolton Hill neighborhood. (Nationwide Environmental Title Research, LLC.)

On the Cover: Taken in the late 1800s, employees of the United Electric and Railways Company pose at a stop in front of the main entrance to Druid Hill Park at the intersection of Cloverdale and Madison Avenues. Streetcars stopped at terminals that were in and around the neighborhood and served as the main source of transportation until after World War II. (Commission for Historical and Architecture Preservation.)

IMAGES
of America

RESERVOIR HILL

Kelly Dale Terrill

ARCADIA
PUBLISHING

ISBN 978-0-7385-9761-4

Published by Arcadia Publishing
Charleston, South Carolina

Printed in the United States of America

Library of Congress Control Number: 2012938517

For all general information, please contact Arcadia Publishing:
Telephone 843-853-2070
Fax 843-853-0044
E-mail sales@arcadiapublishing.com
For customer service and orders:
Toll-Free 1-888-313-2665

Visit us on the Internet at www.arcadiapublishing.com

To my current friends and neighbors and those who have come before me, I dedicate this book. Reservoir Hill has a history of residents that have changed the world. I hope to inspire each of us to continue to tell the story of our past and how that makes us part of something special today.

Contents

ACKNOWLEDGMENTS

This project would not have been possible without the help and assistance of the many people who gave their time and energy. I would like to thank the following people and organizations: Robbye Apperson, Richard May, Catherine Scott of the Baltimore Museum of Industry, Rachel Kassman at the Jewish Museum of Maryland, John Gantrell from the *Afro-American*, Jerry Kelly at the Baltimore Streetcar Museum, Jason Domasky at Baltimore County Public Library, Jeff Korman and Michael Johnson at the Enoch Pratt Free Library, the Reverend Dale Dusman, Paul Walker, Lance Moore, Eric Hageman, Tom Hall, Teddy Krolik, Rick Gwynallen and the staff at Reservoir Hill Improvement Council, Cal Buikema, Jenny Ferritti and Francis O'Neill at the Maryland Historical Society (MDHS), Jacques Kelly at the *Baltimore Sun*, Cynthia Lewis, Susan Alder, Barbara Katz, Sig and Barbara Shapiro, Lisa Crowley at the Reginald Lewis Museum, Bernadine Johnson, Polly Duke, Frank Shivers, Gilbert Sandler, Eli Pousson and Johns Hopkins of Baltimore Heritage, Barry Kessler, Mike and Karen Finney, Paul Hartzell, Wendell Garland, Tia Tyree, Austin McDonald, Audrey May, Lissie Cain and Brinkley Gary of Arcadia Publishing, Harry Peaker, Cedric and Darryl Powell, Susan Warren, Andrew Harrison of the Chesney Archives at Johns Hopkins University Hospital, Melissa Heaver of the Fire Museum of Maryland, Florence Gillich from the Yale Medical Library, Richard Behles of the Health Sciences and Human Service Library at the University of Maryland, Howard P. Fink, Russ Moss, Councilman Nick Mosby, Kathleen Kotarba and Eric Holcomb from the Commission for Historical and Architectural Preservation (CHAP), all of my friends and neighbors of the Upper Eutaw Madison Neighborhood Association, and many others.

INTRODUCTION

We had our beginning as country estates. In 1838, Solomon Birckhead built his mansion, called Mount Royal, which looked down to the harbor and the new town of Baltimore. Mount Royal was a large area that stretched from today's Druid Hill Park south to the Bolton estate that touched the outskirts of Baltimore. On the western side of Reservoir Hill was the estate of Walter B. Brooks, called Cloverdale. These estates were at a high point above the city, giving outstanding views and providing an escape for the wealthy who wished to avoid the pollution and crowds of the city.

In 1827, the Baltimore & Ohio (B&O) Railroad was created and soon brought Baltimore to the forefront of a new industry that would revolutionize life in the United States. With Baltimore's harbor being the westernmost of any in the United States, the railroad industry blossomed, as did the city's population. Another area of growth was the city's wealth. Close to Reservoir Hill, the area known as Mount Vernon was settled with railroad magnets and members of the business and political elite. Then in 1860, Druid Hill Park opened its doors to the public with much fanfare. Real estate was quickly subdivided in and around the park, and the estates slowly disappeared.

Druid Hill Park, the third oldest park in the United States, has always been the focus for Reservoir Hill. Its 745 acres of land with lakes, walkways, fountains, and eventually exotic animals brought residents from the entire city by the thousands. Boat Lake was the place for ice-skating in the winter and rowboats in the summer. Next to Boat Lake was the promenade with the Moorish Bandstand at the end. Also nearby is the Victorian conservatory, which is the last remaining one in the city. The most identifiable feature in Druid Hill Park is Druid Park Lake. It forms the northern boundary of Reservoir Hill. Walking around the southern portion of Druid Park Lake, one encounters the Moorish Tower and one of the best views of the city from this highest point in Baltimore.

In 1888, Reservoir Hill was annexed into the city boundaries, and developers took advantage of its location. Large elaborate brownstones were being built up and down streets in the neighborhood. Streetcar lines and barns were constructed, as were churches and synagogues. The southern boundary of the neighborhood, North Avenue, was changing from a residential to a commercial district. Established families were moving in, and an urban landscape was coming together. Among residents, one could find names like Derick Fahnestock, the president of the Baltimore Stock Exchange, or Chauncey Brooks, the president of the B&O Railroad. But it was not too long before things began to change.

The automobile opened up the opportunity for suburban living. In 1905, the Roland Park Company began building large homes north of the city, and some of the elite began moving northward. This opened a window for the upwardly mobile Jewish citizens who had been relegated to live in East Baltimore due to real estate restrictions and religious intolerance. Jewish merchants had gained enormous wealth and had a desire to assimilate with some of the traditions of the Catholic and Protestant communities. Moving to brownstone mansions of Reservoir Hill showed that they had reached a higher social status.

By the 1920s, the streets of Reservoir Hill had become home to some of the most influential Jewish members of society. The owners of the largest department stores in Baltimore, including the Hutlzer, Hecht, and Hochschild families, lived there. Literary giants and nationally known medical professionals became scattered throughout the area. Gertrude Stein and her uncle David Bachrach, the internationally known photographer, lived on Linden Avenue. Several smaller Jewish congregations, such as Mishkan Israel, started. But the congregation of Chizuk Amuno was the largest and had built a synagogue on Eutaw Place by 1922. This synagogue is still a vibrant place as the Beth Am congregation uses the building today.

Reservoir Hill was predominantly a Jewish area in the early to mid-20th century; however, many other residents came from diverse religious backgrounds. Hugh Lennox Bond, the second generation to own the Mount Royal mansion, was a Quaker and an ardent abolitionist. Throughout the years, the area was home to clergy of Episcopal and Lutheran congregations, and Roman Catholic priests were also residents of the neighborhood. The boundary for the southwest corner of Reservoir Hill was Babcock Presbyterian Church, and adjacent to the community was St. Bartholomew's Episcopal Church. Two blocks south of the neighborhood was Corpus Christi Catholic Church, one of the more ornate Catholic churches in Baltimore.

Many long-term residents and historians of Baltimore and Reservoir Hill have traced the beginning of instability in the area to World War II. Large numbers of individuals and families began moving from West Virginia and the South for the many jobs that the war effort created. Reservoir Hill and the surrounding area was prime property for new workers because of its accessibility to public transportation and the sheer size of the housing stock. Many single-family homes were converted into apartments, some of which were at such capacity that city officials condemned them and passed laws to address overcrowding and sanitation. The lure of suburban living and real estate profits resulting for the housing demand began to push the socioeconomic status of the area down. The number of committed homeowners began to wane. Owners and renters were no longer able to maintain properties at a level sufficient for our housing stock.

From its beginning to the 1950s, Reservoir Hill was predominately white. Differing opinions and experiences leave questions as to what extent prejudices or cultural norms played a role in this ethnic makeup. One thing was certain: Baltimore was a segregated city and noted nationally for some of its harsh covenants restricting racial minorities in certain areas of the city. Even so, the Jewish community at large, and also specifically in Reservoir Hill, has always been active in the civil rights movement, and many residents were involved in the integration of the city. Both the Jewish and African American population struggled with inequities and, in many cases, worked together to address the social issues of the day.

One area of Reservoir Hill was home to African Americans, many of who were wealthy. The westernmost streets of McCulloch and Madison were once considered a part of what was called Sugar Hill. As the possibility for African Americans to own their own homes increased, Sugar Hill was the sought out place to live. Over the years, countless influential doctors, lawyers, businessmen, and politicians lived in that neighborhood and the areas directly west of McCulloch Street and Madison Avenue. Thurgood Marshall and Lillie Mae Carroll Jackson both lived in the vicinity. The beginnings of the Baltimore chapter of the NAACP can be traced to meetings and discussions happening in the surrounding area. With the work of Lillie Mae Carroll Jackson, the Baltimore NAACP chapter became the largest in the nation. Also nearby, Pennsylvania Avenue provided the area with shopping and entertainment at a time when African Americans were only able to use separate establishments. Cab Calloway and many other well-known singers and musicians had their start at the Royal Theater on Pennsylvania Avenue.

The 1960s were tough on Reservoir Hill. As white flight was changing the ethnic makeup of the neighborhood, civil unrest ensued. The decade that saw the Civil Rights Act of 1964 later witnessed the death of Dr. Martin Luther King Jr. Anger and frustration over Dr. King's untimely death led to riots. Businesses and homes in the neighborhood were looted and burned. Afterwards, many well-intentioned planners sought to reestablish the neighborhood with urban renewal. Blocks of row houses were torn down, and streets were closed. The northbound and southbound sides of North Avenue were almost completely demolished from Interstate 83 to the western edge of Reservoir Hill. In their place were garden and high-rise apartments. The neighborhood's only school, School No. 61, was replaced with a new building today called John Eager Howard Elementary.

By the 1970s, homesteaders were coming into the city and were trying to reestablish neighborhoods that had suffered from the ills of the 1960s. Baltimore mayor William Donald Schaefer introduced the $1 house program to entice homeowners to move back to the city. Many vacant and abandoned houses were purchased and restored to their original state. Groups were being formed to help organize the community. The Reservoir Hill Improvement Council originated in the late 1970s.

Reservoir Hill benefited from hard work and dedication; however, it never became fully revitalized as did the Inner Harbor and surrounding areas of the city. During the 1980s and 1990s, Baltimore was hit with a drug epidemic that impeded progress and increased crime in the neighborhood. Reservoir Hill's only area businesses, located on Whitelock Street, were torn down after serious deterioration and persistent drug issues.

The 21st-century Reservoir Hill neighborhood is culturally, economically, and socially diverse. Excitement and optimism are on the rise. New and old residents are working together, planning, dreaming, and building on the uniqueness of the neighborhood. Vacant lots are becoming community gardens and parks. Abandoned and deteriorated houses are now urban mansions, and blight is slowly disappearing. New development and business ventures are in the making. Our school, John Eager Howard, has received new funding and support from our local university, Coppin State. Reservoir Hill has endured and now leads by example. Learning from the hardships and struggles of the past, we have built a thriving community embodying the best aspects of urban life.

One

The Early Years

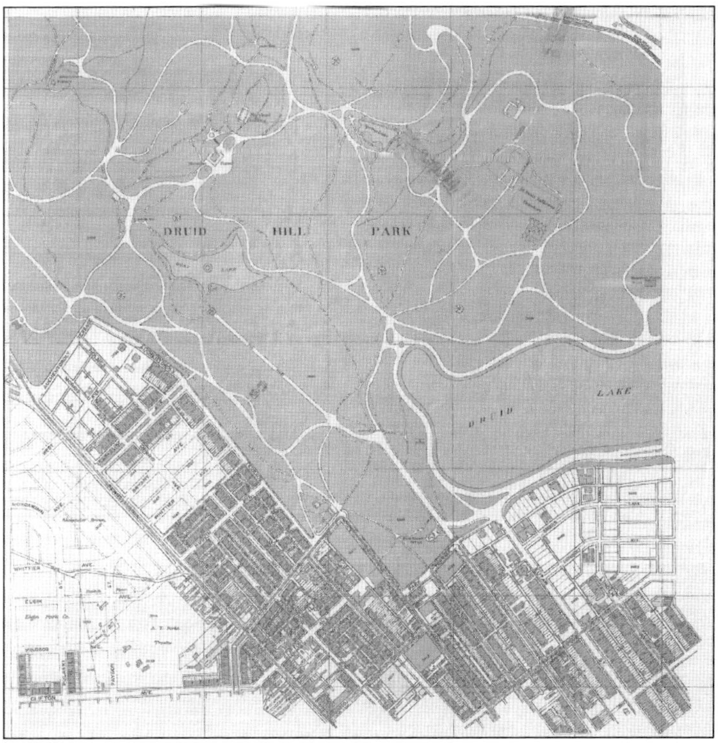

The area now known as Reservoir Hill was once a part of a 1,000-acre estate owned by Charles Carroll of Carrollton. Carroll was a signer of the Declaration of Independence and Maryland's representative at the Continental Congress. Shown here in 1914 is the northwest corner of Reservoir Hill, the adjacent neighborhood of Auchentoroly Terrace and Druid Hill Park. (CHAP.)

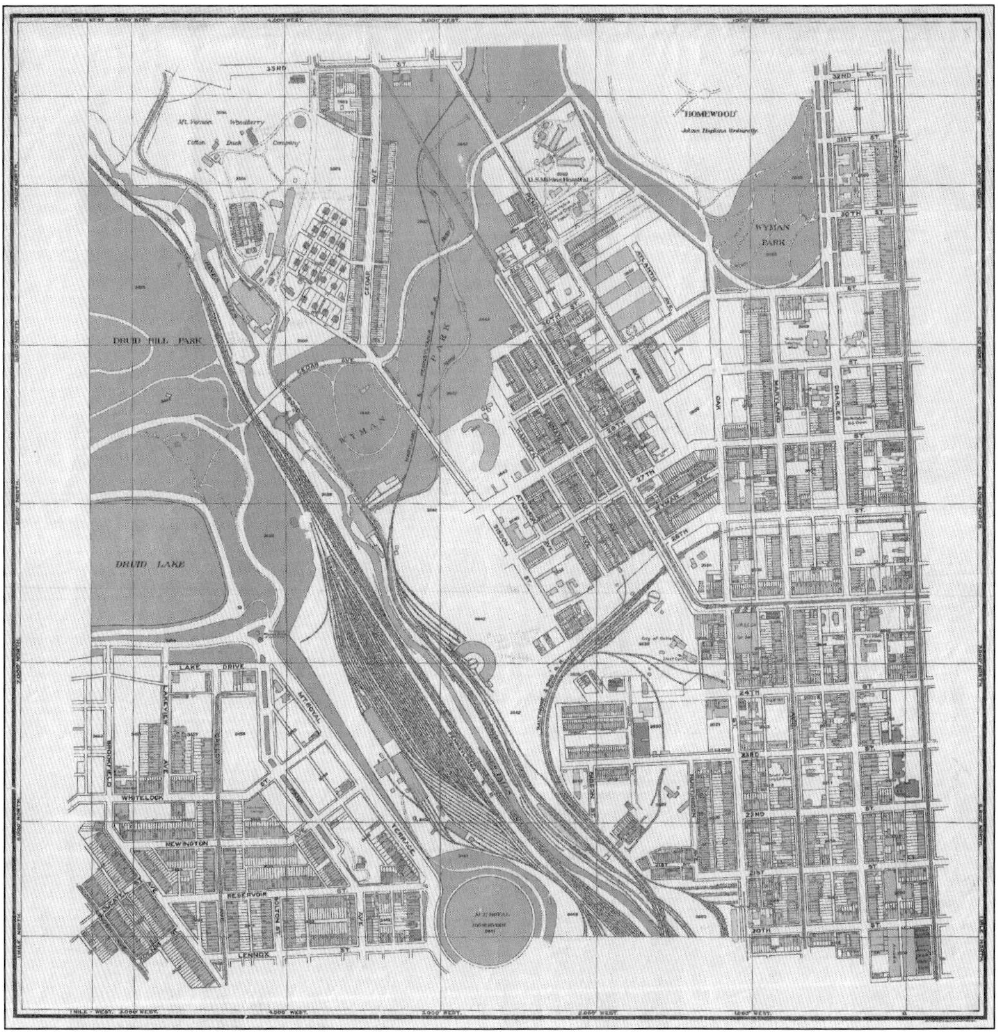

In 1888, Baltimore City annexed the Reservoir Hill area, and the city was booming. Areas directly south of Reservoir Hill had been almost completely developed, and there was a need for more upscale housing for the prosperous citizens of the city. Estates were sold and developed with large brownstones and elaborate synagogues and churches. Druid Hill Park was a magnet for the entire city's population, and the land in the surrounding area became highly sought after. Pictured is the 1914 Bromley Map of the Reservoir Hill neighborhood. By this date, most present-day streets had been developed with exception to the northeast corner. (CHAP.)

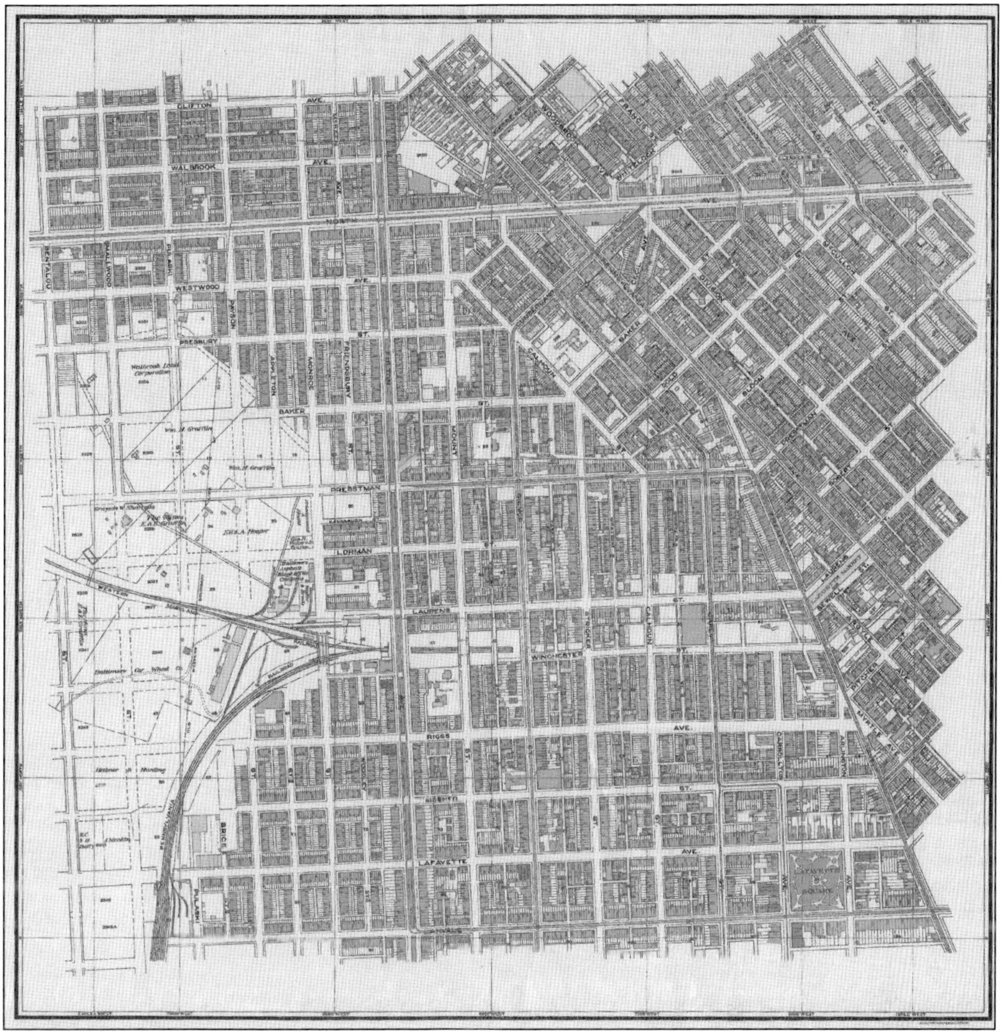

Seen in the top right-hand portion of this photograph is the southwestern corner of Reservoir Hill in 1914. The two largest roads that make a *T* in the photograph are North and Fulton Avenues. Both streets still serve as busy thoroughfares in West Baltimore. Note all the areas on the west that are yet to be developed. (CHAP.)

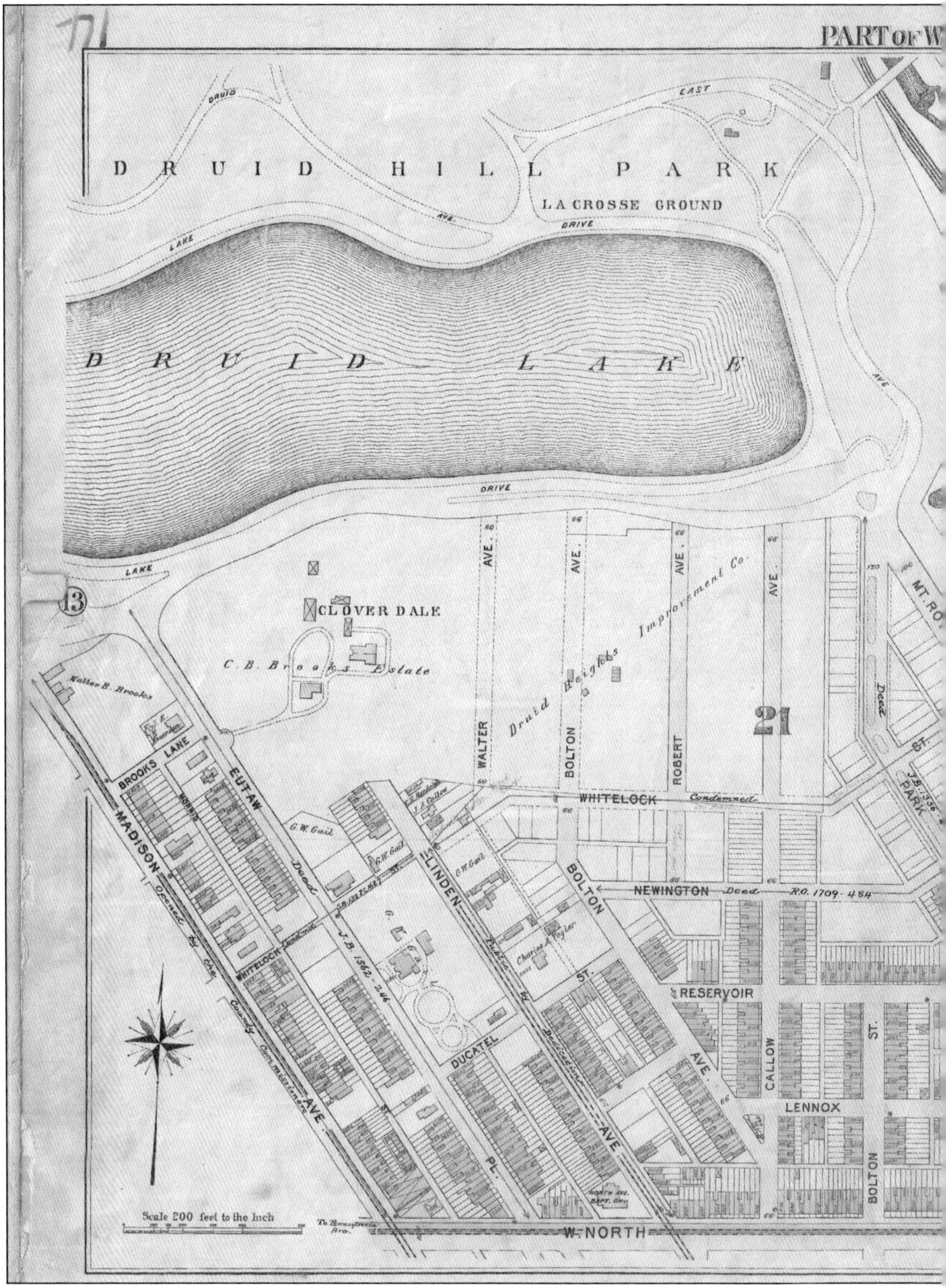

This 1905 Baltimore City Atlas of the Reservoir Hill area shows that the northeast portion of the neighborhood is undeveloped and still home to large country estates. The area owners who purchased much of Reservoir Hill from the original Charles Carroll estate were William Callow, Thomas Bond, George Gail, F.W. Felgner, Robert Whitelock, Chris Vogeler, E.H. Horne, and

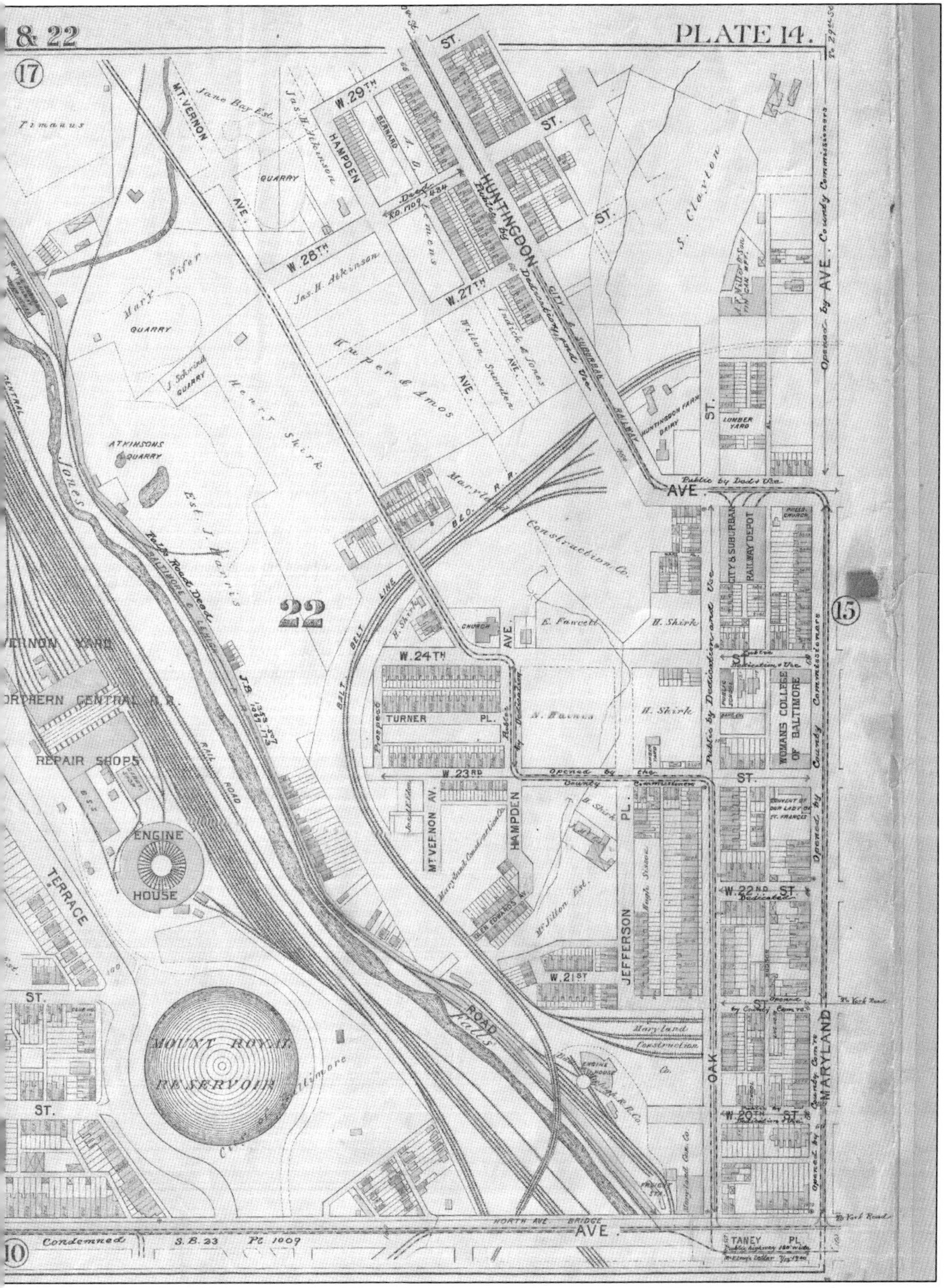

Chauncey Brooks. These men built country estates to be away from the city's core but close enough to get there by the limited transportation options available. The streets in Reservoir Hill that are named after these men are their most recognizable legacy. (CHAP.)

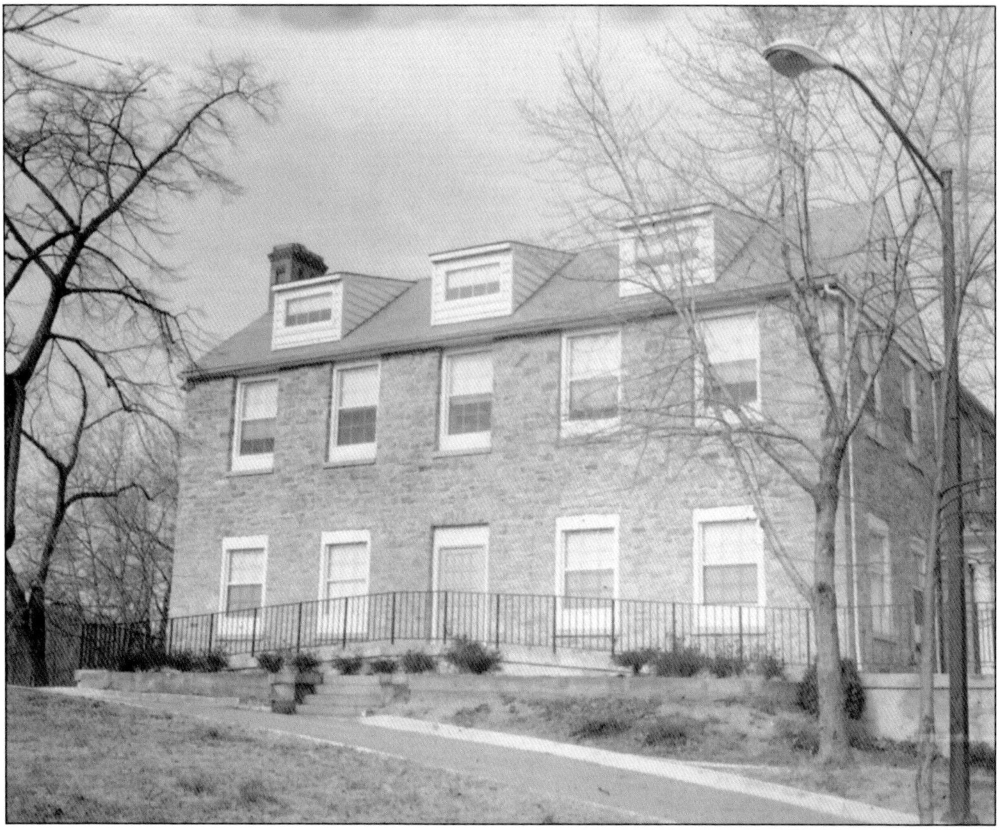

The Mount Royal estate was built in 1792 for Solomon Birckhead, a Quaker, whose daughter Christiana married into the Bond family. Hugh Lennox Bond and his descendants occupied the home for over a century. Bond was a stalwart supporter of President Lincoln and of emancipation. He was chief judge in the US 4th Circuit Court, where he was nicknamed "the Curse of the KKK" for his harsh sentences. In the early 20th century, the estate became known as the Norwegian Seamen's Home. Today, the Bond House serves as the home for the Reservoir Hill Improvement Council and the Head Start program. (Above, BCPL; below, CHAP.)

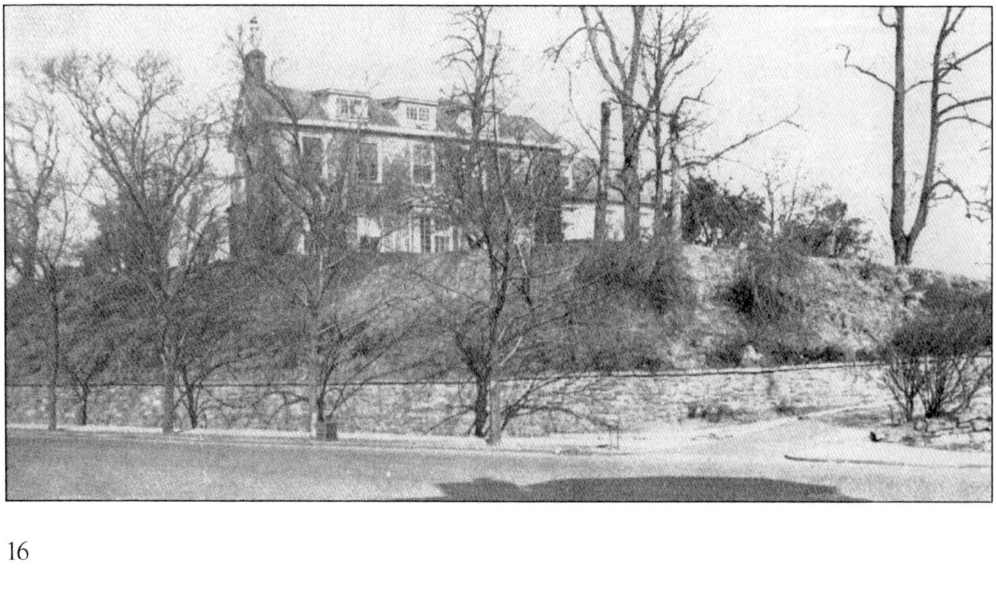

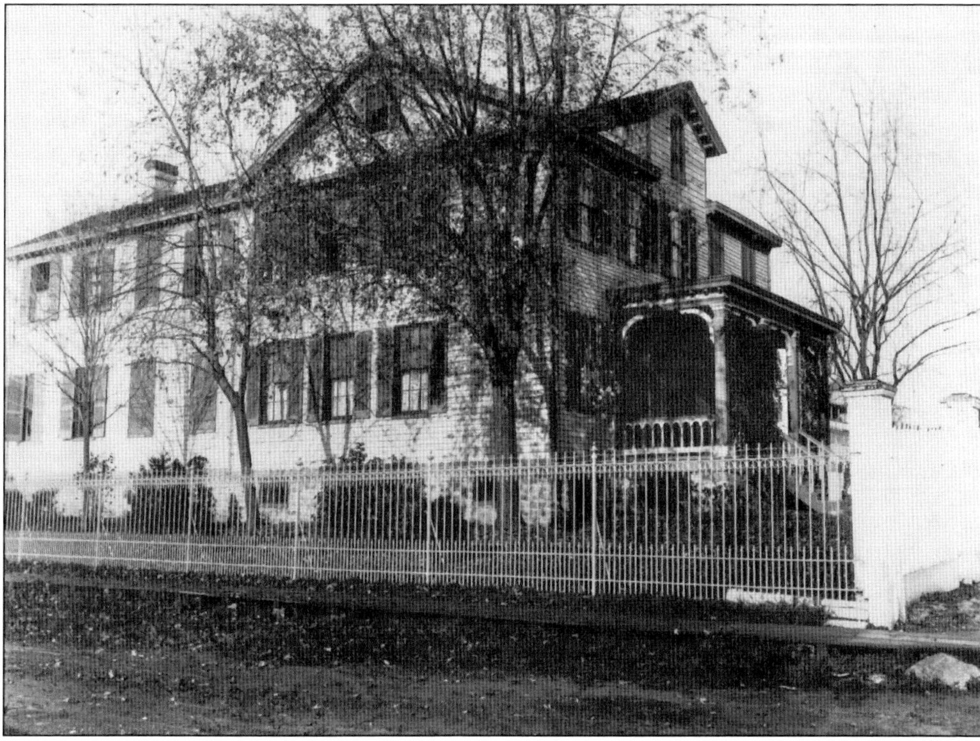

The George W. Gail estate was located between present-day Eutaw Place, Linden, Whitelock, and Ducatel Avenues. George W. Gail was owner and founder of one of the most well-known businesses in Baltimore, the Gail & Ax Tobacco Company. The company was sold in 1891 to the American Tobacco Company, whose owner was James Duke, founder of Duke University. The Gail Mansion was artistic and three stories high with a total of 35 rooms. Besides having the ordinary rooms of a residence, it also had a gymnasium and pool and billiard rooms. Also on the property were a stable, carriage house, and greenhouses. The home was sold and demolished in 1906 to make way for the present-day homes on Linden Avenue and Eutaw Place. (Both, MDHS.)

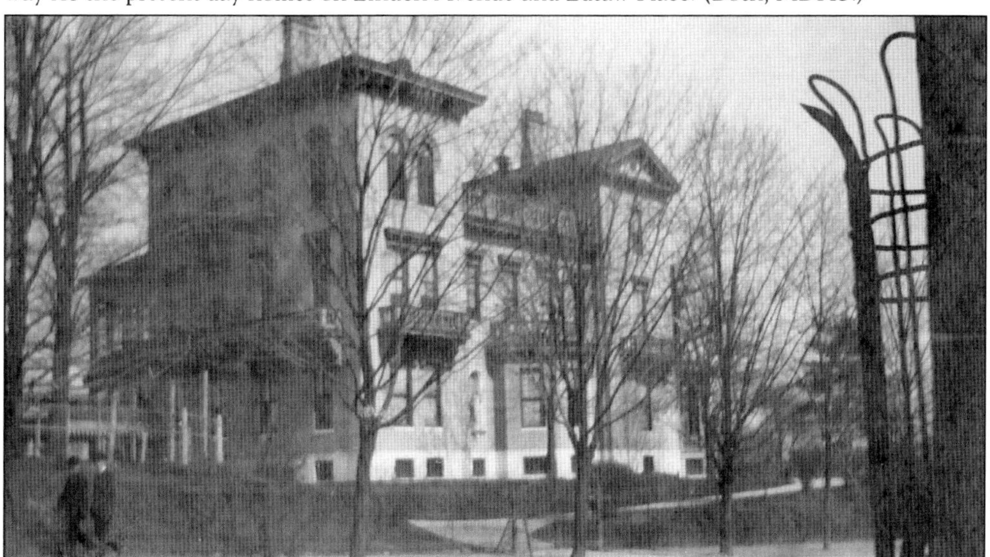

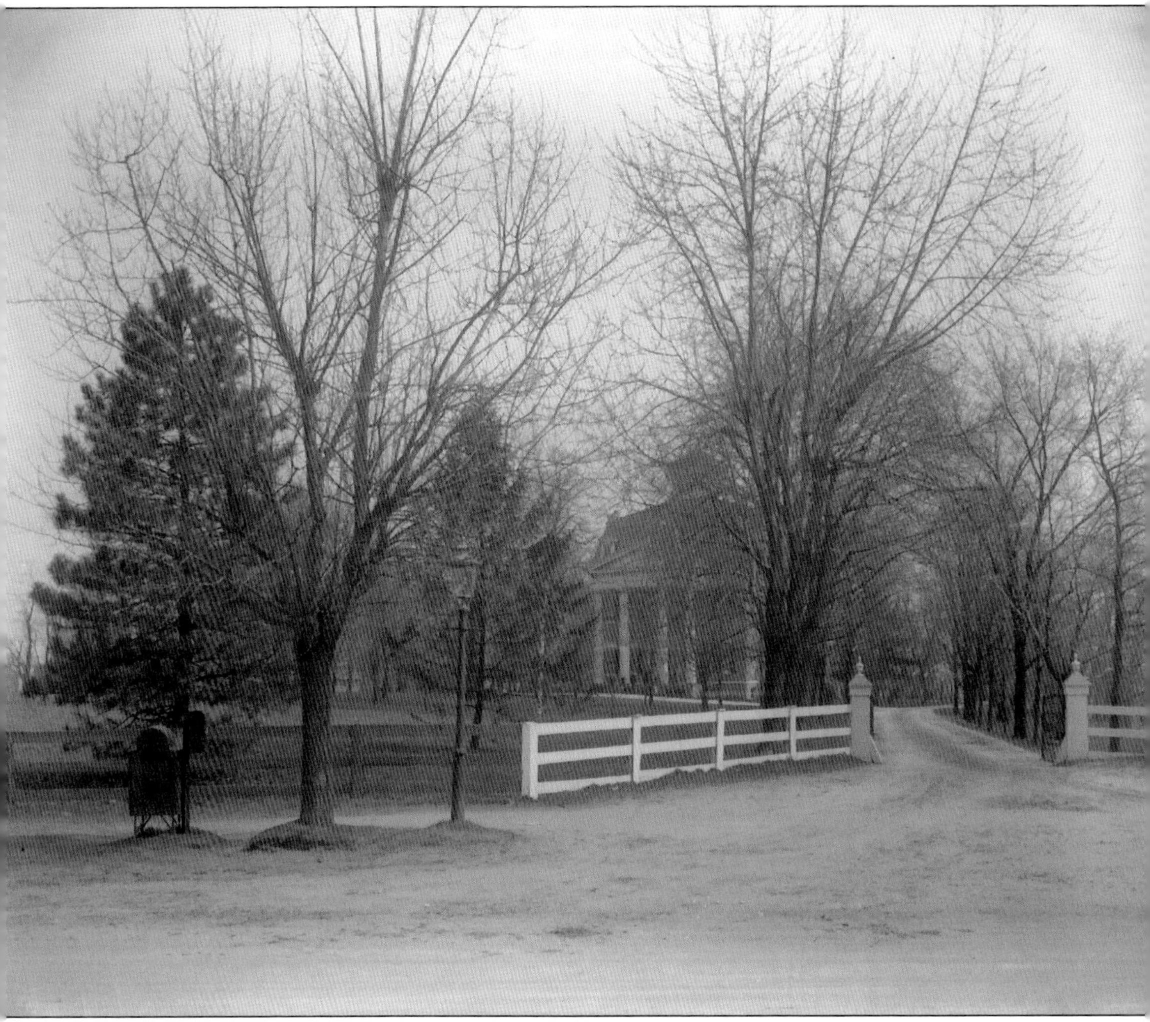

One of the oldest and largest estates in Baltimore, Cloverdale consisted of an area bounded by Eutaw Place, Druid Park Drive, Whitelock Street, and Callow Avenue in its later years. Bought and settled by Chauncey Brooks in 1838, it stood until 1913, when it was demolished to make way for Chauncey Avenue and Brooks Lane. Six generations of the Brooks family members called the Colonial mansion home. One interesting note is that the Whatcoat Memorial Episcopal Burying Grounds were located inside the estate grounds near the present-day Madison entrance to Druid Hill Park. The bodies were moved to other locations during the development of Druid Hill Park. Chauncey Brooks, president of the B&O Railroad, was one of the best-known businessmen in the country at the time. The *Baltimore Sun* characterized the Brooks Mansion as "center of social life for the city and was the scene of many brilliant and historic assemblages." (MDHS.)

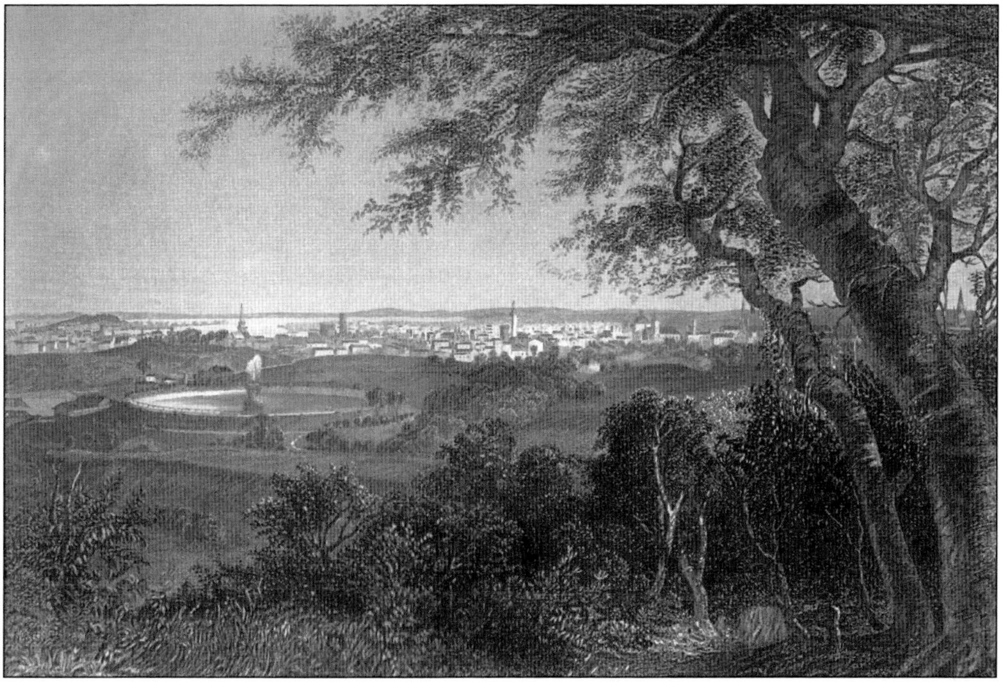

One of the early additions to the area was Mount Royal Reservoir, which eventually gave the Reservoir Hill neighborhood its name. It was a circular reservoir that was built in 1861 and held around 25 million gallons of water. It was the main source of water for West Baltimore until Druid Hill Lake was completed in 1864. The land used for Mount Royal Reservoir was a part of the Mount Royal Milling Company, located next to the Jones Falls. The Mount Royal Reservoir was razed in 1923, and the land was converted into parkland after discussion of using the land for a stadium for the Baltimore Orioles. (Above, author's collection; below, Dale Dusman.)

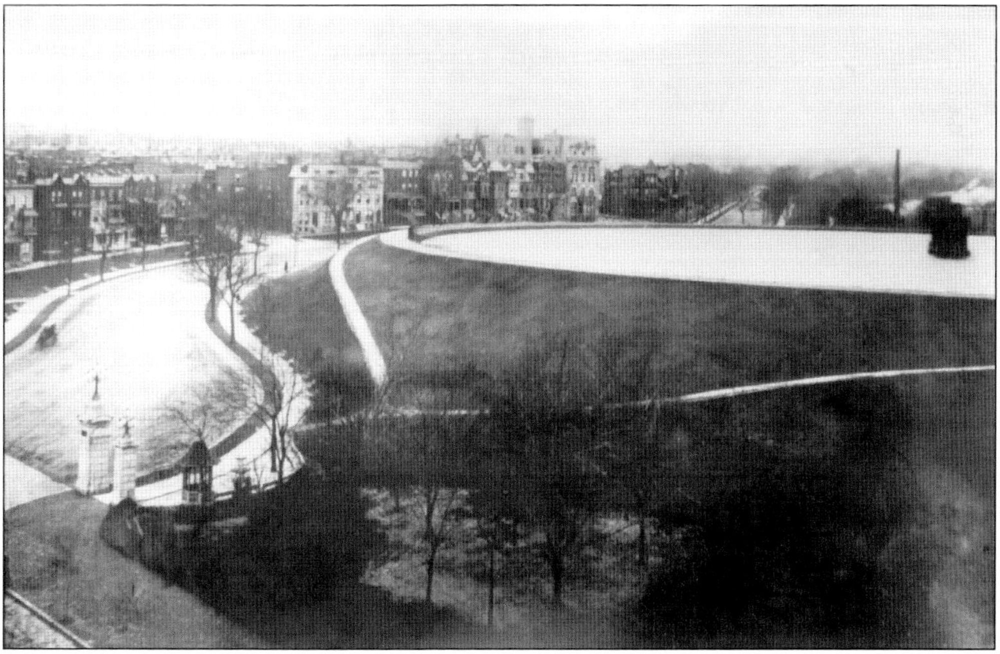

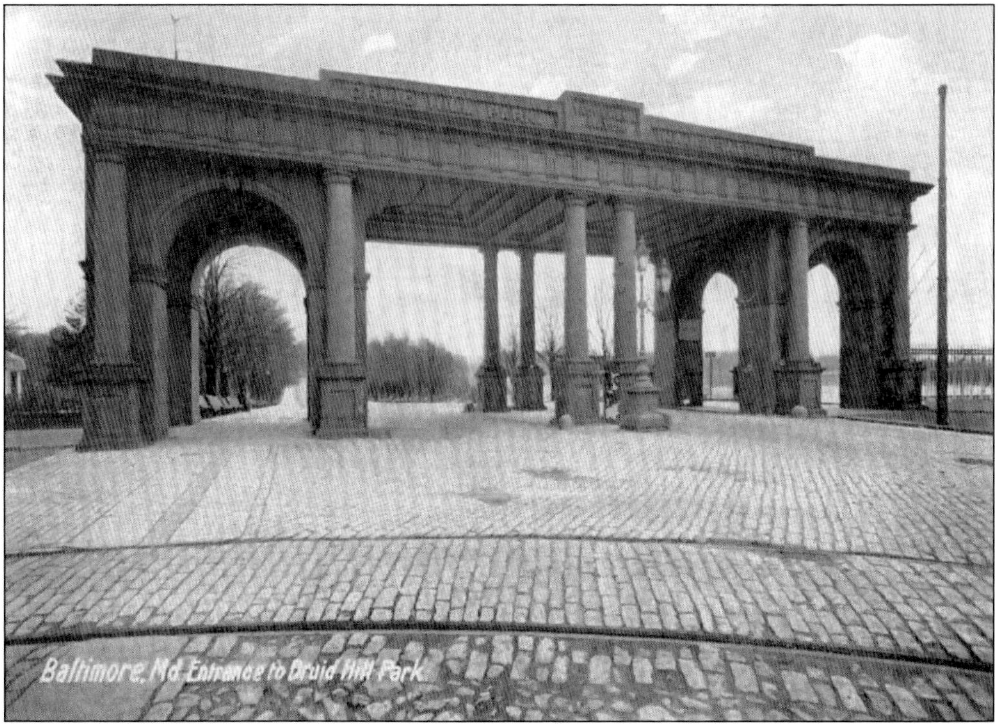

Druid Hill Park opened in 1860 in what was originally the Nicholas Rogers estate. Much detail was put into the entrances to the park and its landscape to include gates, lights, and fences. The Madison Avenue gate was completed in 1868 and is made of sandstone. The architect was George A. Frederick, who designed what is now known as the Rawlings Conservatory as well as other famous structures in Baltimore city parks. The Madison Avenue gate still stands today and is slated for restoration in 2012. (Above, Susan Adler; below, Lance Moore.)

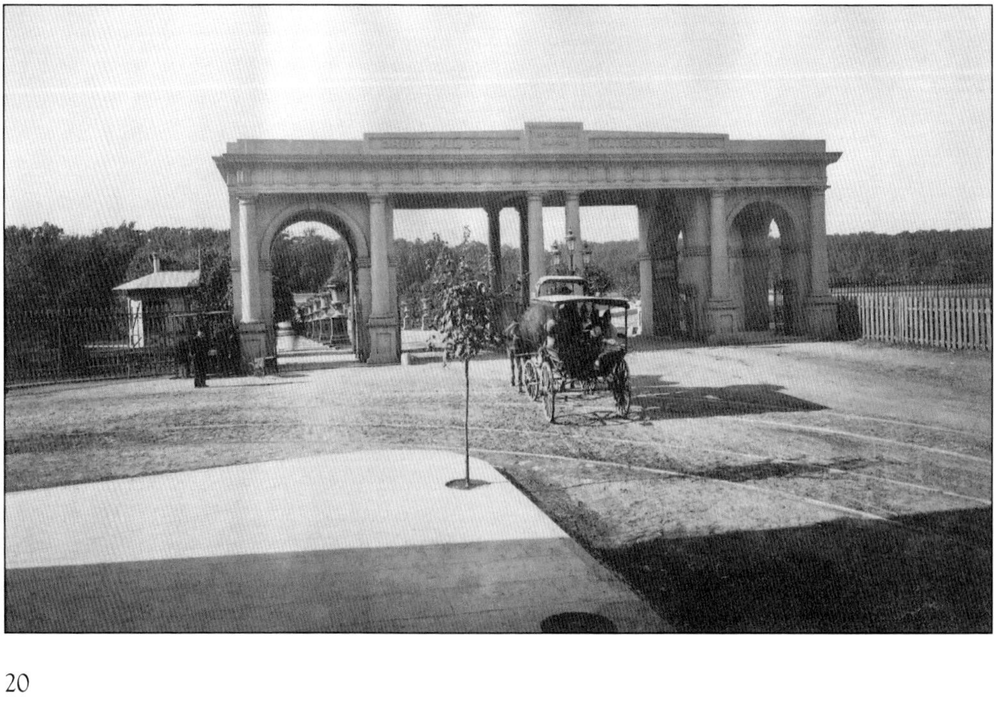

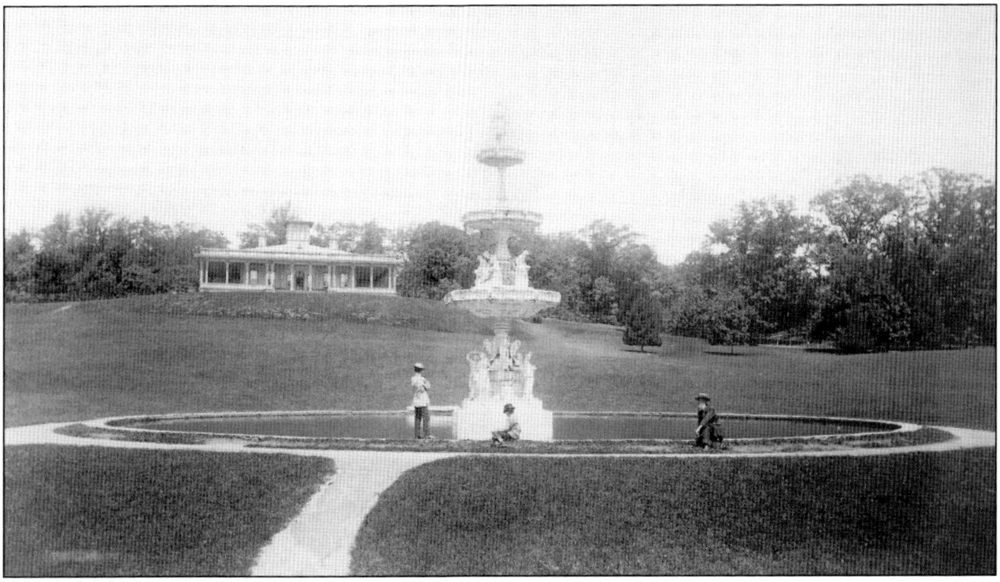

The Nicholas Rogers estate was a large parcel of land that consists of mostly what is today Druid Hill Park. The Rogers Mansion, known today as the Mansion House, is one of the few mansions still standing in the Reservoir Hill area. It was built in 1801 and converted into a public pavilion in 1863. The original entrance was removed and a 20-foot-wide open porch was added on all four sides. It has served many purposes over the years, including a restaurant and a private school. Today, the Mansion House is the headquarters for the Maryland Zoo. (Above, Susan Adler; below, Library of Congress.)

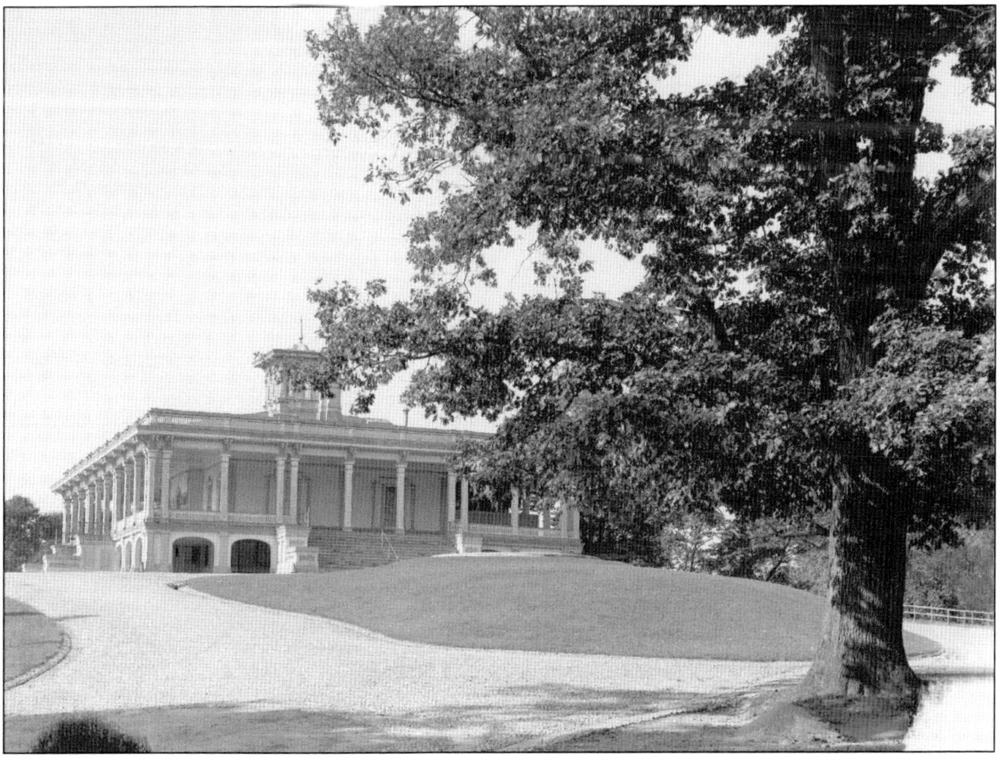

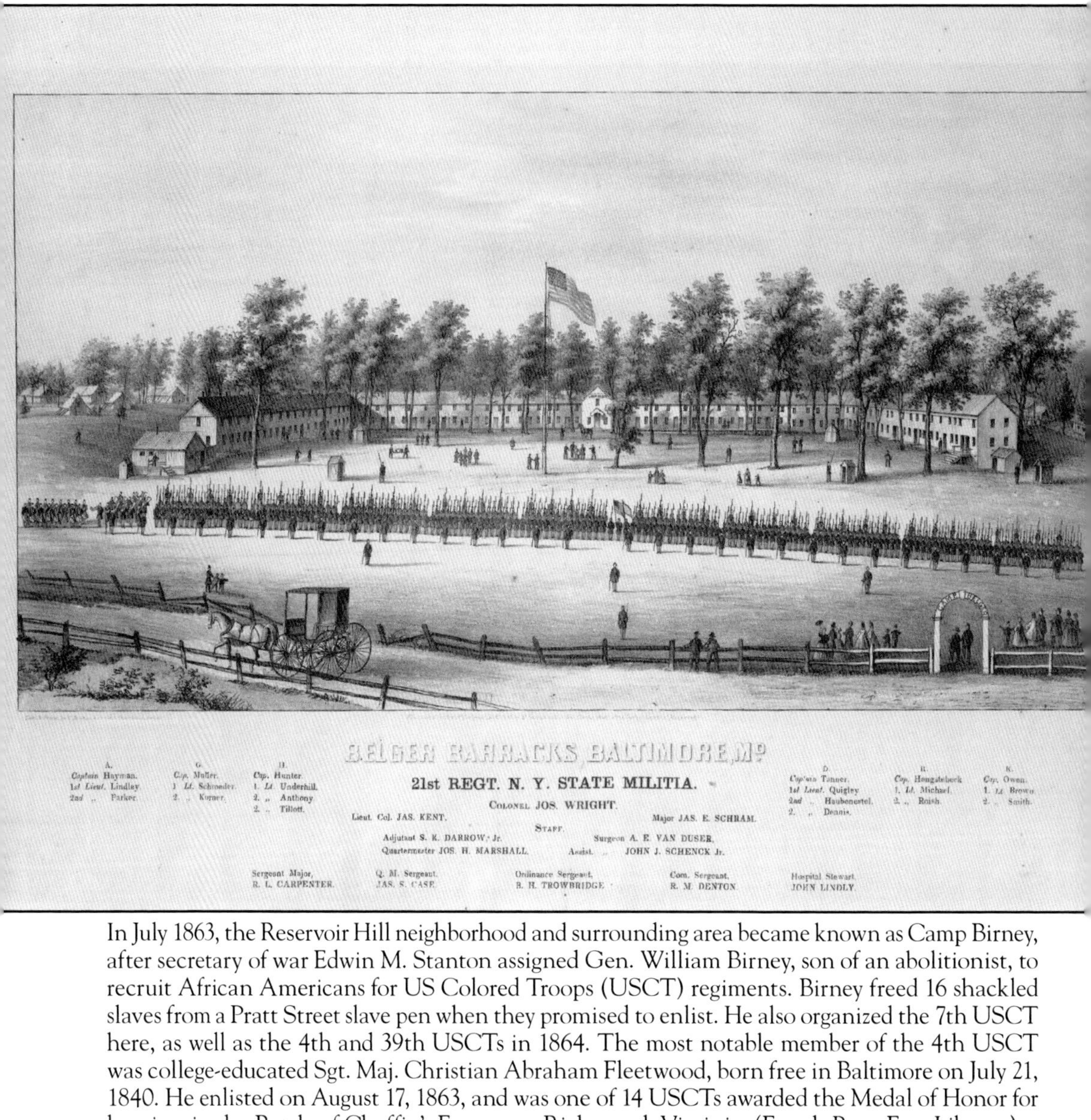

In July 1863, the Reservoir Hill neighborhood and surrounding area became known as Camp Birney, after secretary of war Edwin M. Stanton assigned Gen. William Birney, son of an abolitionist, to recruit African Americans for US Colored Troops (USCT) regiments. Birney freed 16 shackled slaves from a Pratt Street slave pen when they promised to enlist. He also organized the 7th USCT here, as well as the 4th and 39th USCTs in 1864. The most notable member of the 4th USCT was college-educated Sgt. Maj. Christian Abraham Fleetwood, born free in Baltimore on July 21, 1840. He enlisted on August 17, 1863, and was one of 14 USCTs awarded the Medal of Honor for heroism in the Battle of Chaffin's Farm near Richmond, Virginia. (Enoch Pratt Free Library.)

Two

STREETS AND LANDMARK BUILDINGS

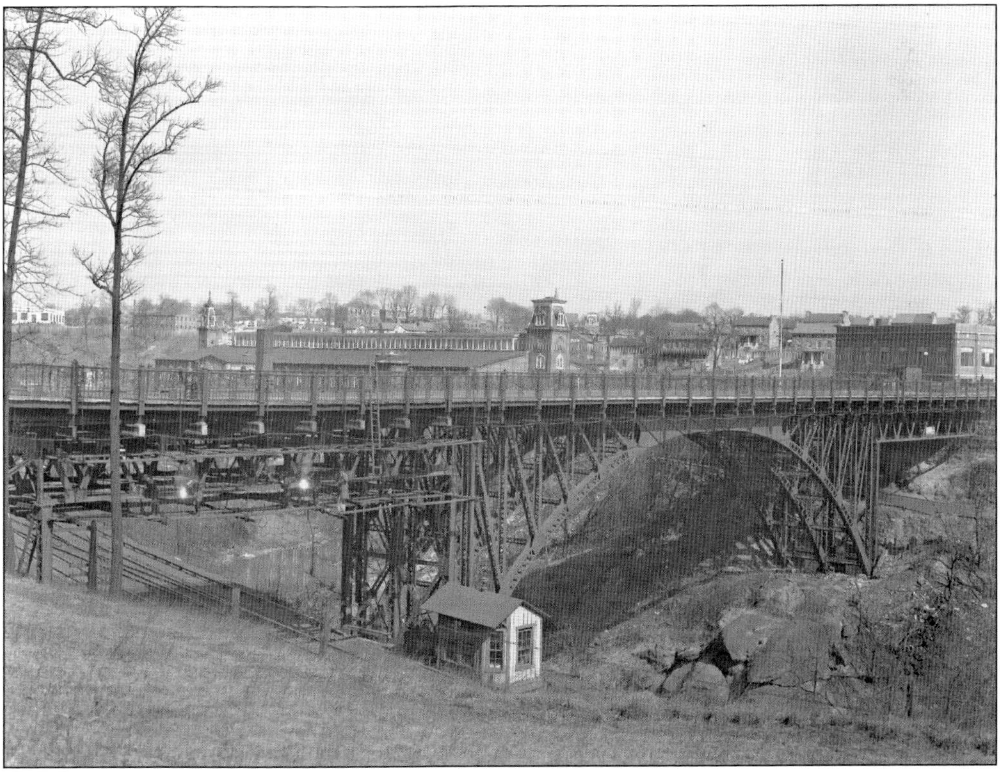

Cedar Avenue Bridge was one of the only connections from Reservoir Hill to the areas east of the Jones Falls until the Twenty-ninth Street Bridge was built in 1936. It was a substantial and ornamental bridge, supported by massive masonry piers and abutments. It was constructed by the King Iron Bridge Company of Cleveland, Ohio, and completed in 1890. It was demolished in the late 1950s during construction of the Jones Falls Expressway. (Baltimore Museum of Industry, BGE Collection.)

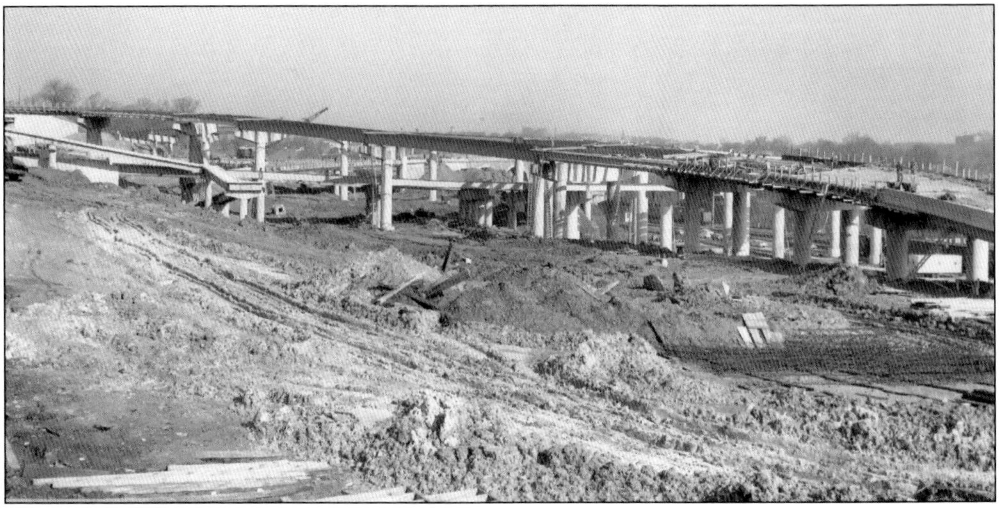

The Jones Falls Expressway, officially Interstate 83, was by far the biggest road construction project in Baltimore City and was responsible for major physical changes in the Reservoir Hill Area. The first portions of the Jones Falls Expressway (JFX) opened on December 16, 1961. Seen here is construction of the Twenty-eighth Street Bridge and its connection with Lake Drive. (Cal Buikema.)

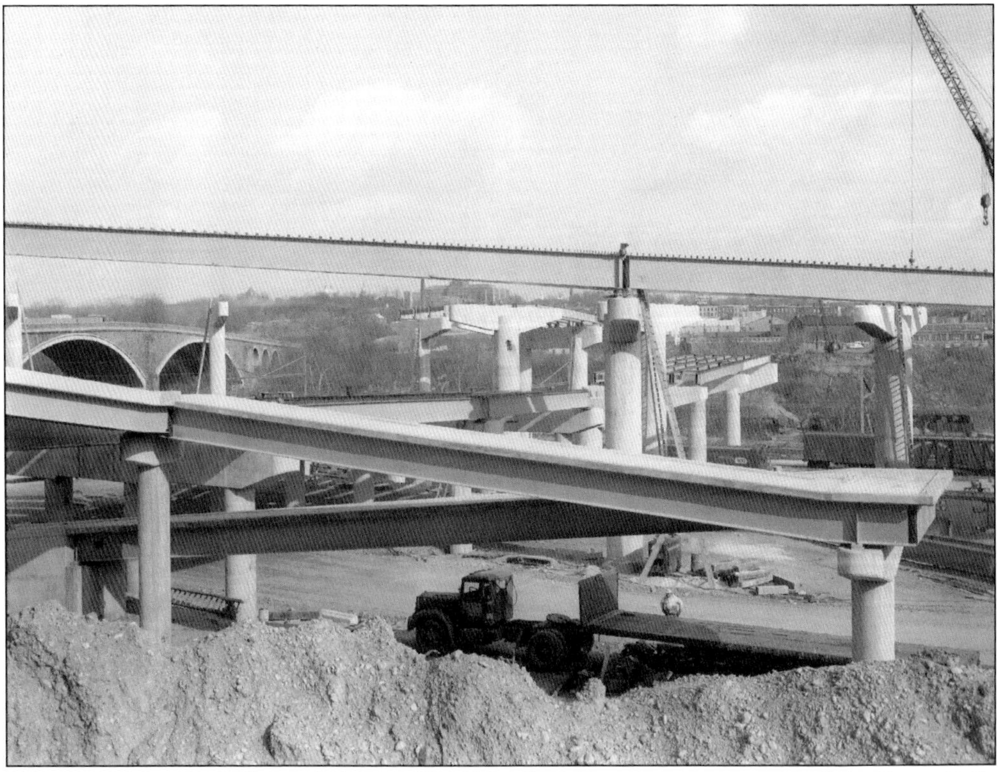

Then-mayor D'Alesandro and the local neighborhood associations supported the Jones Falls Expressway during its initial inception. Traffic bottlenecks were common in the city, and many city officials believed a new freeway would revitalize the downtown area. Here is another view of the Twenty-eighth Street Bridge and the pedestrian bridge under construction. (Cal Buikema.)

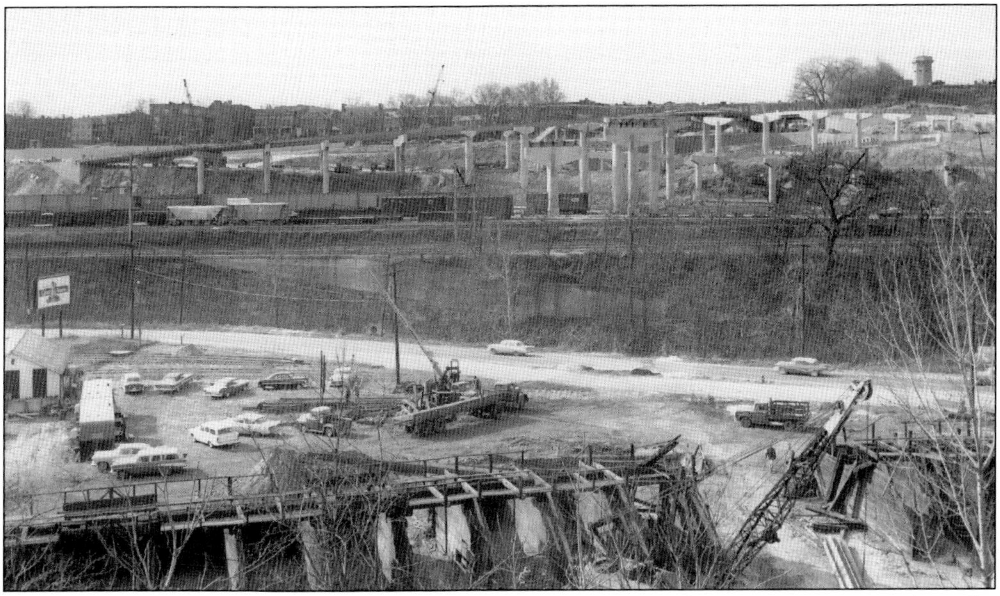

Once the planning got underway for the exact layout of the JFX, fierce opposition rose from the park board, Mount Royal Improvement Association, and Park Royal Association for the portion running on the eastern edge of Reservoir Hill. The proposed layout would remove about 40 acres of Druid Hill Park and eliminate the eastbound lanes of Mount Royal Avenue. This picture shows the construction of the JFX next to present-day Mount Royal Terrace. (Cal Buikema.)

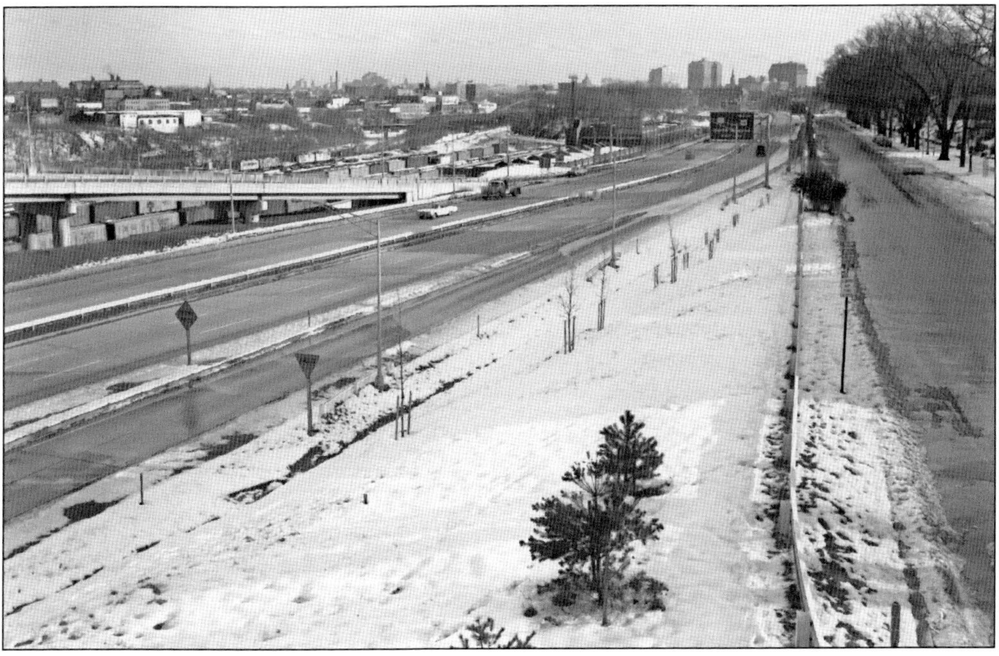

Despite opposition to the layout of the Jones Falls Expressway, construction was completed and traffic was connected from the Baltimore Beltway, Interstate 695, and downtown Baltimore. The freeway was completed in sections with the last portions opened farther outside the city limits. Seen here is the Jones Falls Expressway during the first days of its completion around the Reservoir Hill area. (Baltimore Museum of Industry, BGE Collection.)

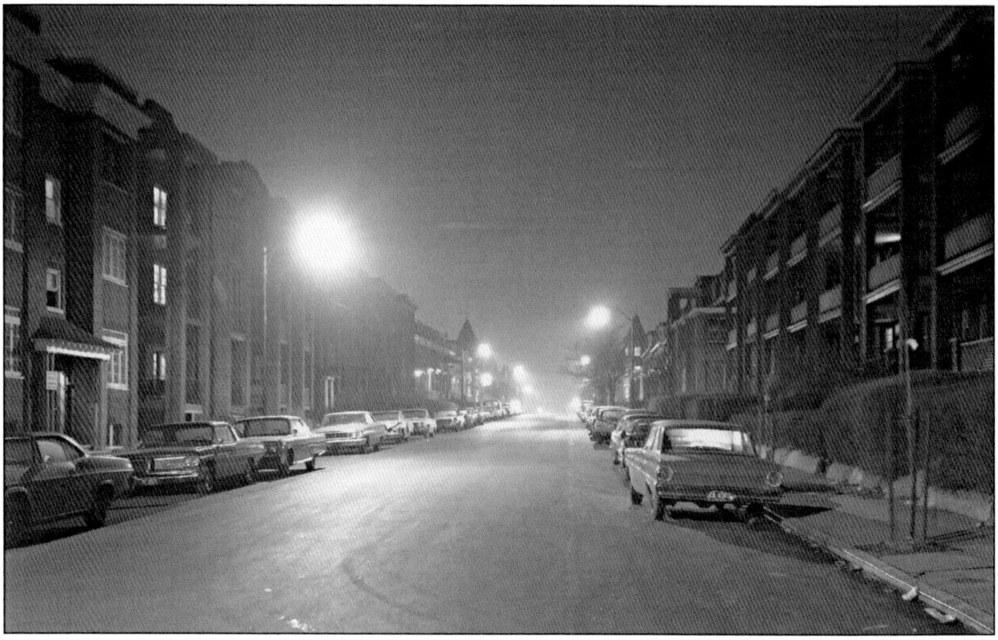

The invention of the car changed the entire city and impacted the Reservoir Hill neighborhood as less people were using mass transit. Roads were becoming crowded, and freeways were being built. Here are two photographs from the late 1950s. The photograph below is of Reservoir Street looking east, and above is of Callow Avenue looking south. Reservoir Street has been known for its outstanding backyard gardens for decades. The residence at 609 Reservoir Street won first prize in a citywide contest in 1929 from the Women's Civic League. Today, the annual home and garden tour showcases many addresses on Reservoir Street and surrounding streets. (Both, Baltimore Museum of Industry, BGE Collection.)

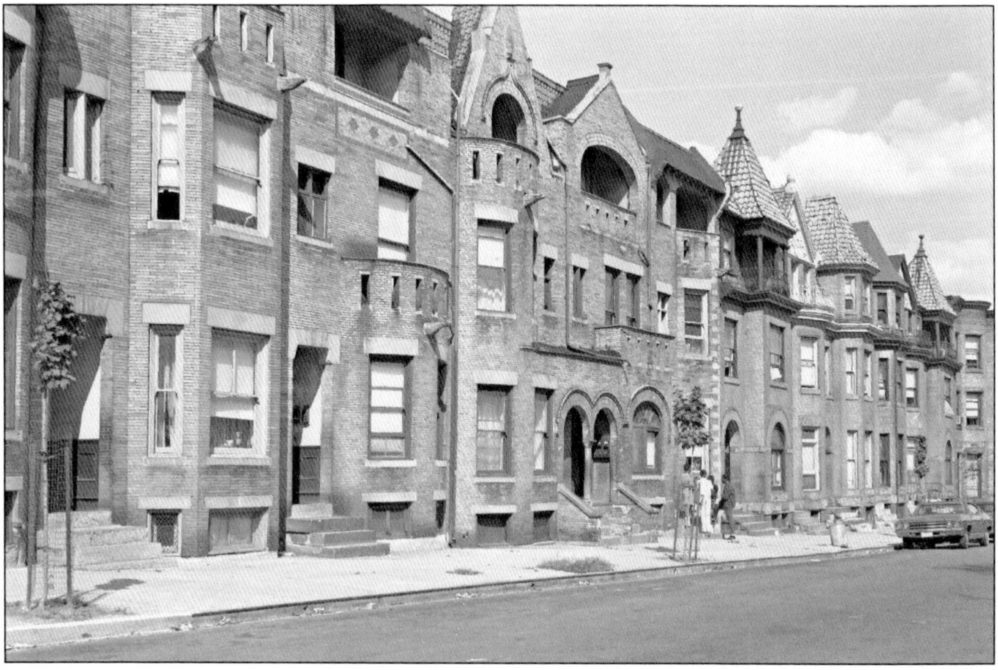

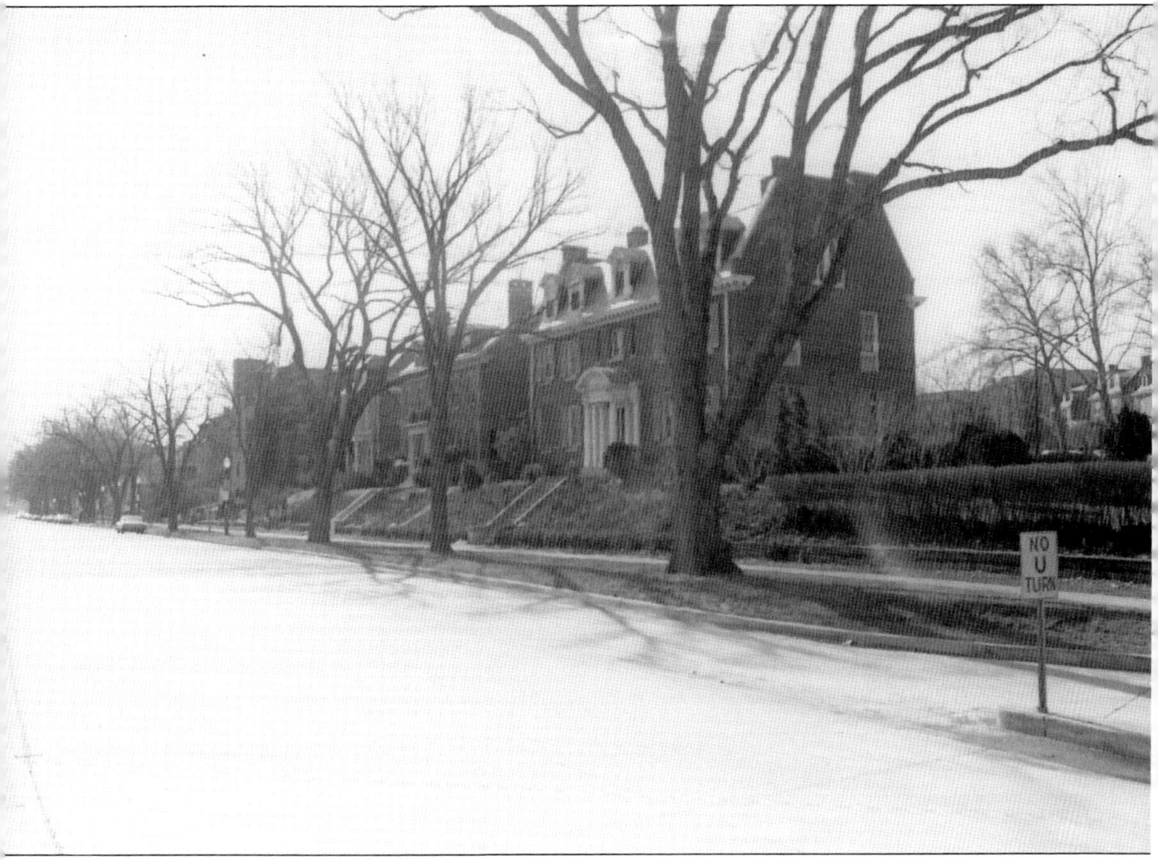

Mount Royal Terrace is the easternmost street in Reservoir Hill. Originally, the landscape in front of the houses would have been a terrace leading down toward the Jones Falls. It was also considered the grand entrance to Druid Hill Park. The intersection of Boundary (North) Avenue and Mount Royal Terrace included beautiful Victorian homes around the perimeter of Mount Royal Reservoir. Today, Mount Royal Terrace is a one-way street, and traffic is much lighter than the days prior to the Jones Falls Expressway. (CHAP.)

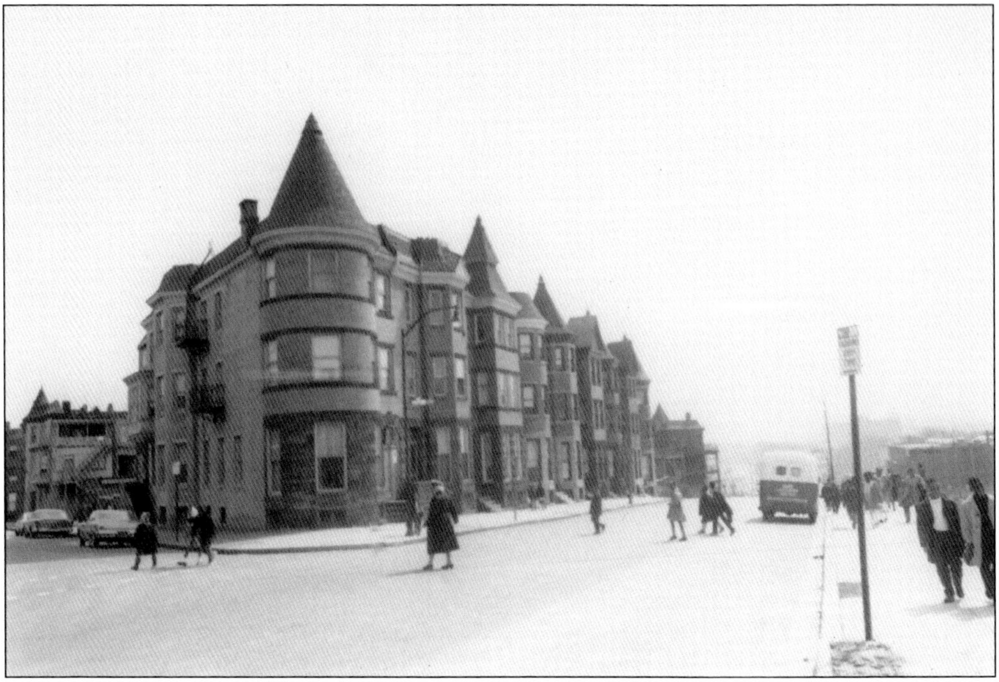

Pictured above is Brookfield Avenue north of Lennox Street. Directly to the right of this view of Brookfield Avenue was School No. 61, the only school in Reservoir Hill. Pedestrian traffic was busy on this day in 1961. Below is a photograph of Newington Avenue, a street in the heart of Reservoir Hill that runs east and west between Brookfield and Mount Royal Terrace. The street consists of three-story row houses except for an apartment complex at the corner of Mount Royal Terrace and Newington Avenue. (Both, CHAP.)

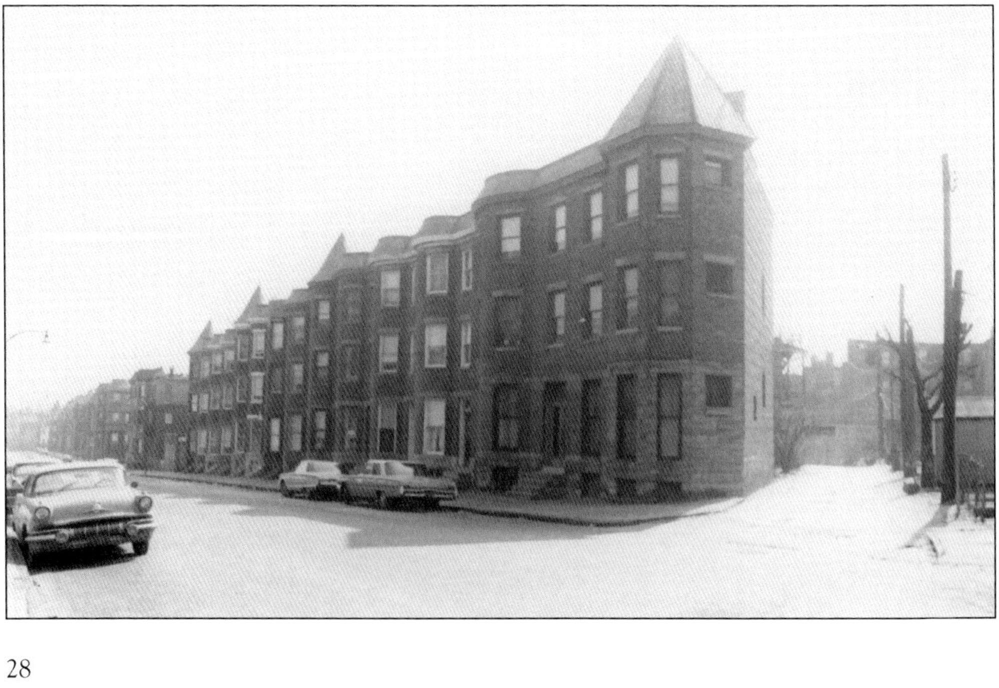

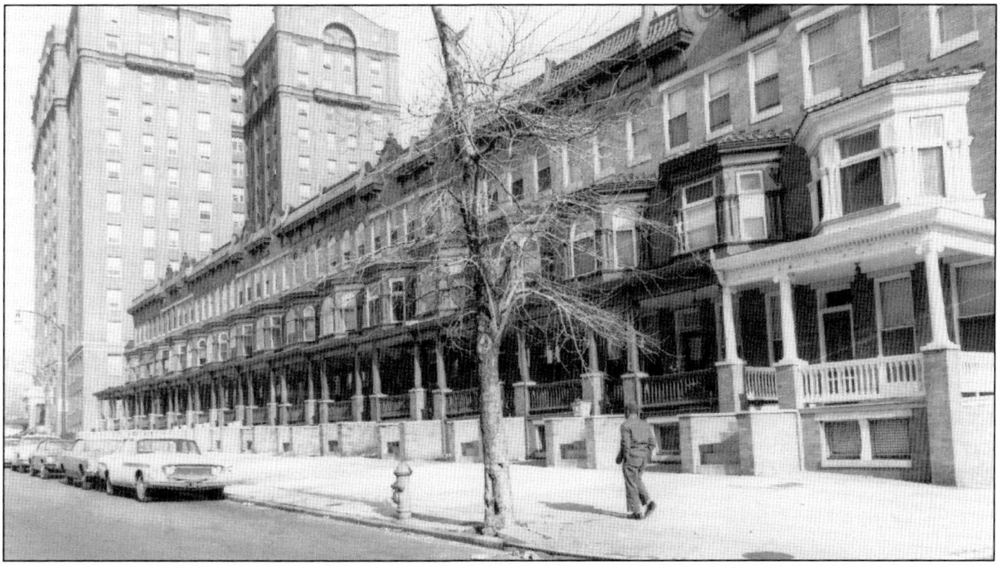

Below is a photograph of the 2400 Block of Eutaw Place, built by famous Baltimore developer Ed Gallagher. Gallagher had been building standard-size row houses in Baltimore until this construction on Eutaw Place. Following the 2400 block of Eutaw Place, he went on to build some of the more elaborate homes next to Patterson Park in East Baltimore. Above, the 2500 Block of Madison Avenue shows the Temple Gardens Apartments and a uniform block of "daylight row houses" that were becoming fashionable by 1915. A daylight row house was defined as one with a front porch and was "a city house with suburban advantages." (Both, CHAP.)

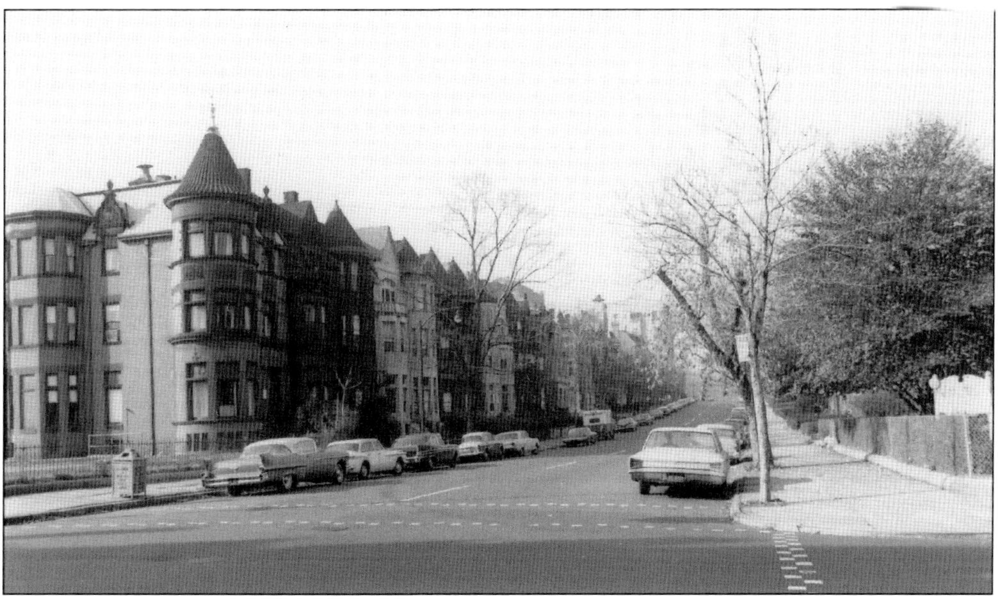

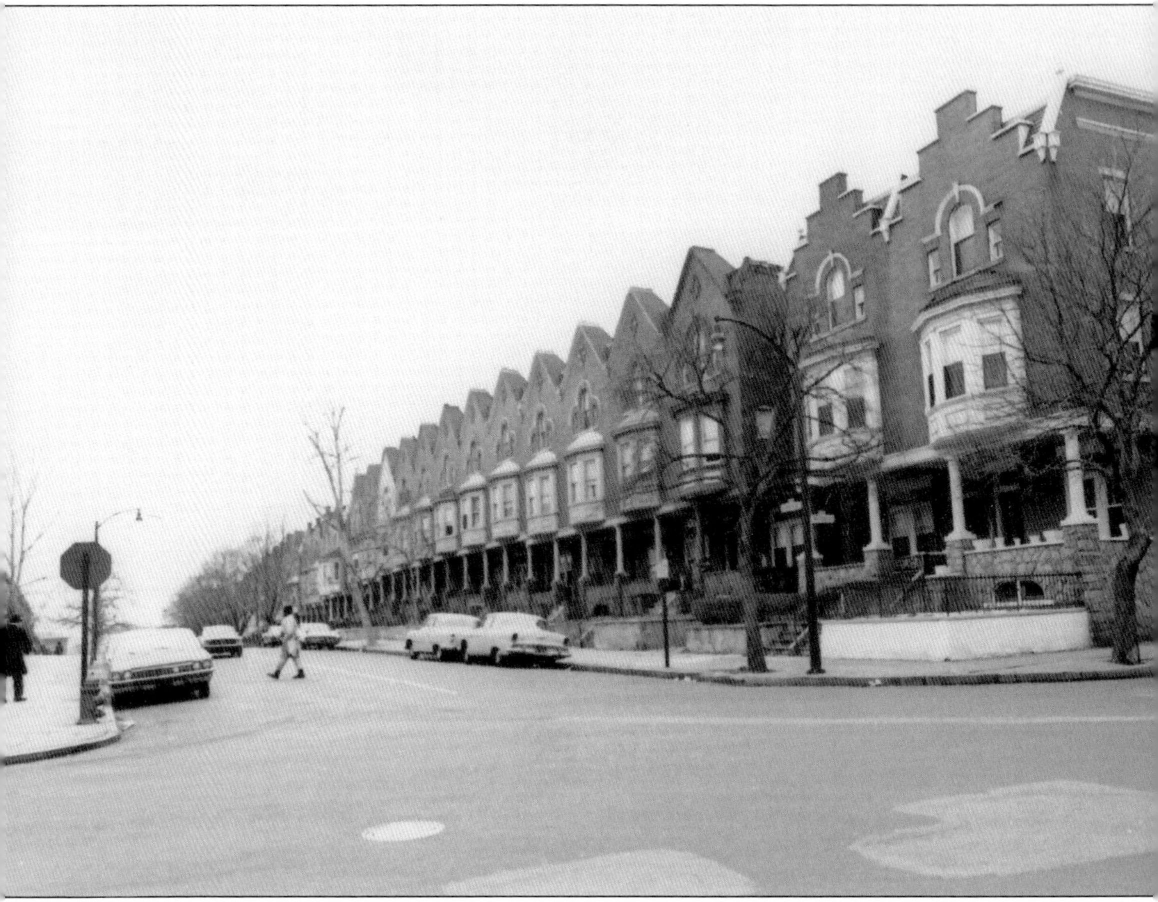

Above is the intersection of Linden Avenue and Whitelock Street looking south toward North Avenue. The row houses pictured here on Linden Avenue look virtually the same today. Linden Avenue travels north and south through Reservoir Hill and continued south into the Bolton Hill neighborhood until the 1960s. Today, Linden Avenue and Park Avenue are the only two north-south streets in Reservoir Hill that remain open to two-way traffic. (CHAP.)

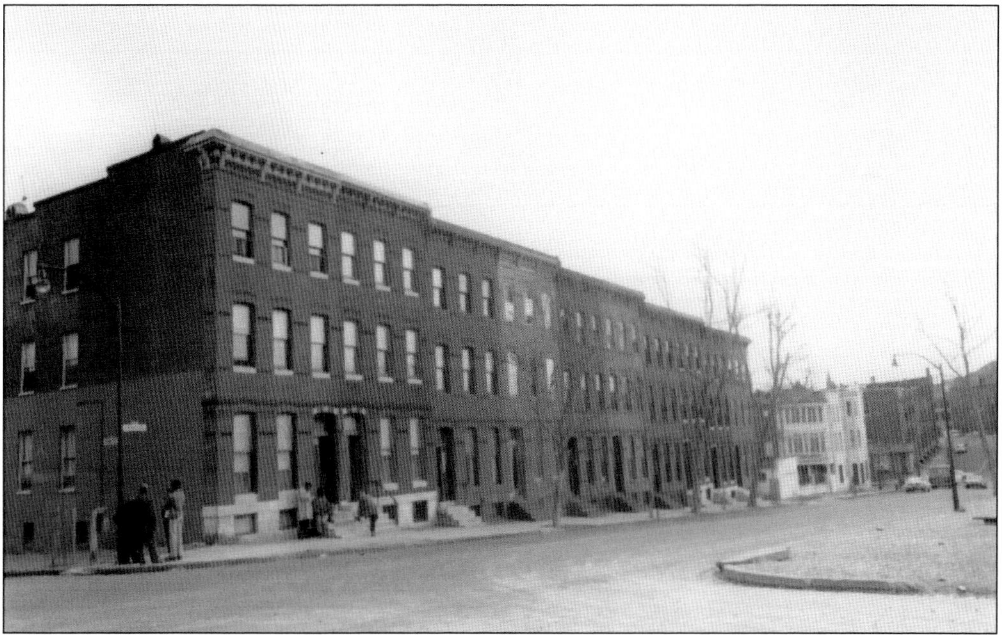

Above is the intersection of Lennox Street and Park Avenue looking south to North Avenue and into the Bolton Hill neighborhood. The row houses on the east side of Park Avenue still stand today; however, the large building at the intersection of North and Park Avenues has been razed. The west side, as seen in the photograph, was already cleared to make way for the Madison Park North Apartment Complex. Below is a photograph of Lake Drive and Lakeview Avenue where today's Lakeview Towers now stands. The unique building shown in the picture has gone through additions, including Georgian columns not seen in Reservoir Hill or most of Baltimore. (Both, CHAP.)

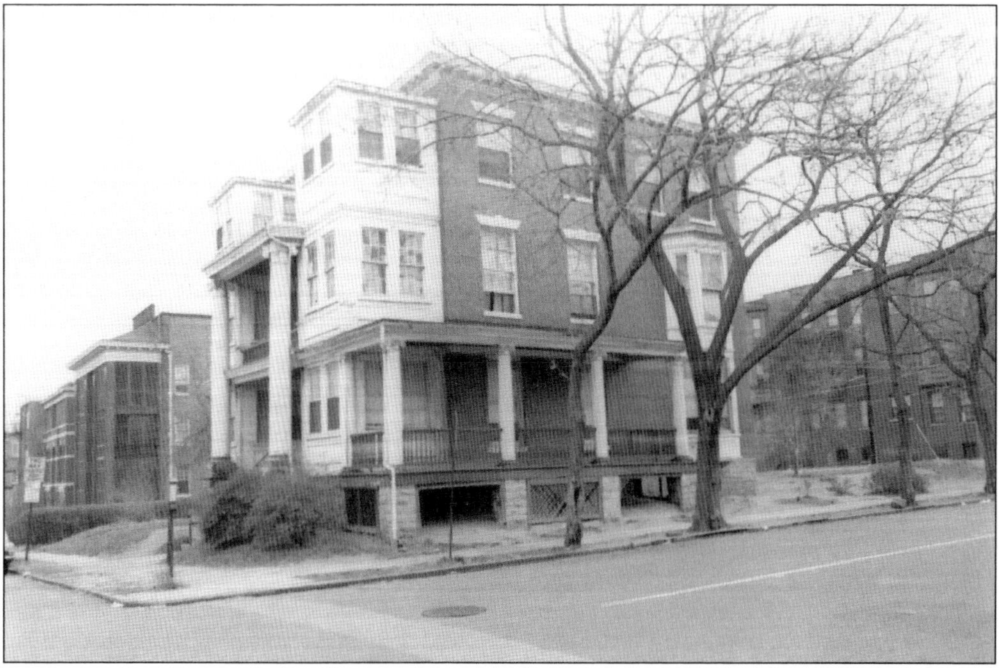

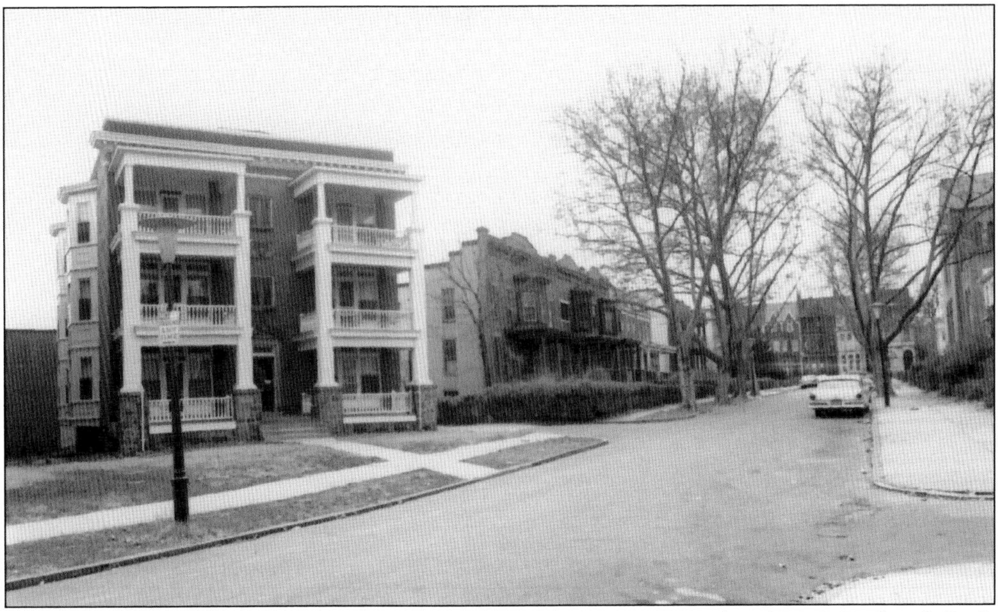

Chauncey Avenue and Brooks Lane are named after Chauncey Brooks of B&O Railroad. Both streets were created after the Brooks estate was sold in 1913 and developed thereafter. With many area Jewish families not able to afford the larger, more elaborate homes of Eutaw Place, Jewish families initially purchased the row houses on these two streets. One of Maryland's most successful and well-known citizens, David Cordish, grew up on Brooks Lane. Another factor that affected the nature of Brooks Lane and Chauncey Avenue was its proximity to Chizuk Amuno, a conservative Jewish synagogue. Many residents were active members of Chizuk Amuno, at which their social and religious lives revolved around. (Both, CHAP.)

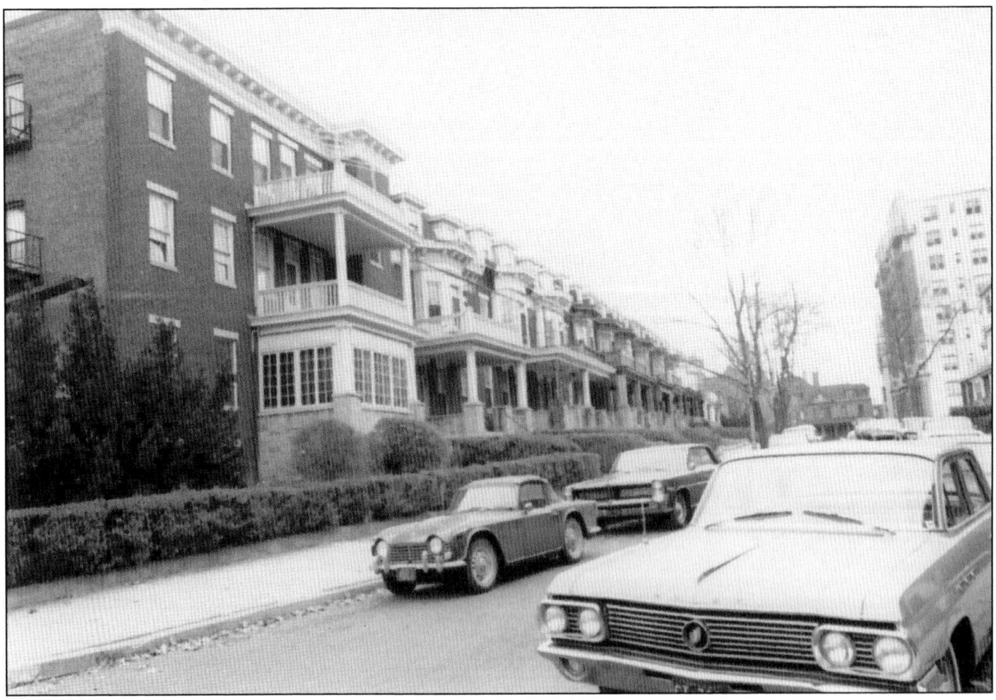

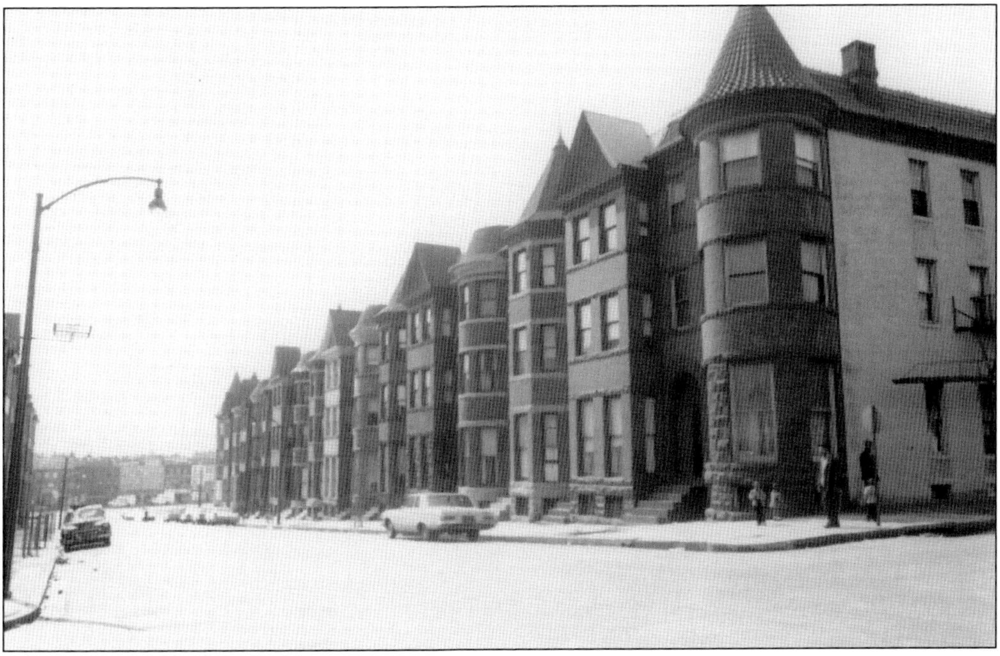

Above is the intersection of Bolton and Reservoir Streets looking south toward North Avenue. In this picture, one can see the cleared area south of Bolton Street where urban renewal plans were underway to construct the Madison Park North Apartment Complex. Eventually, all the homes seen on the south side of North Avenue were demolished. Shown below is Lennox Street looking west toward Park Avenue. The 700 block of Lennox Street was once where Babe Ruth would play catch with Lennox residents while the Yankees were in town. Babe Ruth was born in Baltimore and had many ties to the city. (Both, CHAP.)

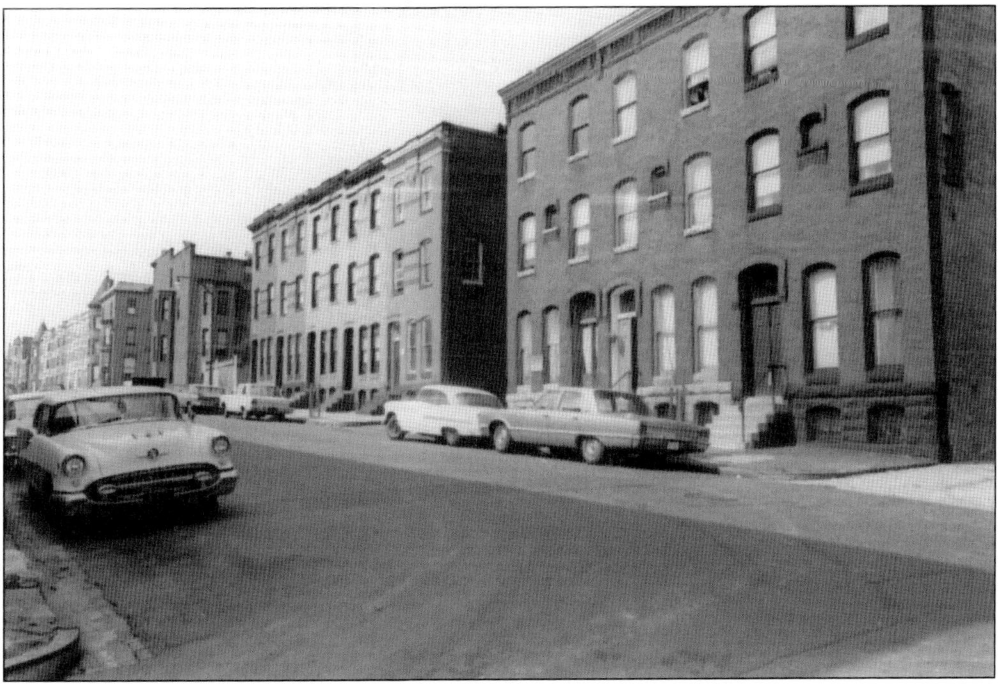

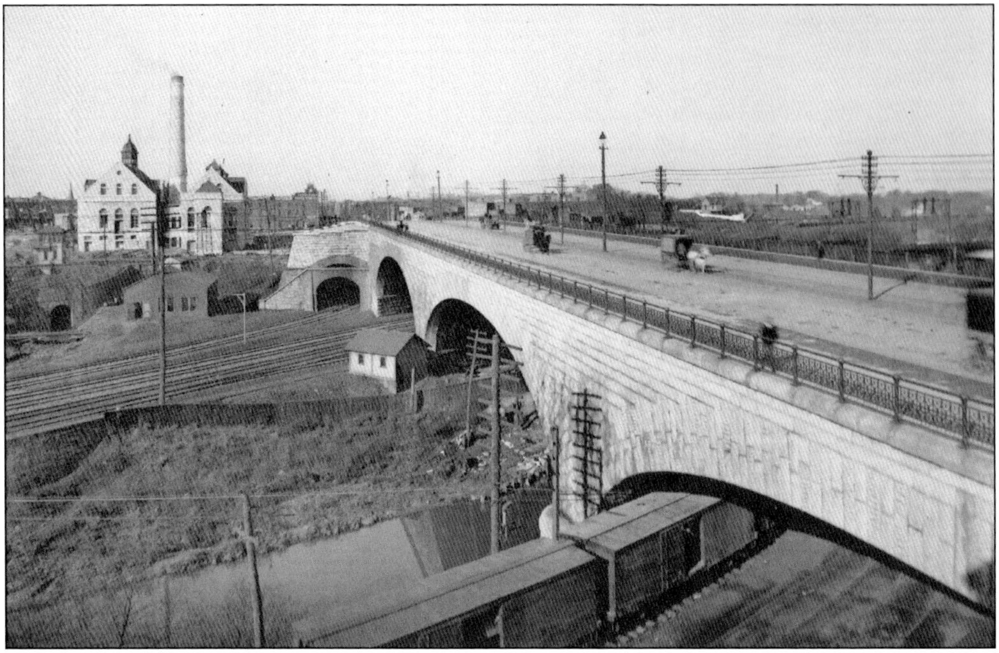

Above is the North Avenue Bridge in 1899, which connected East and West Baltimore. At that time, North Avenue was still mostly residential but that would quickly change in the next couple of decades. North Avenue, once the northern boundary of Baltimore, was, for the first half of the 20th century, a very busy street and one of the larger commercial corridors in the city. As the suburbs grew and the city population decreased, North Avenue suffered. The first major construction on North Avenue in decades began in 2012 with a residence hall for Maryland Institute College of Art (MICA). Below is the Seville Apartments at Lake Drive and Linden Avenue, which was demolished in the 1960s. The land has been vacant for decades but is now slated for residential construction. (Both, CHAP.)

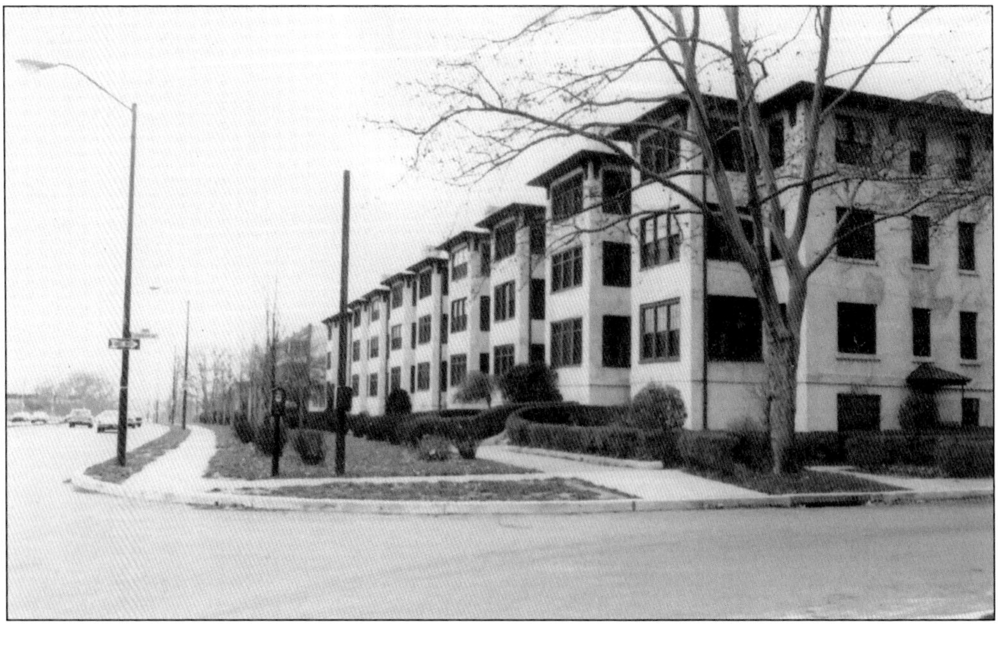

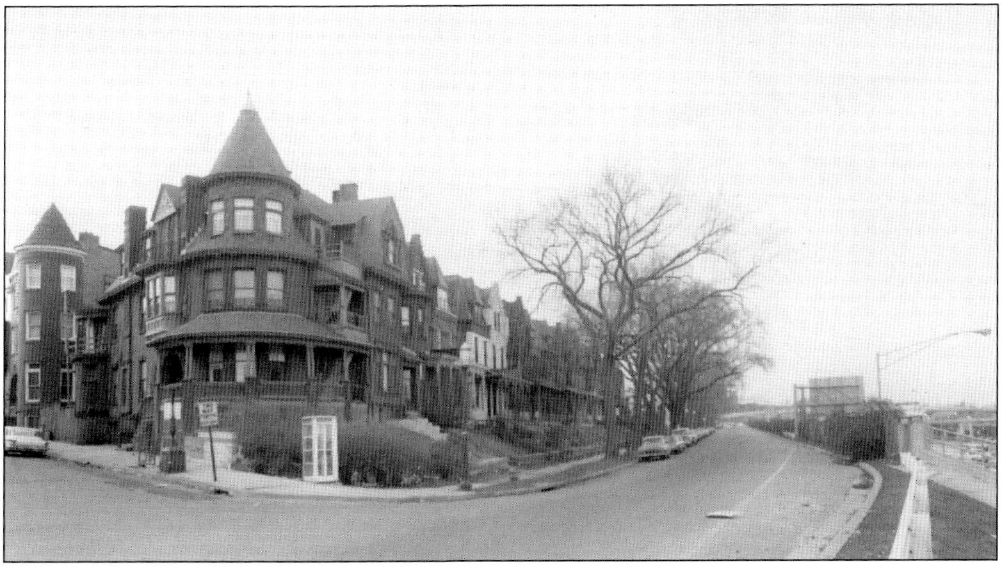

Home of J. Kemp Bartlett, 2100 Mount Royal Terrace, was the center of the deal making that gave Woodrow Wilson, 28th president of the United States, the nomination and subsequently the presidency. The 1912 Democratic Convention was held at the 5th Regiment Armory on Mount Royal Avenue. Williams Jennings Bryan, Democratic presidential candidate, former secretary of state, and law partner to J. Kemp Bartlett, was the connection to 2100 Mount Royal Terrace and its use in the Wilson nomination discussions. Today, 2100 Mount Royal Terrace is the Woodrow Wilson Bed & Breakfast. (Above, BCPL; below, Dale Dusman collection.)

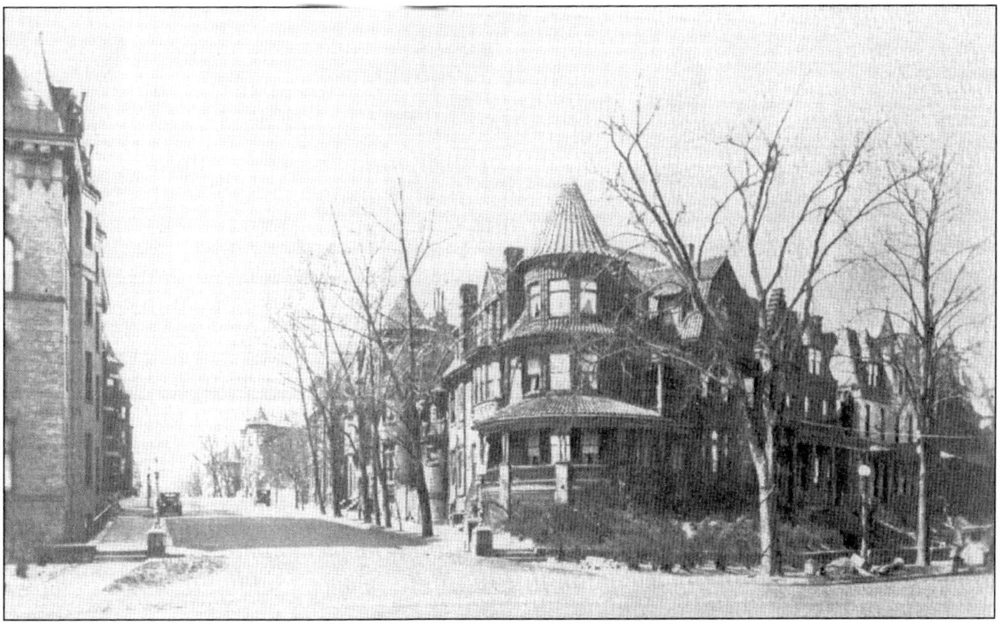

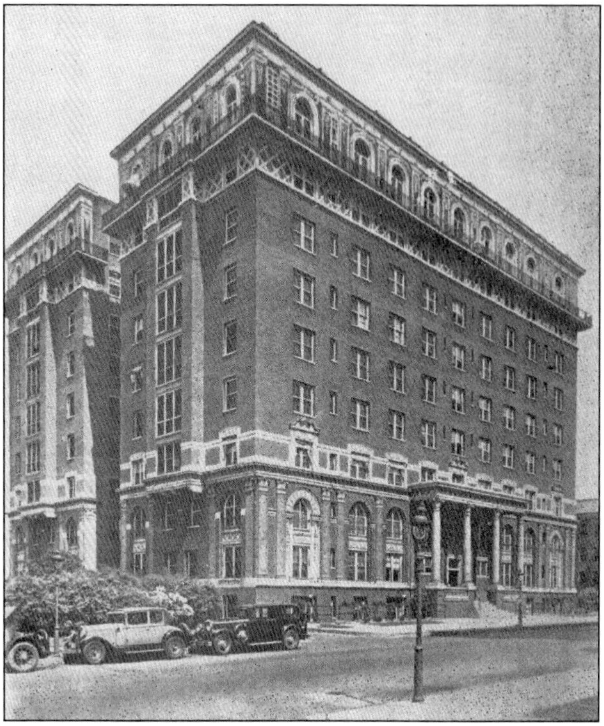

The Esplanade Apartments opened in 1912 with much fanfare. The height of comfort and luxury was throughout every apartment. Heavy hardwood trim and floors, Istrian-stone mantels of special design, and glass doors were some of the features. Each apartment also had refrigerators and freezers, which were new technology at the time. (Dale Dusman collection.)

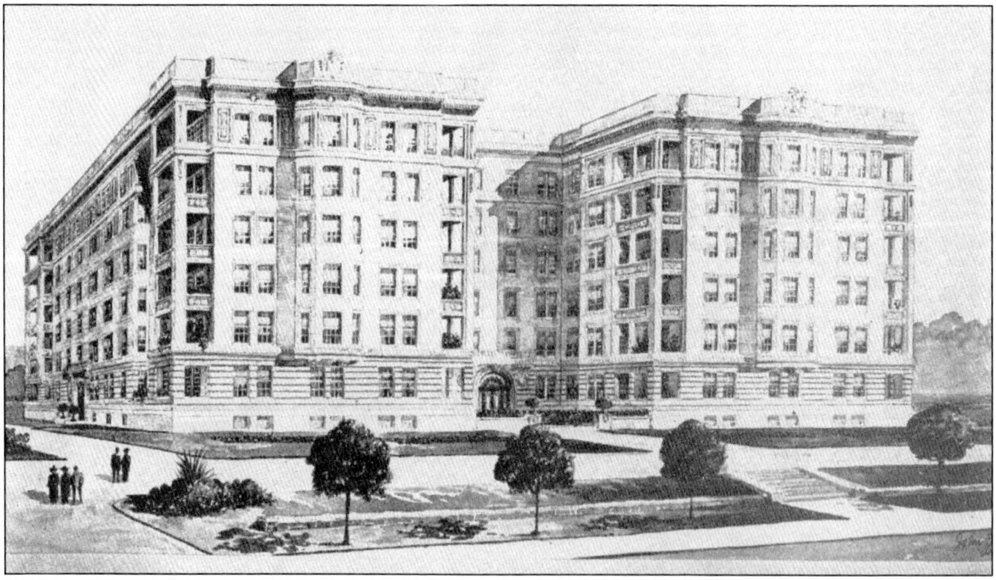

The Riviera Apartments, a combination of Beaux Arts and Renaissance Revival details, are some of the most ambitious structures designed by John Freund Jr., a Baltimore architect who created smaller apartment houses in Reservoir Hill and many churches throughout the city. The Riviera is representative of Baltimore's apartment-building boom of the early 20th century and an integral part of the luxury-housing district constructed along Lake Drive during the first two decades of the 1900s. Among the features considered noteworthy at the time of construction were 10-foot-high ceilings and parquet floors in the apartments and porches that could be converted into glass-enclosed conservatories. (Dale Dusman collection.)

The Emersonian Apartments were completed in 1916 to attract those who wanted to live in a large suburban home but wanted the amenities of city life. Each apartment took up half the floor of these two buildings, which were separated by a courtyard. All apartments had five porches and a kitchen balcony, resembling a rear porch of a suburban home. Also unique was that all garbage at the property was incinerated on site. The architect was Joseph Evans Sperry who was the architect for many of Baltimore's best landmarks. (Dale Dusman.)

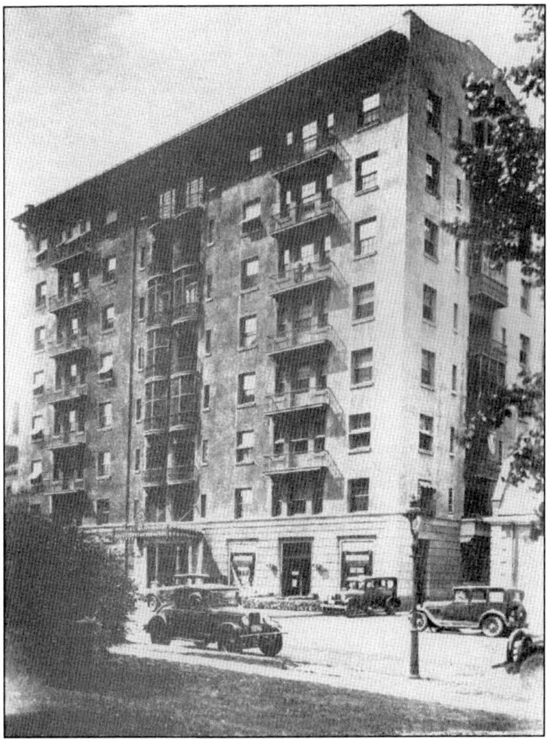

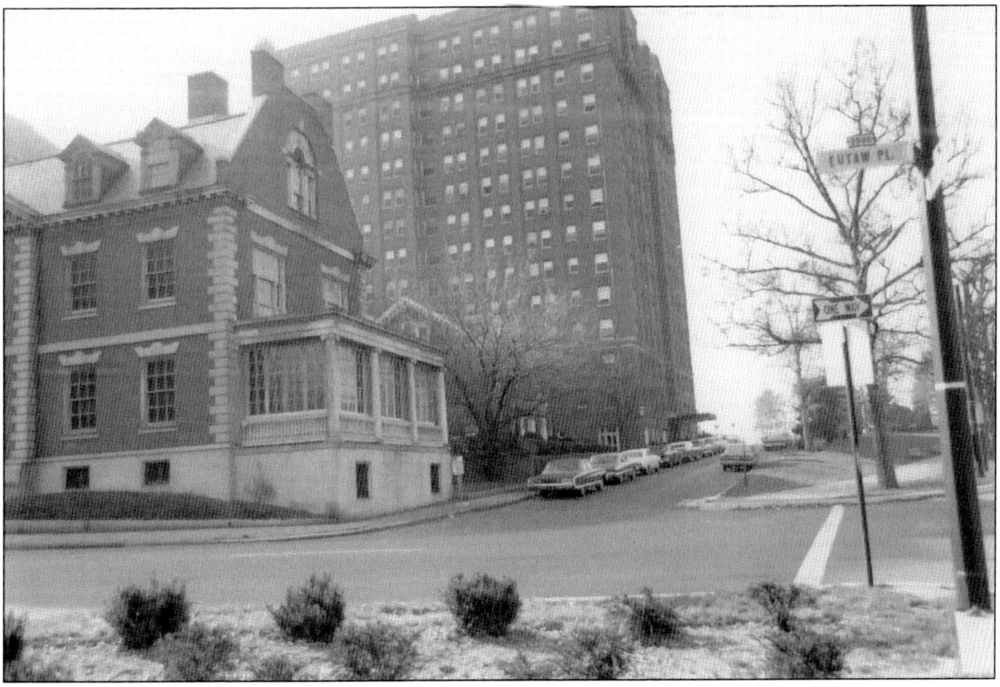

Completed in September 1926, Temple Gardens, located at Lake Drive and Madison Avenue, had 104 apartments with all the newest technology. It is made of brick with terra-cotta and cast stone trimming. For many years, Temple Gardens stood as the highest point in Baltimore. (CHAP.)

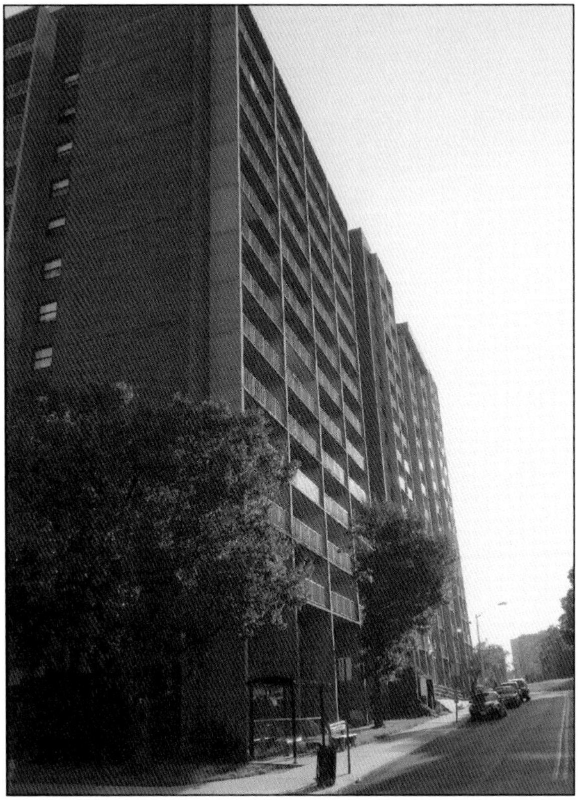

Lakeview Towers, to the left, was a public housing project built for the elderly. It has 305 units and is located on Lake Drive between Park and Lakeview Avenue. The first tower was opened in 1969 and the second in 1979. (Author's collection.)

The French Renaissance–style Mount Royal Pumping Station was completed in 1899 and took water from Lakes Montebello and Clifton and sent it to the High Service Reservoir in Druid Hill Park. It was state of the art at the time of completion and was studied by engineers from all over the country and Europe. It was located close to the intersection of Mount Royal and North Avenues. (Baltimore Museum of Industry, BGE Collection.)

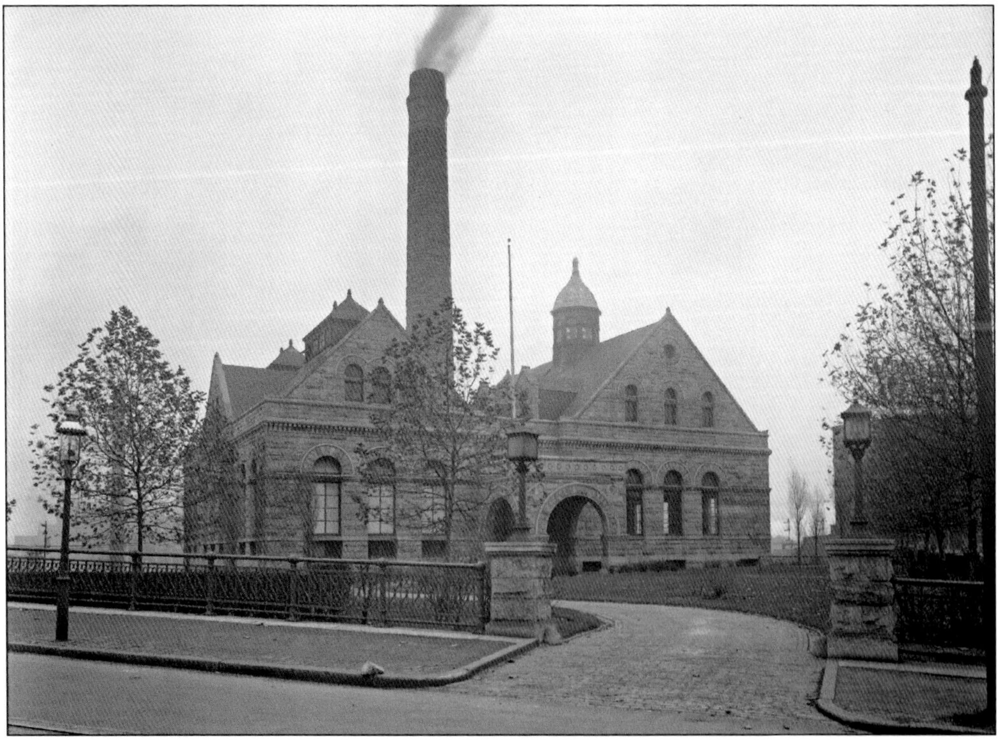

Three

TRANSPORTATION

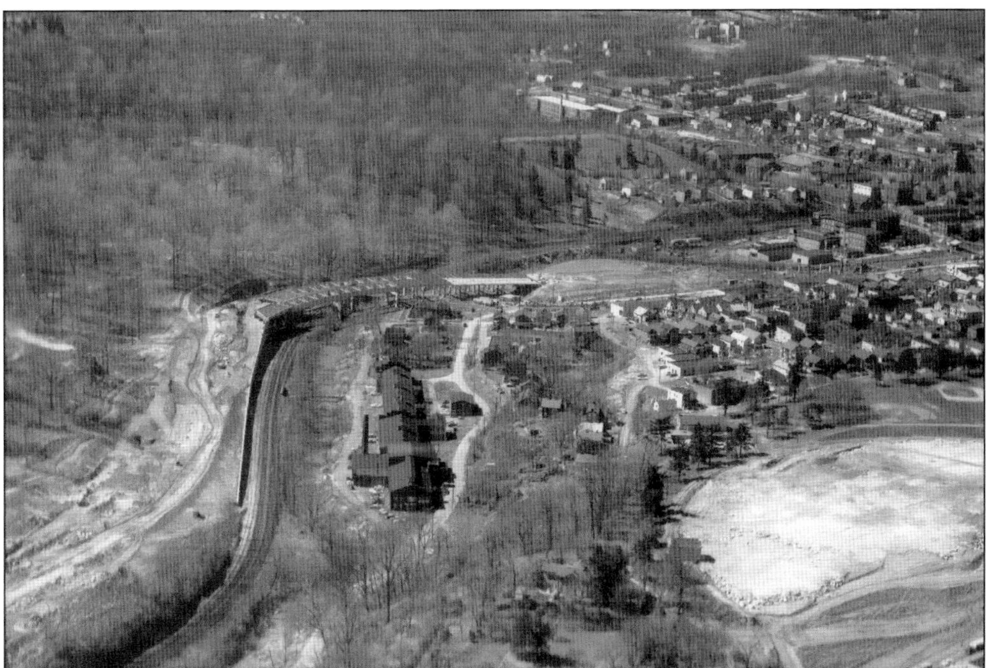

The Jones Falls Expressway (JFX) changed the landscape of the eastern portion of Reservoir Hill. The JFX is the only major freeway into Baltimore from the north. Shown here is the regrading of the land and removal of a portion of the eastern embankment of Druid Hill Lake. (Cal Buikema.)

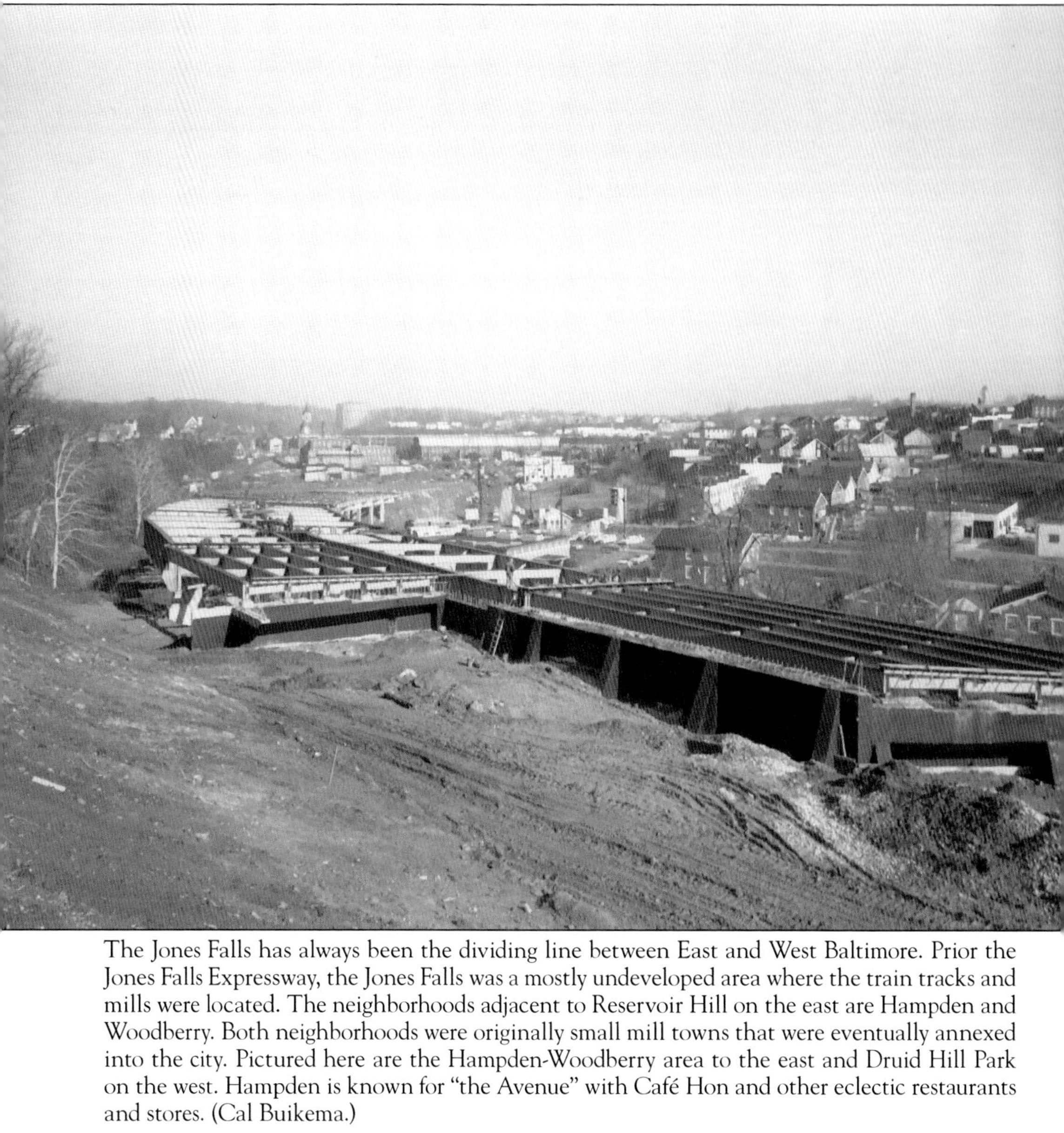

The Jones Falls has always been the dividing line between East and West Baltimore. Prior the Jones Falls Expressway, the Jones Falls was a mostly undeveloped area where the train tracks and mills were located. The neighborhoods adjacent to Reservoir Hill on the east are Hampden and Woodberry. Both neighborhoods were originally small mill towns that were eventually annexed into the city. Pictured here are the Hampden-Woodberry area to the east and Druid Hill Park on the west. Hampden is known for "the Avenue" with Café Hon and other eclectic restaurants and stores. (Cal Buikema.)

Reservoir Hill had three streetcar lines and one bus line that served the neighborhood. They were the B bus line and the 12, 16, and 32 streetcars lines. Streetcars were a large part of transportation for Baltimore until the 1960s, when the last streetcar line stopped. They were replaced with buses and some discontinued. Remnants of the streetcars lines can still be seen in the neighborhood as tracks appear from underneath asphalt and old streetcar terminals dot the area. Here are the cards distributed by the Baltimore Transit Company for the B line and the 12 line. (Both, Baltimore Streetcar Museum.)

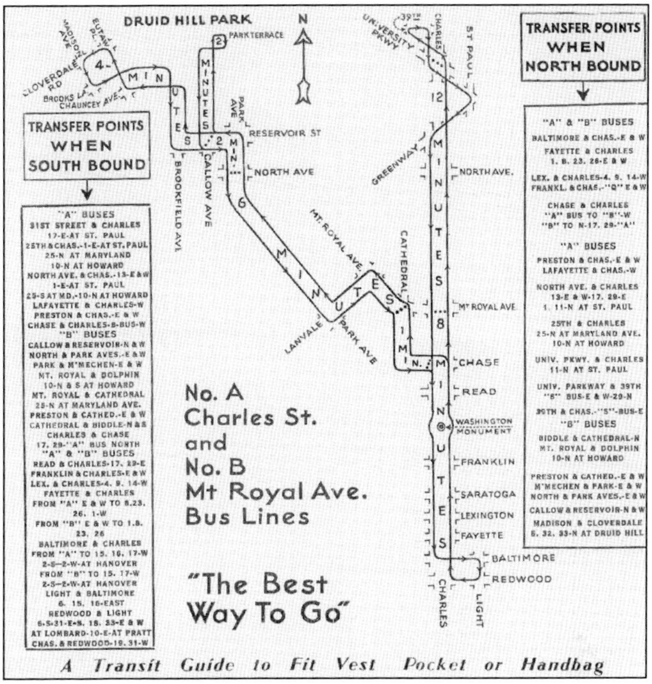

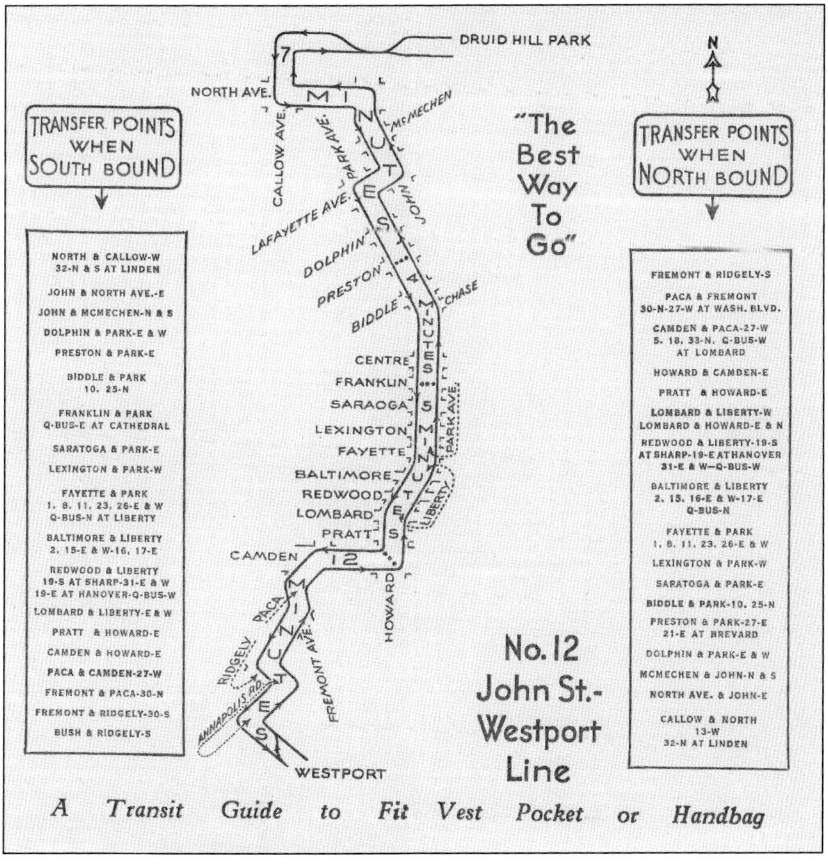

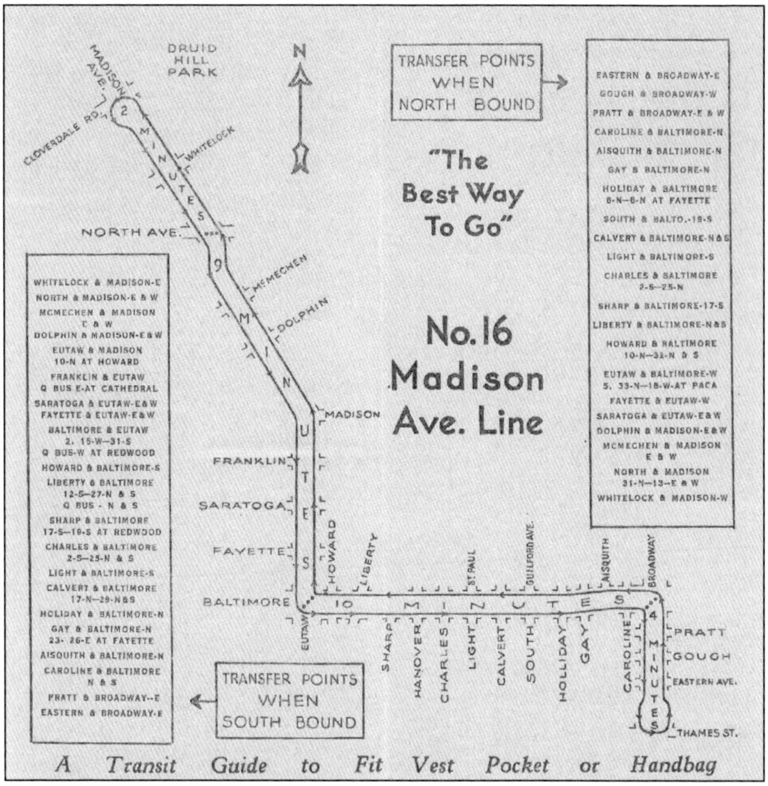

Streetcars could travel throughout the city including Druid Hill Park. One of the accomplishments of Mayor Thomas Swann was the creation of the park tax. The tax was nine percent of the total cost of each fare. The tax-generated revenue for city parks was essential for keeping the parks maintained. By 1931, the park tax was in jeopardy and eventually eliminated. The card to the left is for the 16 streetcar line. (Baltimore Streetcar Museum.)

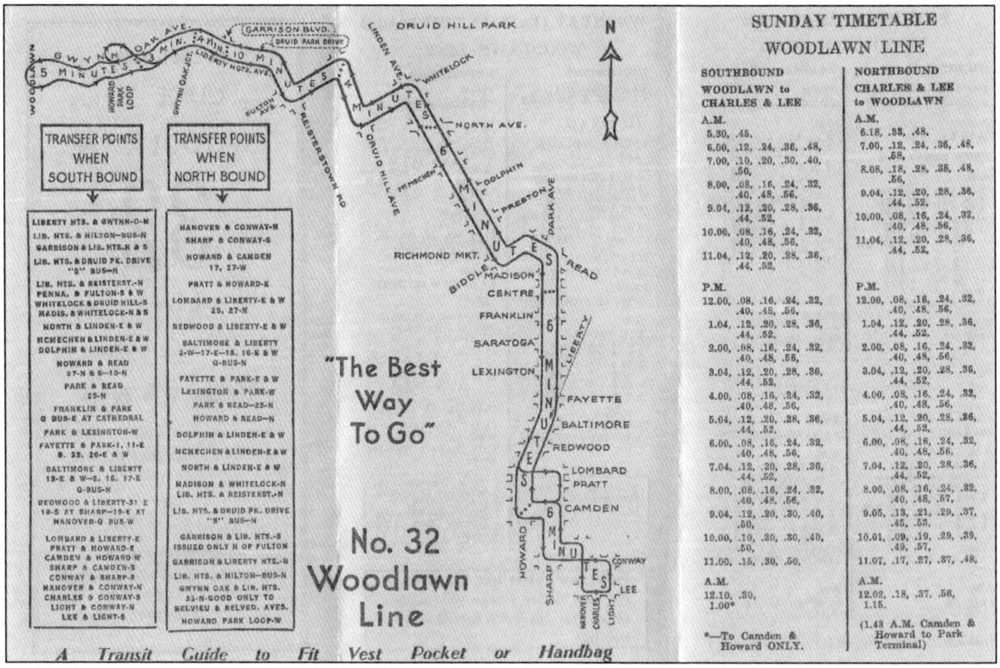

Streetcars and their tracks were originally owned by many different companies. Later, they consolidated and were run as United Railways and Electric Company and then the Baltimore Transit Company. The above card is for the 32 streetcar line. (Baltimore Streetcar Museum.)

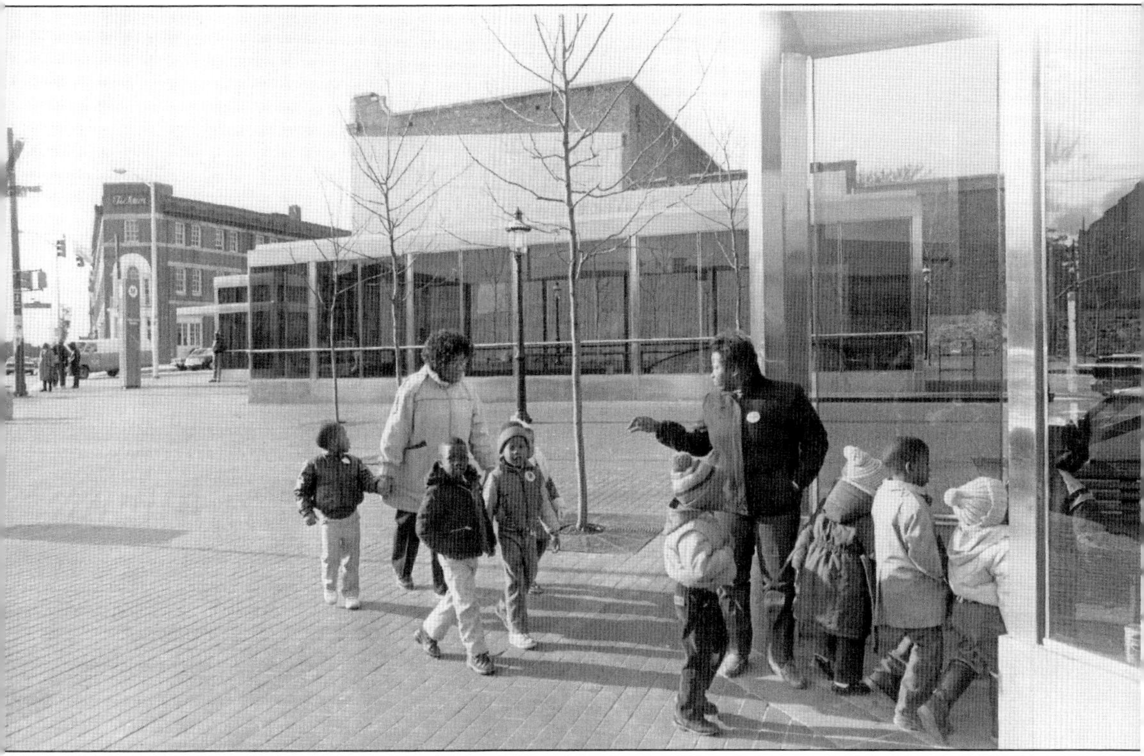

Baltimore has a subway system, though it is not as extensive as other northeastern cities. A master plan was published in 1965 and included six rapid transit lines radiating from the center of downtown Baltimore. The Maryland General Assembly funded only one of the six transit lines—the one that goes north and west from downtown to Owings Mills, Maryland, with stops at Lexington Market and Johns Hopkins Hospital. Fortunate for Reservoir Hill, there is a stop on the subway two blocks from the neighborhood at Pennsylvania and North Avenues. It was completed and opened on November 21, 1983. Preliminary plans are in place for a new red line that would run east and west and connect with the current northwest line. Pictured is the Penn-North subway station at its opening. (Tribune Photo Archives.)

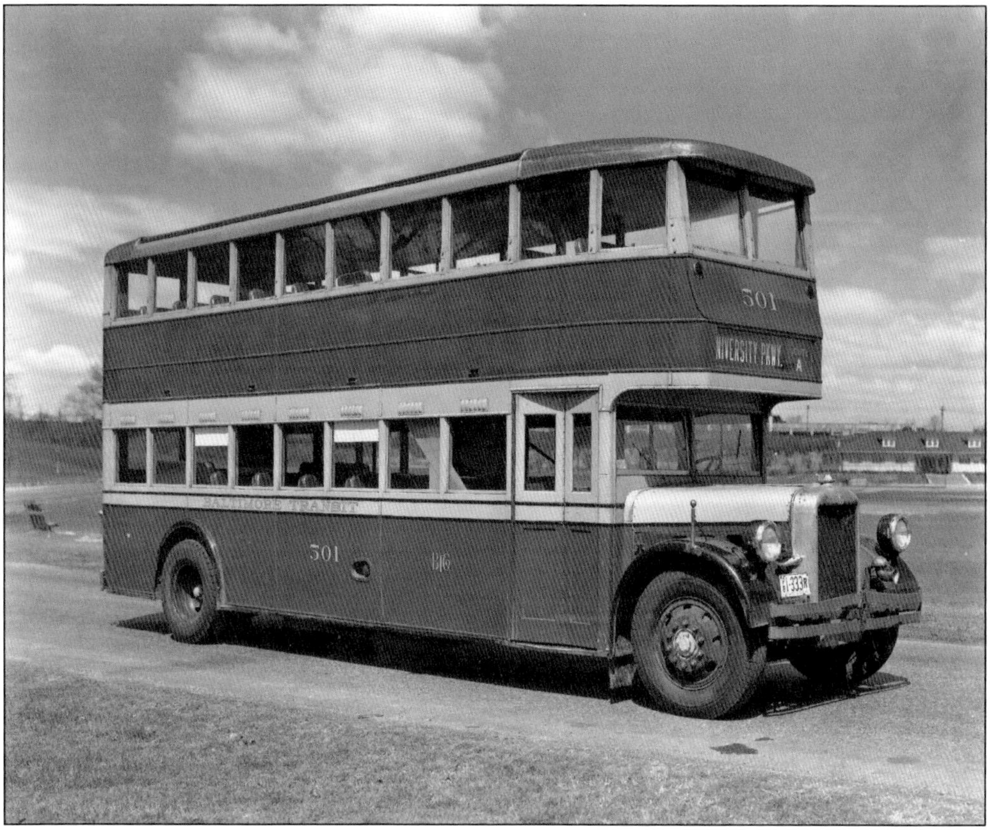

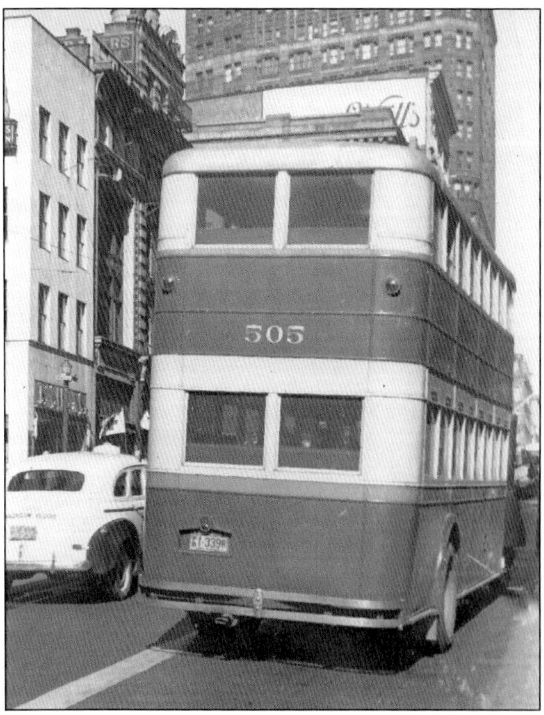

Buses were becoming more and more popular after World War II. The B bus line went through Reservoir Hill. It went up around the Park Avenue and Whitelock Street area and also to the Madison Avenue and Druid Lake Drive area. It was a double-decker bus that could take passengers to the heart of downtown at Charles and Light Streets. Today, bus route No. 5 takes a similar path, albeit with more modern buses. (Both, Baltimore Streetcar Museum.)

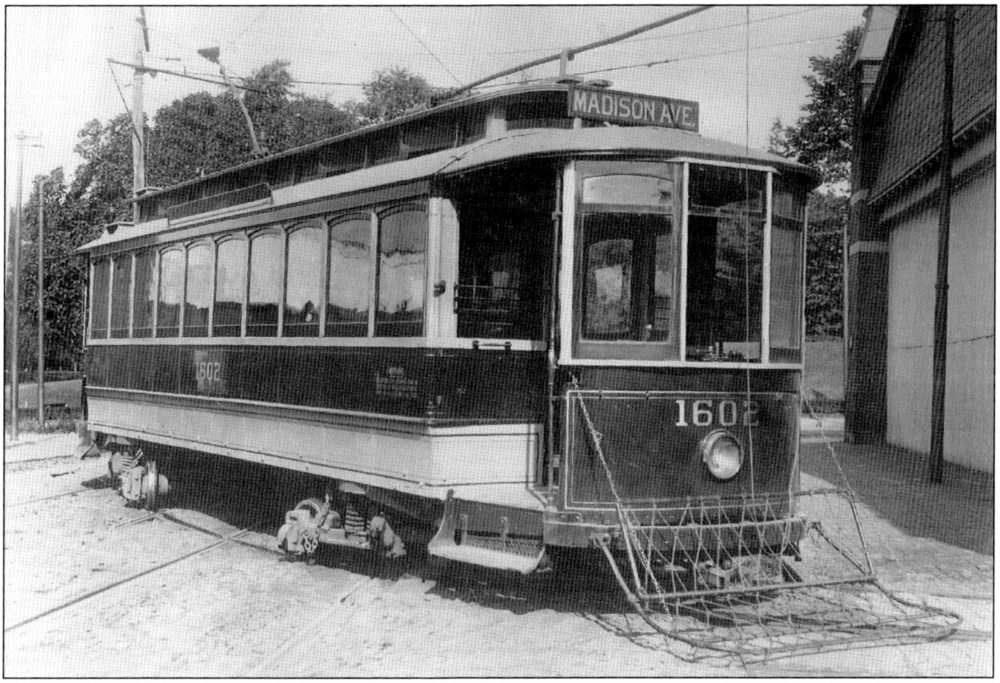

Streetcars began in 1859 when the city council granted the first horsecar franchises. By 1883, the first electric streetcar came into existence in the Hampden neighborhood located directly east of Reservoir Hill. A host of companies ran streetcar lines until 1899, when all Baltimore Streetcars were consolidated into the United Railways and Electric Company. Seen here are pictures of the Madison Avenue car barn located at the intersection of Madison and Druid Hill Park. Today, the Maryland Institute College of Art owns the building. The second floor was removed, and some other minor changes were made, but the building still has many of the original characteristics. (Both, Baltimore Streetcar Museum.)

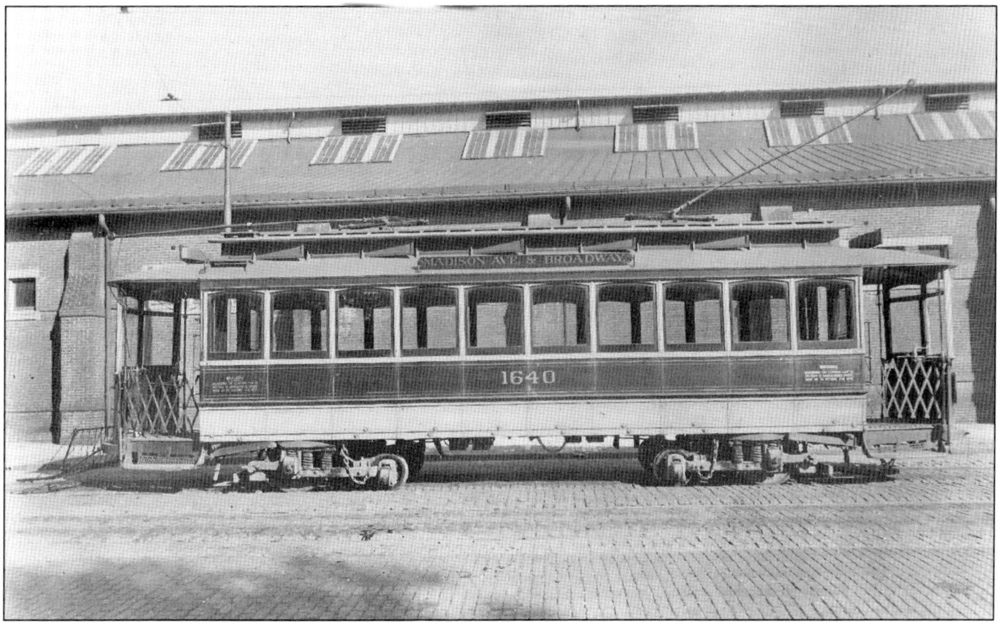

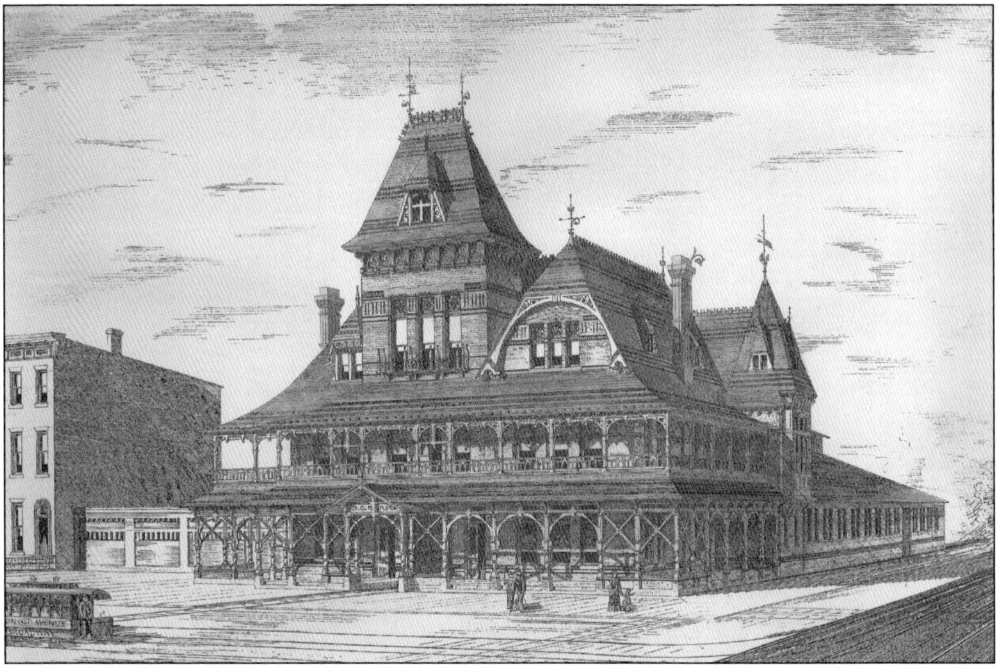

Car barns were architectural masterpieces and were typically covered with ornate stone and brickwork. Madison Avenue car barn was one of the first to be built in the city, and the location was chosen because of its proximity to the entrance to Druid Hill Park. All together, there were five streetcar terminals in the Reservoir Hill area. Seen here are an artist's rendering and a photograph of the Madison Avenue car barn in the late 1800s. (Above, Mike and Stacey Finney; below, Baltimore Streetcar Museum.)

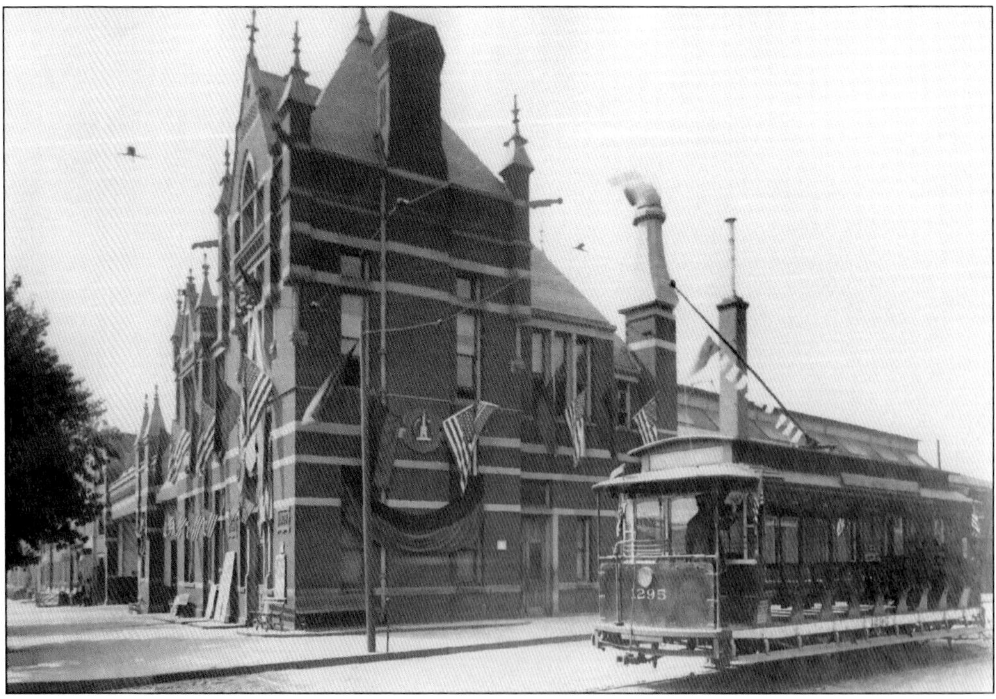

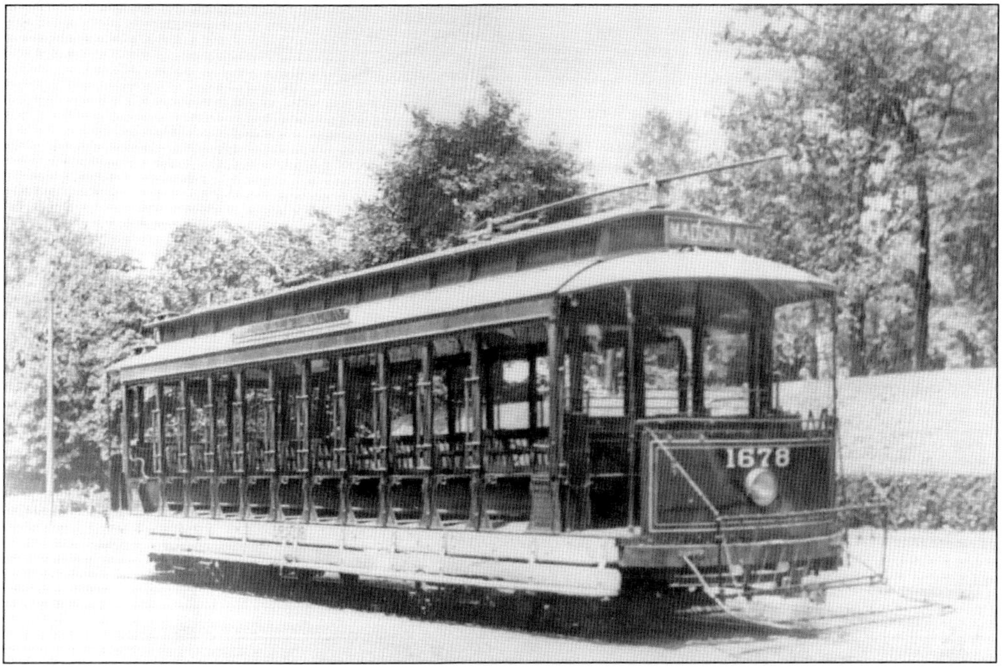

While streetcars were primarily used for public transportation, they also served a recreational use. In the late 1800s, there was a streetcar line within Druid Hill Park that would take guests to the different pavilions, which are still present today. It gave city residents a way to relax and enjoy the scenery of the park. Most of the pavilions are still used for recreation and park events, including one at the entrance of the Maryland Zoo in Baltimore. Both cars shown here are located at the edge of the park near the Madison Avenue entrance to Druid Hill Park. (Both, Baltimore Streetcar Museum.)

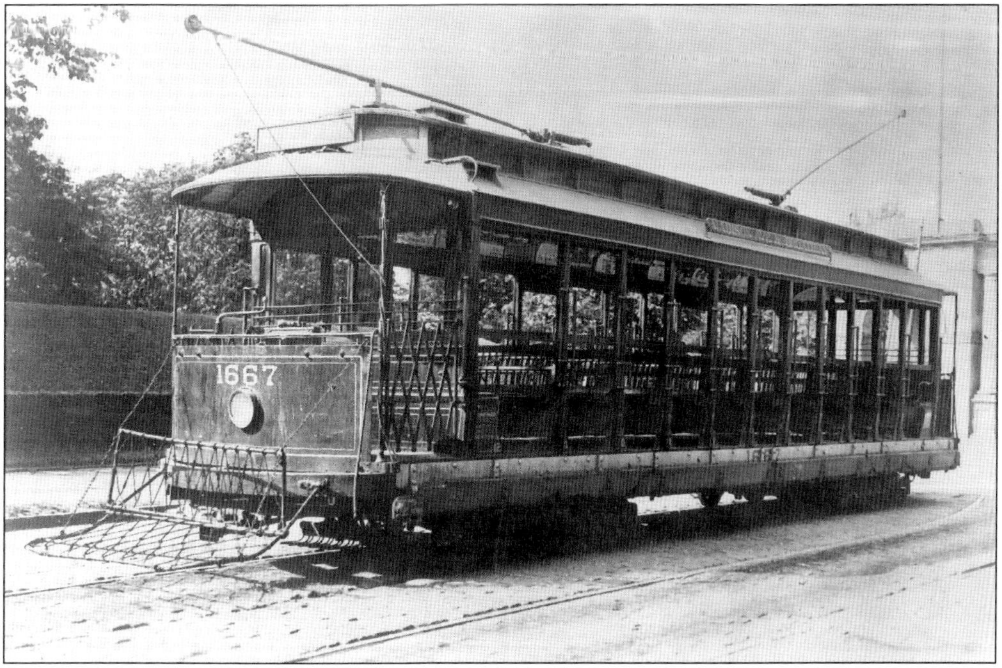

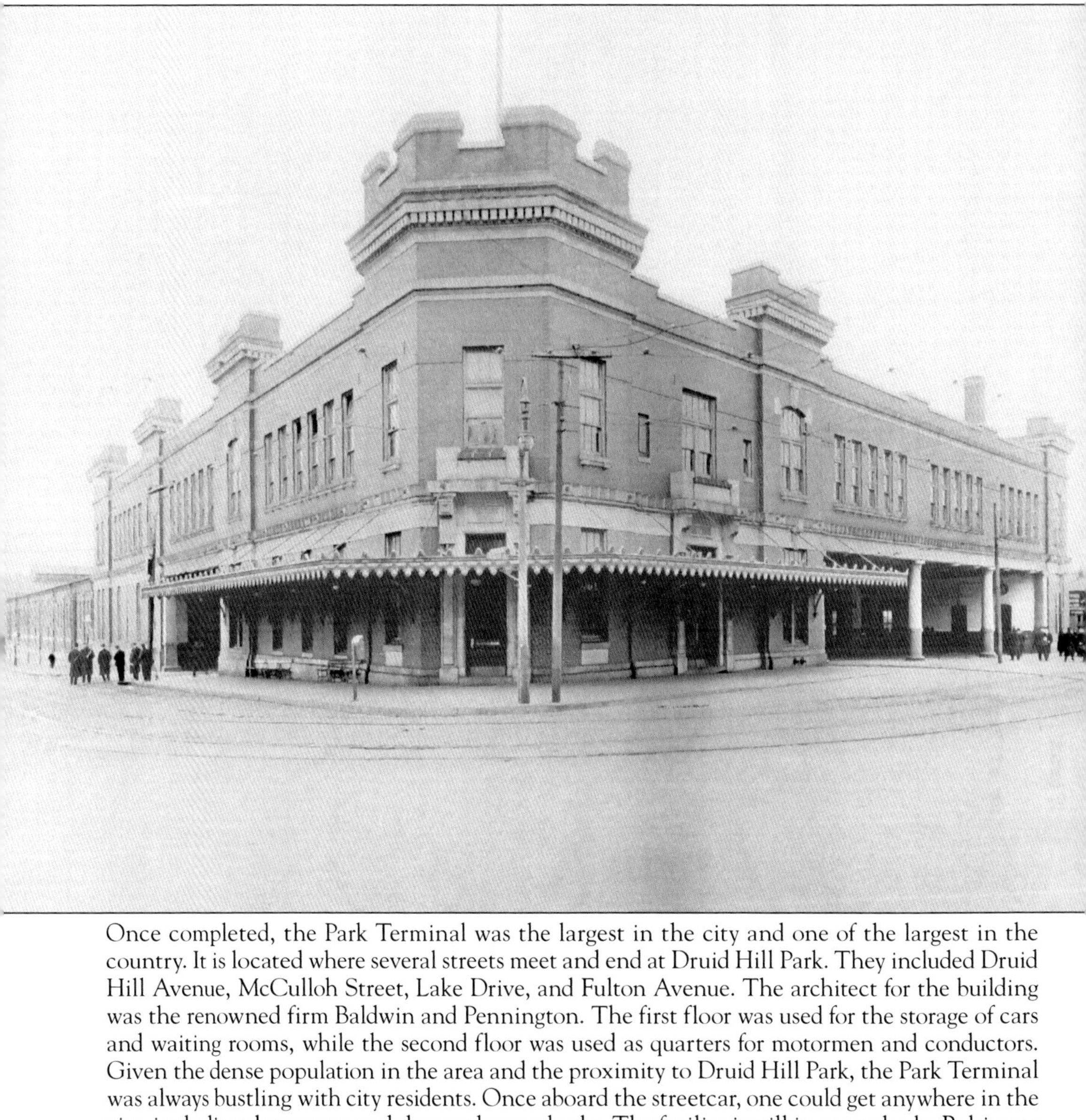

Once completed, the Park Terminal was the largest in the city and one of the largest in the country. It is located where several streets meet and end at Druid Hill Park. They included Druid Hill Avenue, McCulloh Street, Lake Drive, and Fulton Avenue. The architect for the building was the renowned firm Baldwin and Pennington. The first floor was used for the storage of cars and waiting rooms, while the second floor was used as quarters for motormen and conductors. Given the dense population in the area and the proximity to Druid Hill Park, the Park Terminal was always bustling with city residents. Once aboard the streetcar, one could get anywhere in the city, including downtown and the northern suburbs. The facility is still in use today by Baltimore City Department of Transportation. (Baltimore Streetcar Museum.)

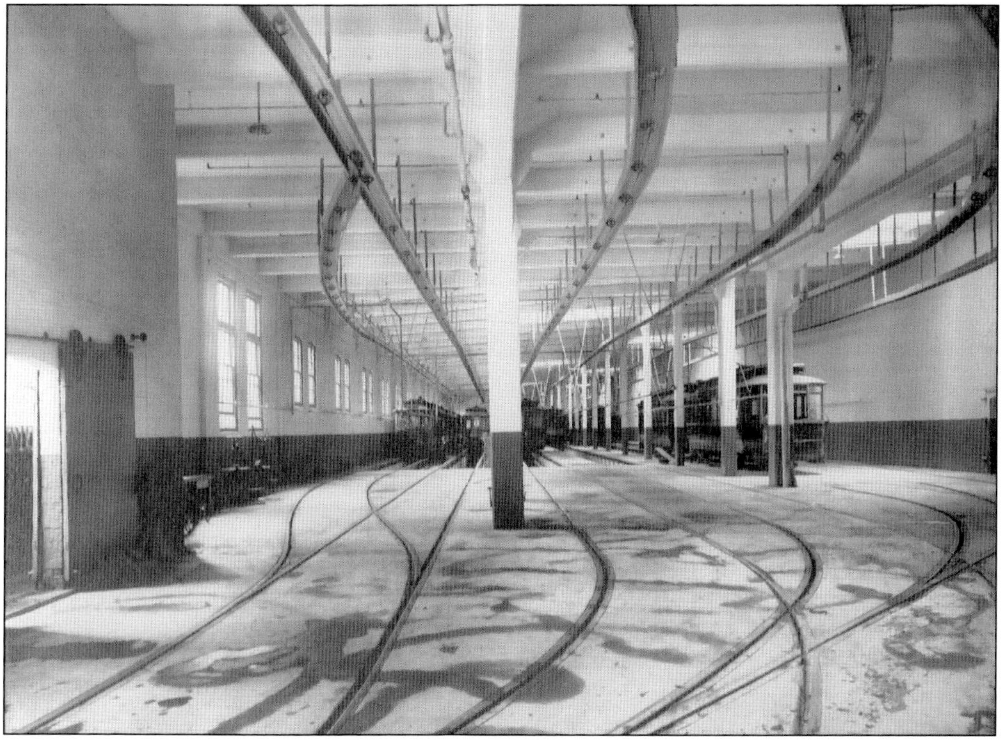

At one point, five different streetcar lines went through Park Terminal. Inside was a technologically advanced distribution of streetcar lines. The building was constructed to be fireproof after sparks had caused previous city car barns to burn. Pictured here is the interior of the first floor of Park Terminal. (Baltimore Streetcar Museum.)

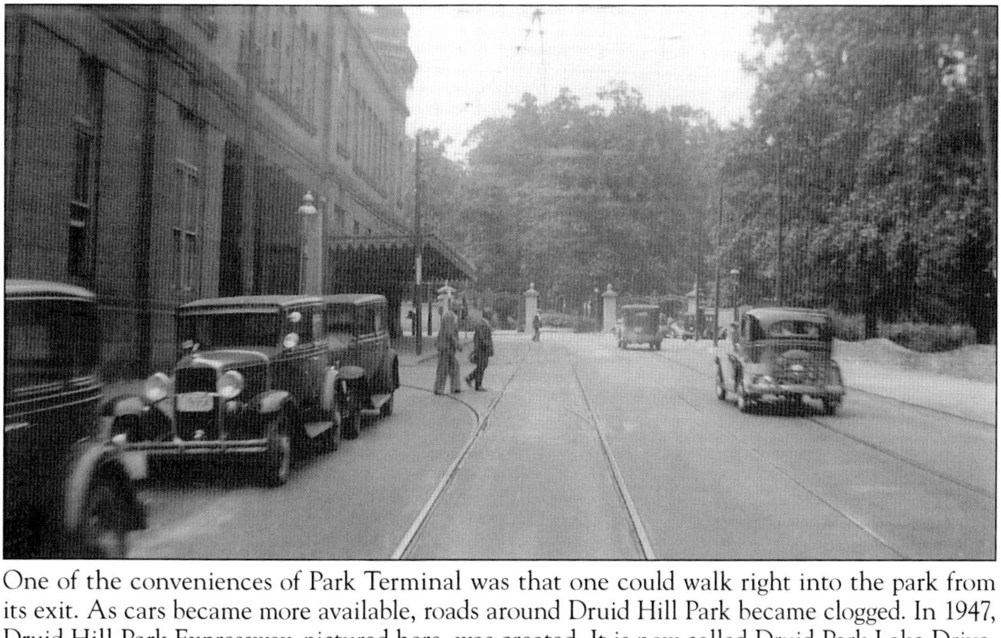

One of the conveniences of Park Terminal was that one could walk right into the park from its exit. As cars became more available, roads around Druid Hill Park became clogged. In 1947, Druid Hill Park Expressway, pictured here, was created. It is now called Druid Park Lake Drive. (Baltimore Streetcar Museum.)

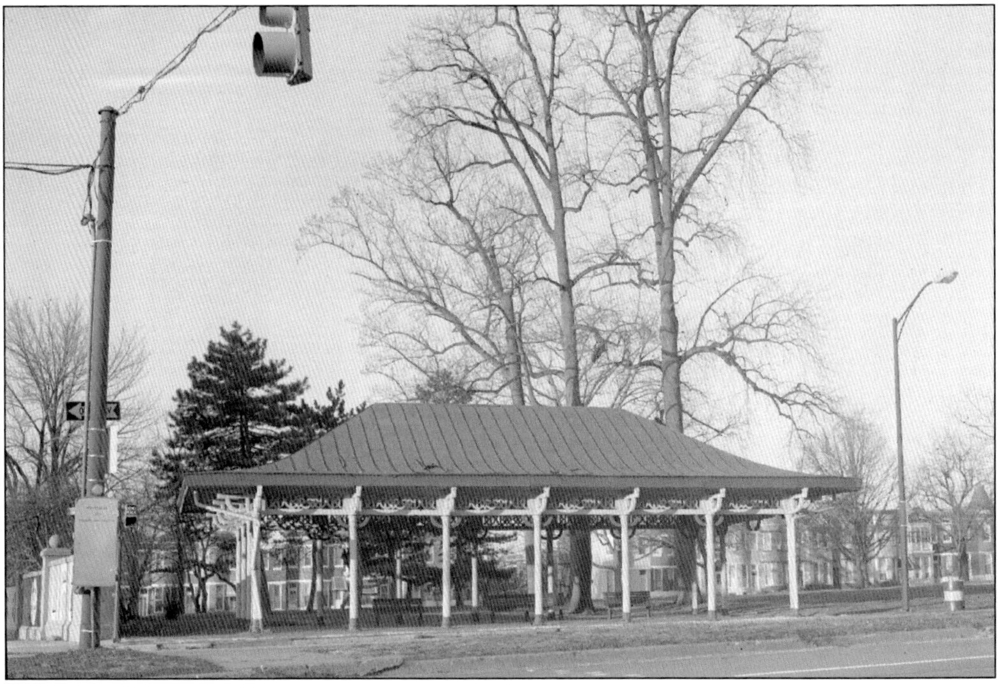

Pictured here next to Park Terminal was the Chinese Pavilion, which has now moved into Druid Hill Park off of the Madison Avenue entrance. Now a relatively quiet intersection, it once had thousands of city residents leaving Park Terminal to visit Druid Hill Park. (BCPL.)

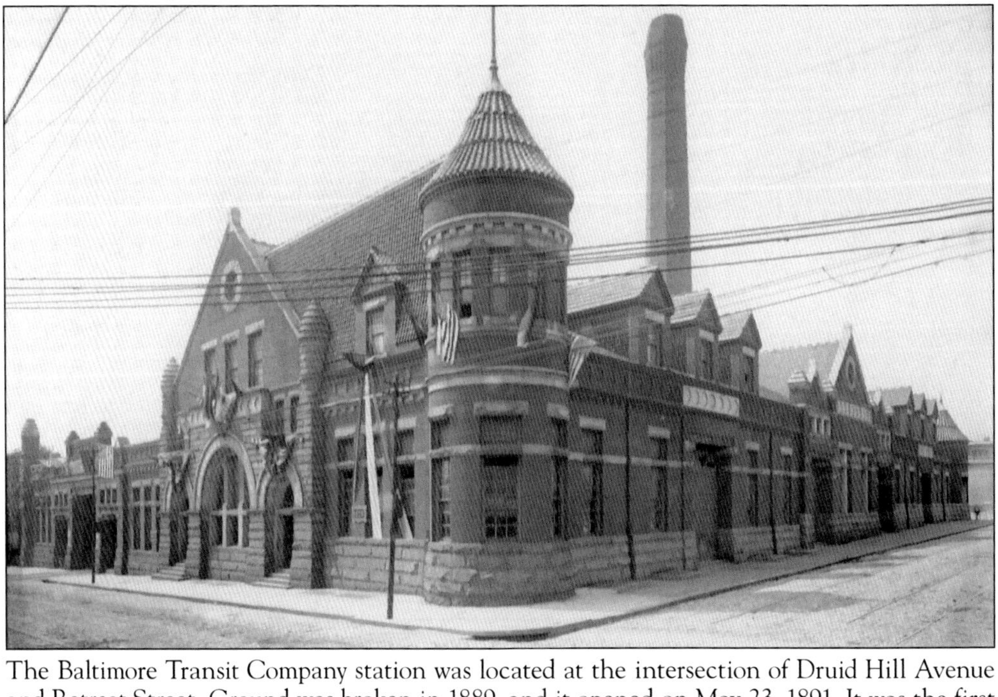

The Baltimore Transit Company station was located at the intersection of Druid Hill Avenue and Retreat Street. Ground was broken in 1889, and it opened on May 23, 1891. It was the first of the rapid transit barns to open in the city. Unfortunately, much of the building was lost to fire in 2005. (Baltimore Streetcar Museum.)

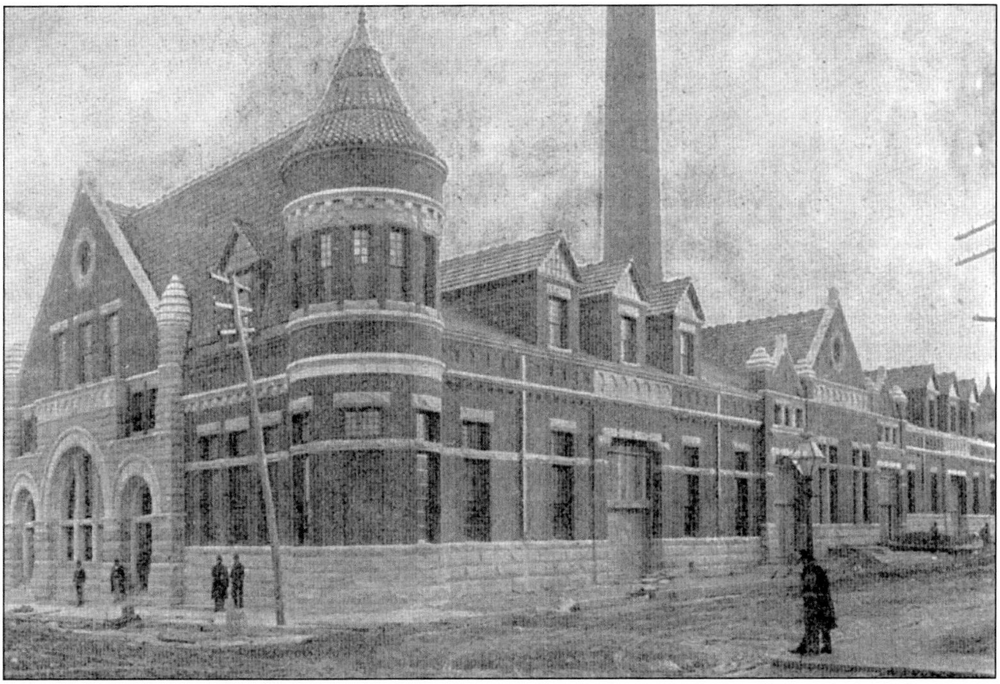

The imposing Baltimore Traction Company transit station at Druid Hill Avenue and Retreat Street was a relic from the days when Baltimoreans thought streetcars were the transit technology of the future. When built, it housed the cable machinery, blacksmith shop, and storage room for 38 cars. (Baltimore Streetcar Museum.)

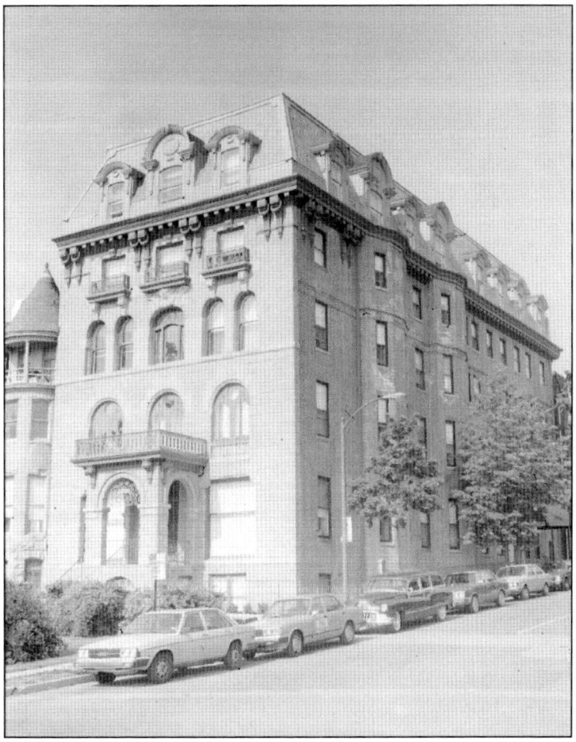

Bicycles became very popular at the turn of the 20th century. In 1881, 21 bicyclists came together to form the Maryland Bicycle Club. The club started out in a small building at North Avenue and John Street. In 1884, they moved to their new clubhouse at Mount Royal Terrace and Reservoir Streets. The building still stands and is used as a luxury apartment complex. (BCPL.)

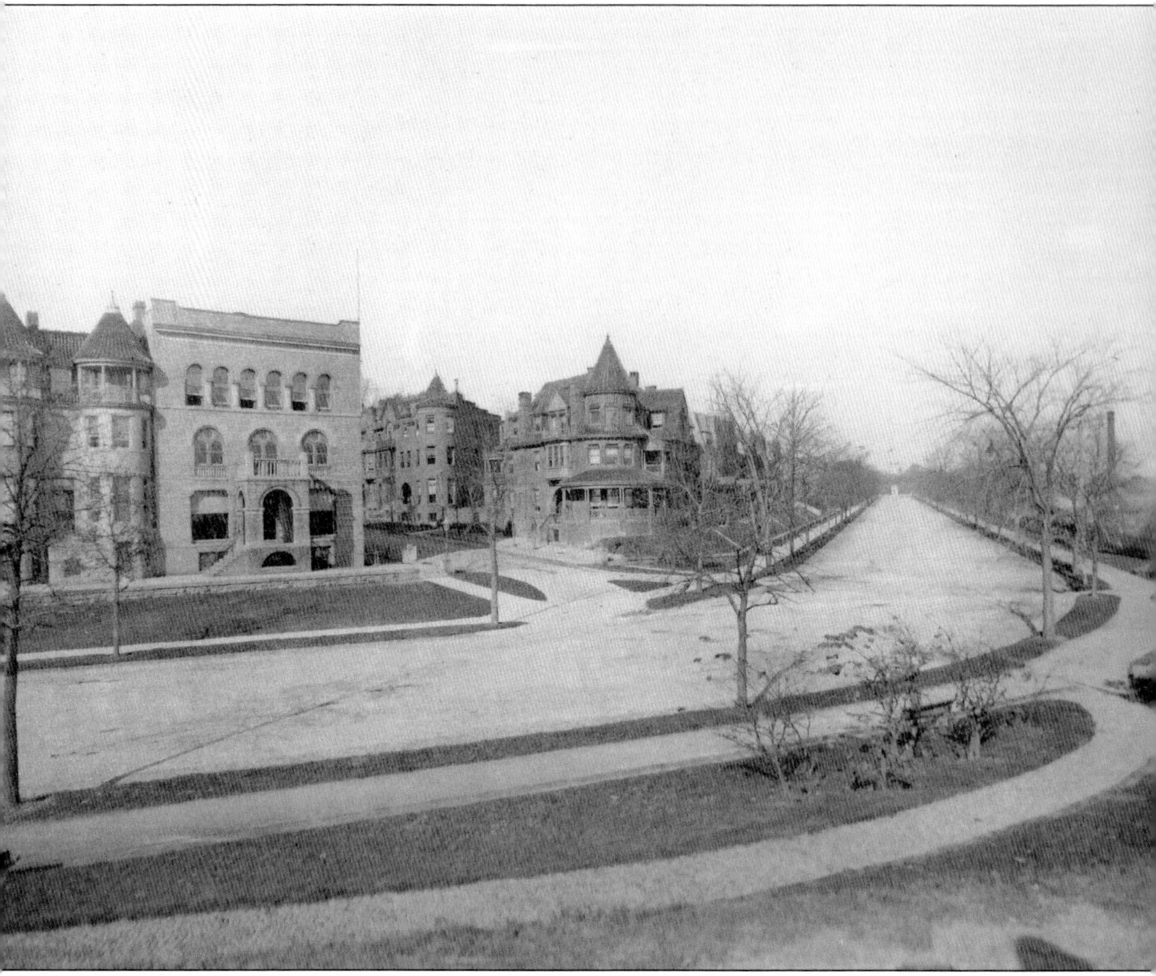

Pictured here is a photograph of Mount Royal Terrace and the Maryland Bicycle Club at the intersection of Mount Royal Terrace and Reservoir Street. Though the Maryland Bicycle Club maintained its presence on Mount Royal Terrace, the club opened a new location on Park Heights in 1900. For members and the public, it sponsored bike races, which ranged from 5 to 100 miles long. Though most races were local, they did race overseas in Europe and in other parts of the United States. The Maryland Bicycle Club building is the one with six identical windows on the third floor. Later, two more floors were added to the building. In 2012, it went under an exterior facade restoration project. It is a part of the Mount Royal Terrace Historical District. (CHAP.)

Four

Fountains, Gardens, and Monuments

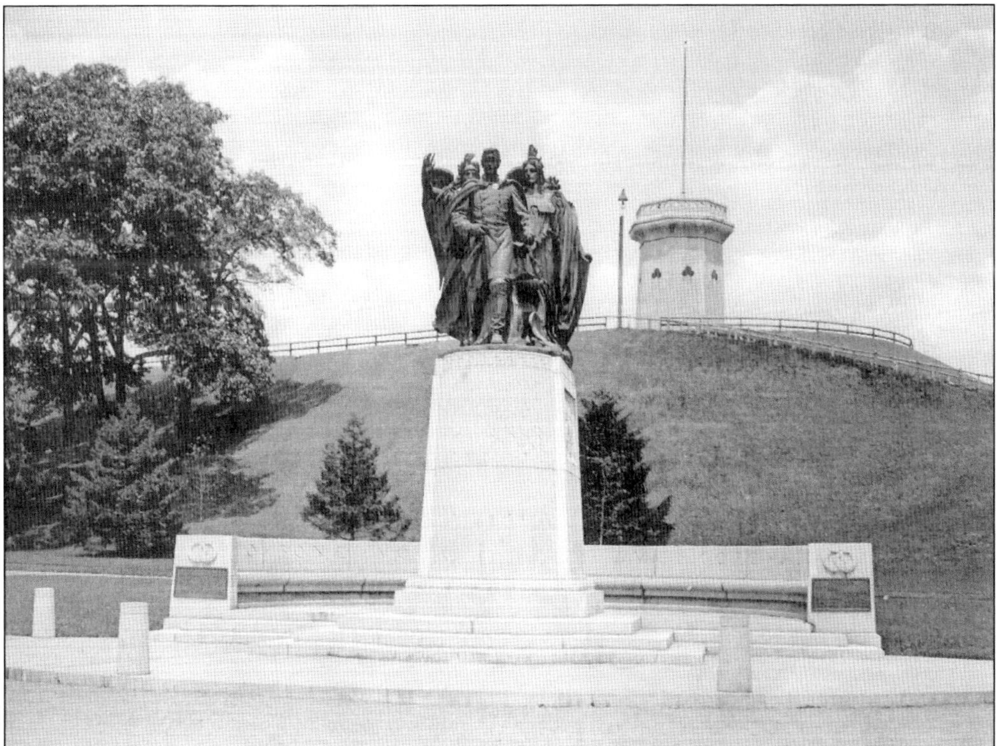

The Union Soldiers and Sailors Monument, sculpted by Adolph Weinman, was erected on November 7, 1909, at the end of Mount Royal Terrace at Druid Lake. It commemorates all branches—infantry, cavalry, artillery, and navy—as was decided by a state legislative act and approved by then-governor Warfield. In 1959, the monument was relocated to the southeast corner of Wyman Park off Charles Street close to the Baltimore Museum of Art. (Cal Buikema.)

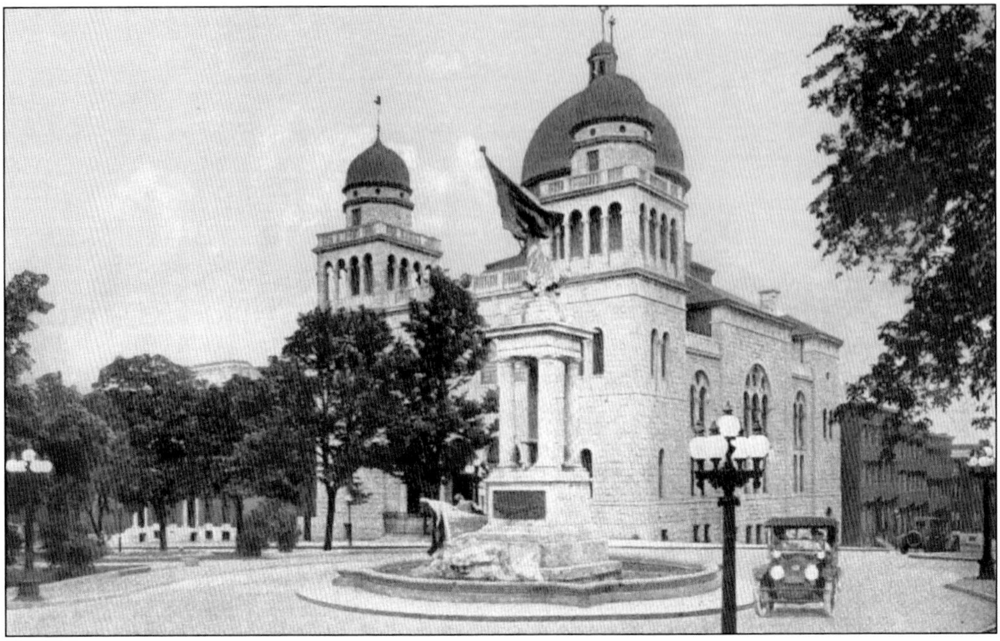

The Francis Scott Key Memorial was designed to commemorate the author of "The Star-Spangled Banner" as part of the "City Beautiful" movement that improved urban areas. Located at Eutaw Place and Lanvale Street, this monument was funded in 1907 by the founder of the Municipal Art Society, Theodore Marburg, at a cost of $25,000. French sculptor Jean Marius Antonin Mercie was commissioned to fashion this bronze figure depicting the poet, Key, standing in a marble boat with a sailor returning from a British ship on which Key had been held during the bombardment of Fort McHenry. (Both, BCPL.)

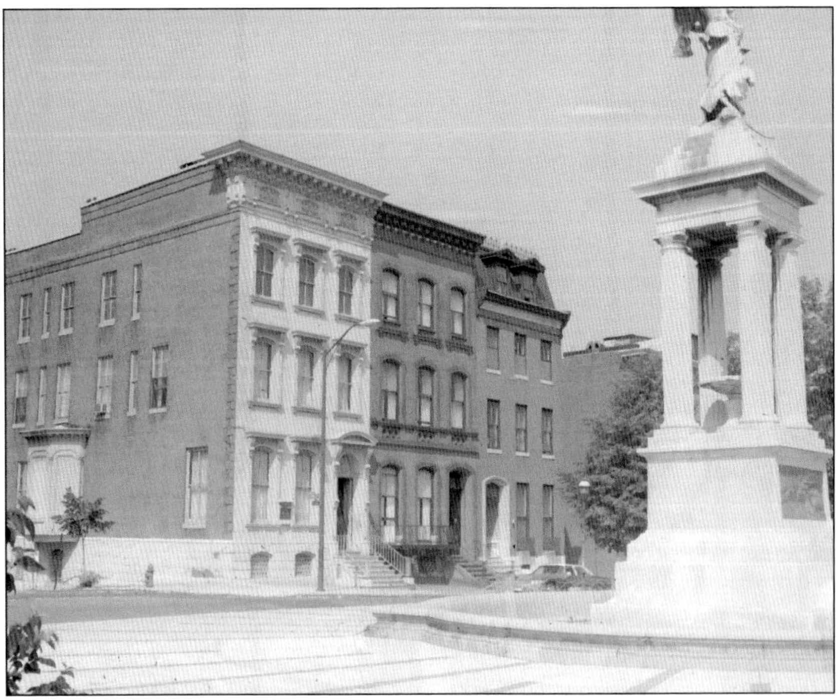

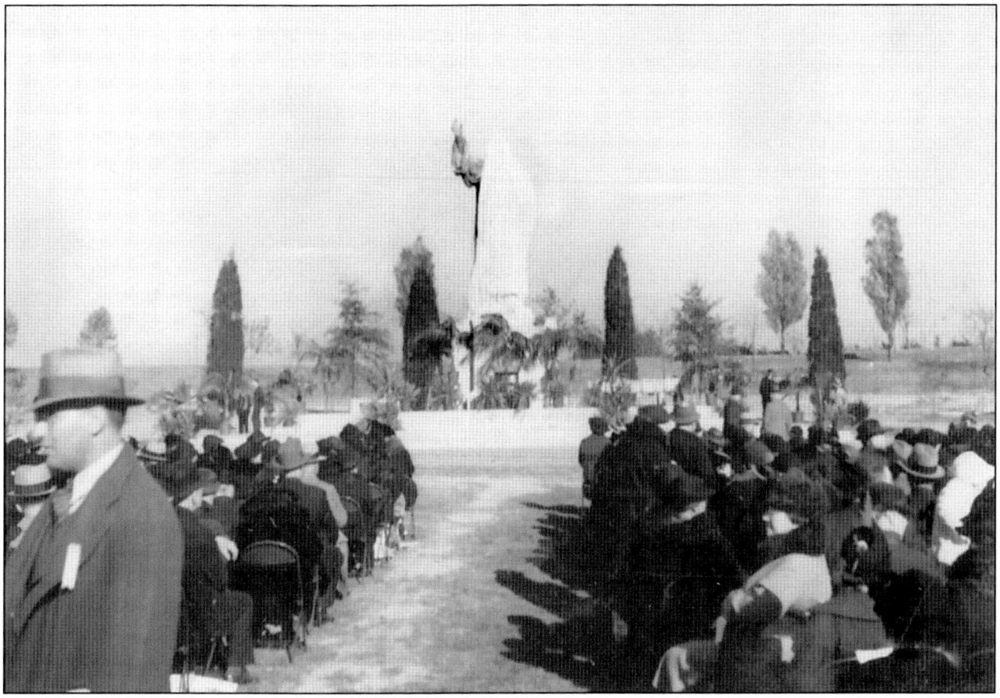

At 18 feet high, the Martin Luther Statue was put in place at the entrance to Druid Hill Park at Mount Royal Terrace above North Avenue on October 31, 1936. This park area was the previous location of the Mount Royal Reservoir. Hans Schuler was the sculptor commissioned for the statue following a donation of $50,000 by Arthur Wallenhorst. A ceremony was held for its unveiling, in which over 8,000 people attended. In 1958, upon construction of the Jones Falls Expressway, the Martin Luther Statue was moved to Lake Montebello in Baltimore. (Both, Dale Dusman collection.)

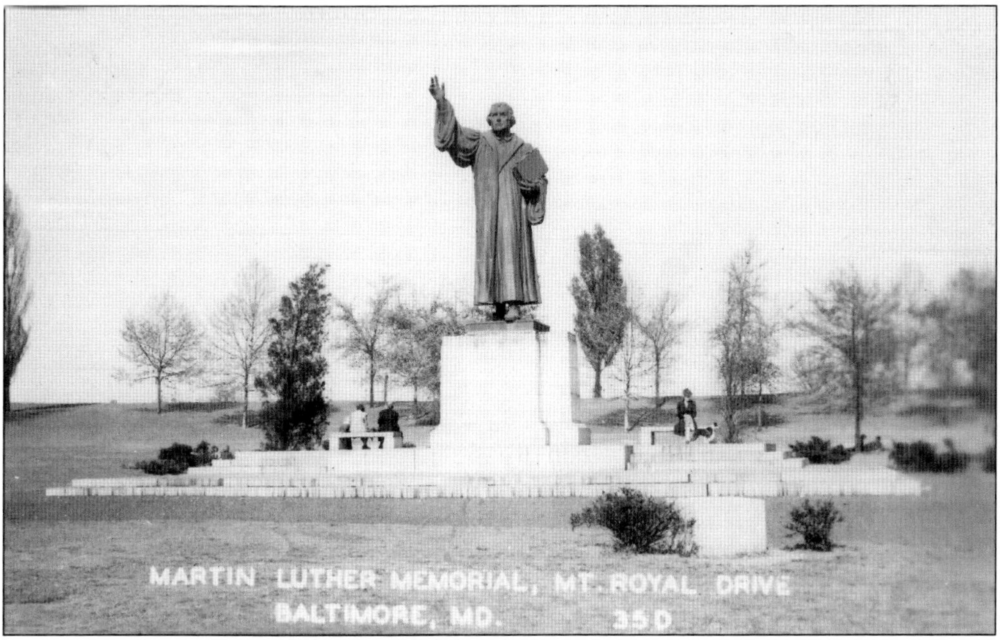

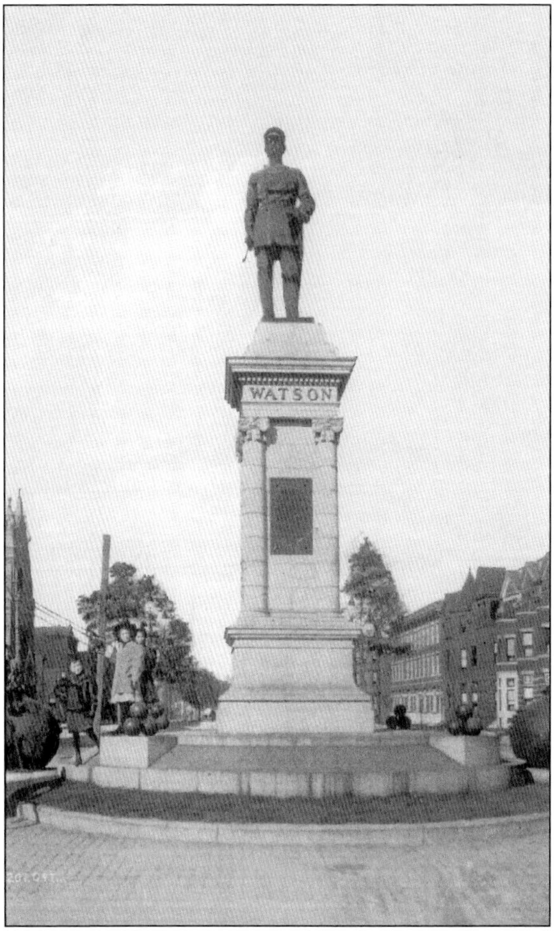

Col. William H. Watson was commander of the Maryland troops and was killed at the Battle of Monterey in 1846. This statue was commemorated in his honor in 1903, commissioned by Edward Berge, and erected by the veterans of the Mexican War as seen at the left. Originally located at Mount Royal Avenue and Lanvale Street, it was moved in September 1930 to make way for the Howard Street overpass. Since then, it has resided in its current location at Mount Royal Terrace and North Avenue. The photograph below is of a fountain that serves as a base for the current location of the statue. In the 1928 picture below are the Wells children of Mount Royal Terrace. (Both, Dale Dusman collection.)

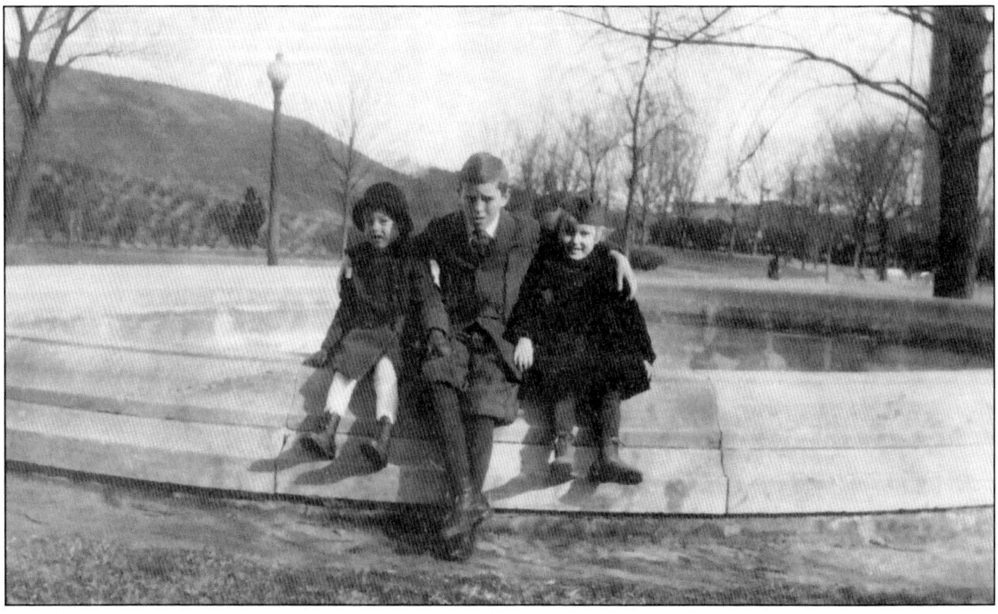

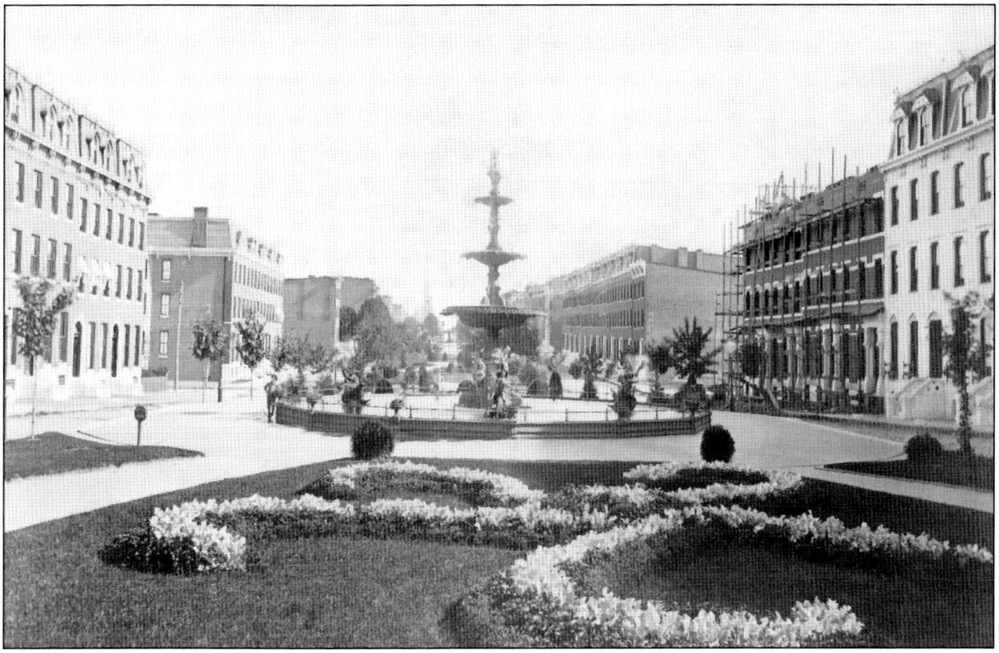

The most elaborate fountain and centerpiece on Eutaw Place was Centennial Fountain. Wealthy residents of Eutaw Place bought the fountain from Mott & Co. of New York after it was showcased at the Philadelphia Exhibition in 1876. Also called the Children's Fountain, it was located at the 1600 block of Eutaw Place and turned on May 19, 1877. The outer basin was 48 feet wide, and the fountain was 50 feet tall with a statue of a woman gracing the very top. Other statues were at the base of the fountain as well as vases for flowers. The fountain broke apart in the weight of ice and snow in 1945 and was removed shortly thereafter. No remnants remain today of this fountain. Above is an 1885 photograph, and below is one from 1910. (Above, Mike Finney; below, Cal Buikema.)

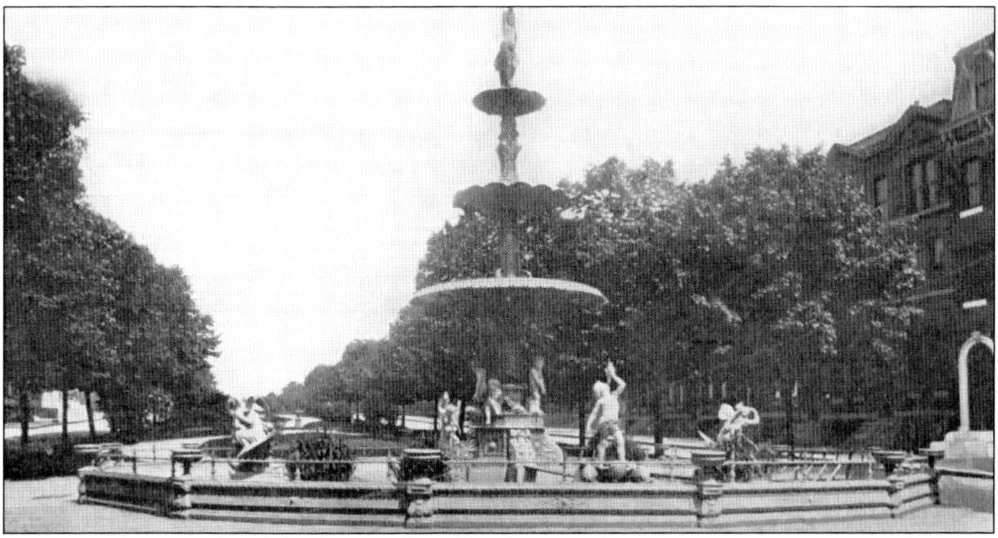

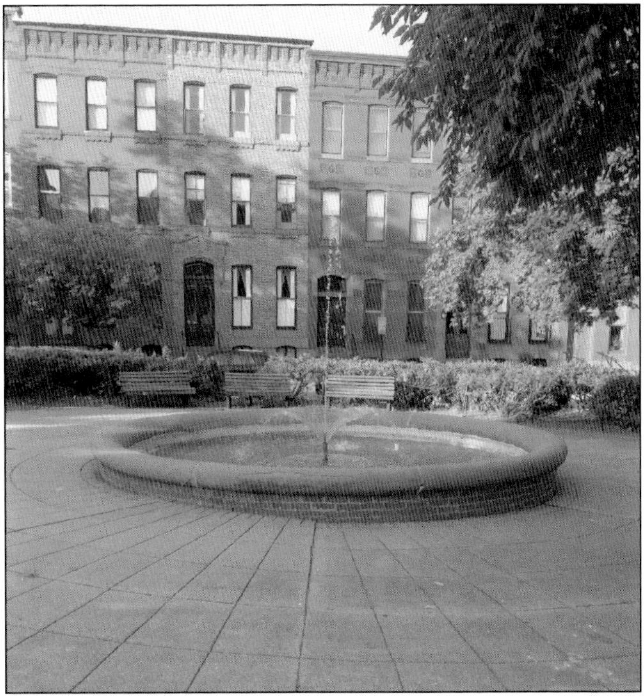

There are four fountains on Park Avenue at 1700, 1800, 2000, and 2400 Park Avenue. While the fountains are of no architectural significance, they show the distinguishing qualities of Park Avenue. Park Avenue has and continues to be one of the notable streets of Baltimore City. It begins in downtown and ends at Druid Hill Park. It goes through the Mount Vernon, Bolton Hill, and Reservoir Hill neighborhoods. (Author's collection.)

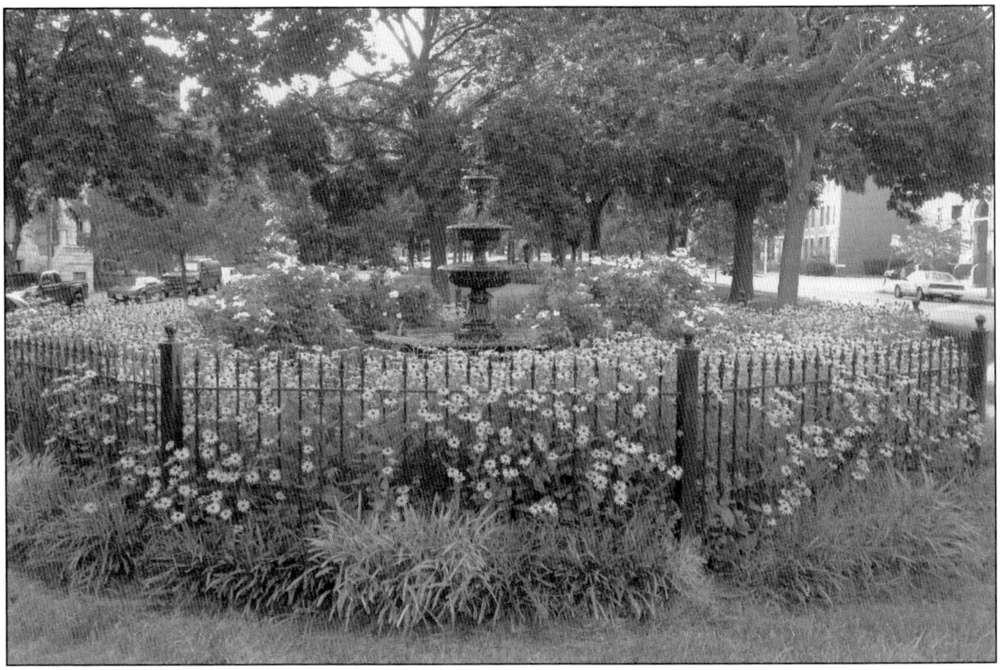

In 2009, a new fountain was added at 1800 Eutaw Place. The fountain was originally at a nursing facility in downtown Baltimore and then was moved to a facility in Baltimore County. Martin Millspaugh and the Midtown Community Benefits District acquired the fountain, and the Bolton Hill Garden Club persuaded Midtown Benefits to donate the fountain to Eutaw Place. Many active members of the Bolton Hill Garden Club, designed and maintain the surrounding gardens. (Author's collection.)

The Lady Baltimore Statue was erected at Mount Royal Terrace and North Avenue in a newly created park in 1980. The statue is from the original St. Paul Street Bridge, which was demolished in 1960. Three identical statues from the St. Paul Street Bridge sat for years at Cylburn Arboretum in North Baltimore. Pictured are guests listening in at the dedication. (Paul Hartzell.)

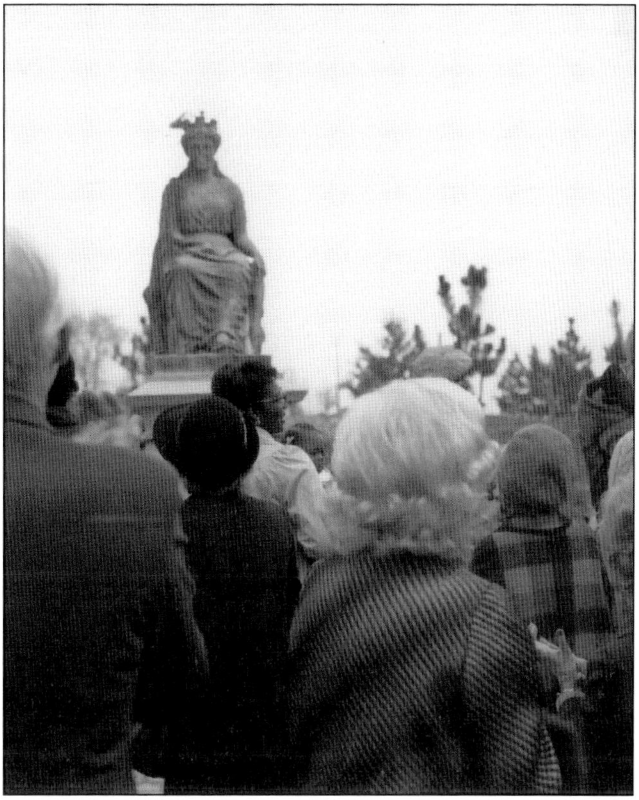

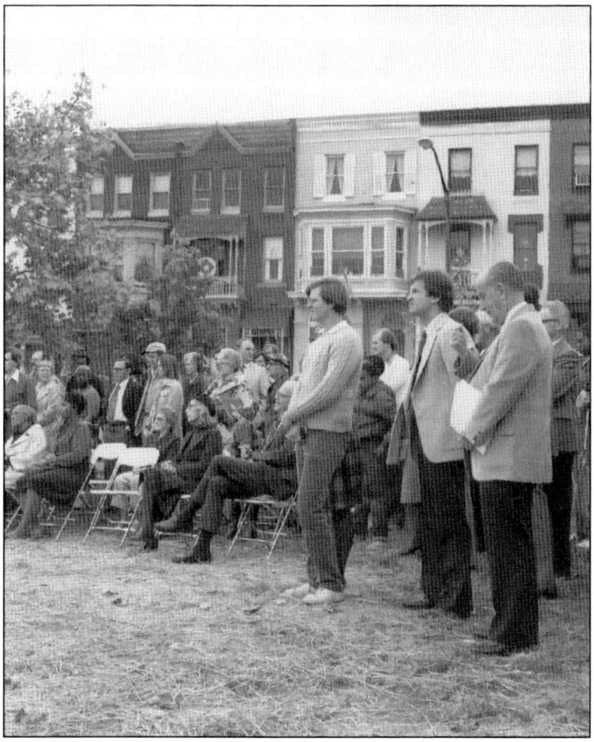

Residents of Mount Royal Terrace were the driving force behind this project. An unveiling was held, and hundreds were present. In celebration of the statue, a reunion was held 20 years after the dedication. The person on the far right is Mayor William Donald Schaefer, who also served as governor and comptroller for the State of Maryland. (Paul Hartzell.)

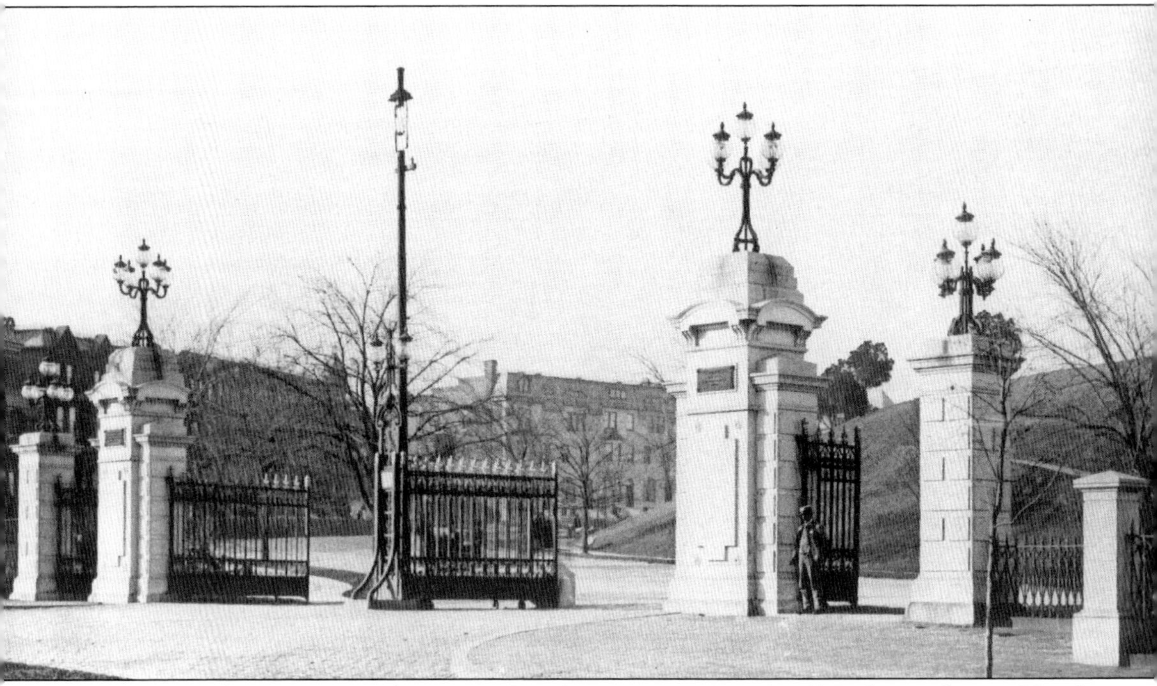

Completed in May 1895, the Mount Royal entrance to Druid Hill Park was designed by the famous Charles H. Latrobe. The central pier, already removed in this photograph, and two side pedestals were made of stone. The crowning ornament of the gate was a 16-foot lamp on top of the central pier constructed by Shultz Gas Fixture and Art Metal Company. It was the largest piece of bronze constructed in the city at that time. All together, the central pier was 35 feet tall, and the span of the entrance was 135 feet. By 1903, the central pier and lamp were removed to widen Mount Royal Terrace. Today, both side pedestals remain after the efforts of Cal Buikema and other residents resurrected the east pedestal. (Cal Buikema.)

Five

Religious, Community, and Family Life

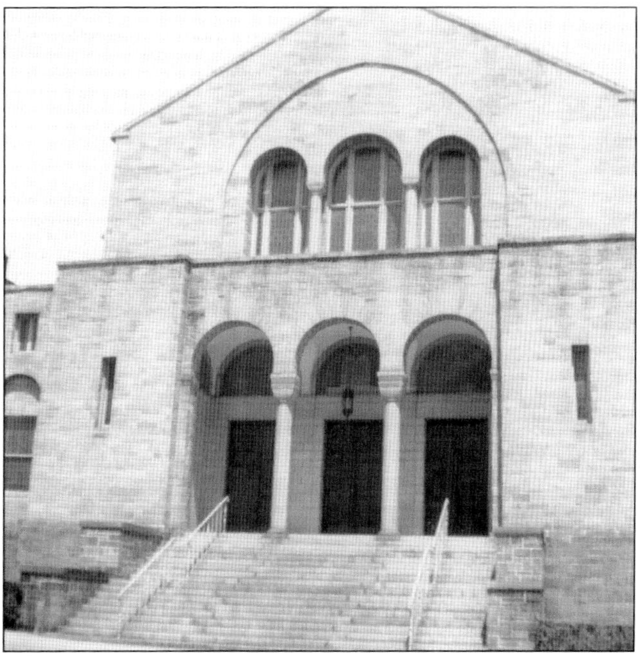

Chizuk Amuno, one of the largest and leading synagogues of Baltimore, moved to its third location on Eutaw Place between Chauncey Avenue and Brooks Lane in 1922. In 1962, Chizuk Amuno built a new synagogue at Stevenson Road and the Baltimore beltway but still continued to use its Eutaw Place location until 1974. Beth Am synagogue and its spiritual leader Dr. Louis Kaplan rededicated the building in 1974. (Jewish Museum of Maryland.)

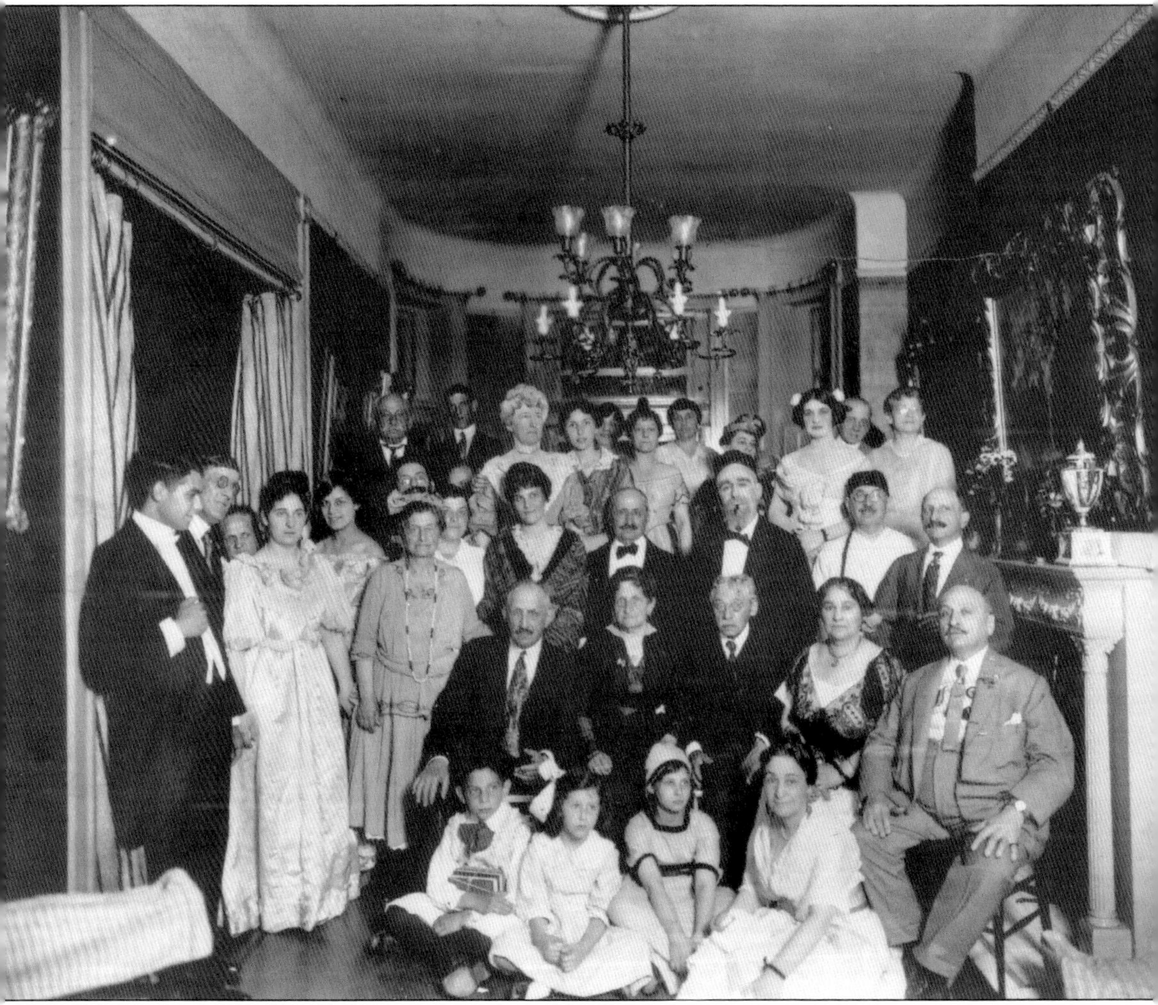

Pictured here is a gathering of the Wiesenfeld-Rosenfeld families in the home of Bernard and Blanche Wiesenfeld on the west side of Eutaw Place between North Avenue and Whitelock Street. Those pictured are, from left to right, (first row, sitting on the floor) Henry Wiesenfeld, Jeanette Myere, Amalia Eseneau Kohn, and Miriam Rosenfeld; (second row, sitting in chairs) Hirian J. Wiesenfeld, Rebecca Wiesenfeld Altmeier, Rebecca's husband, Adelaide Rosenfeld Eiserman, and Benjamin Wiesenfeld; (third row, standing) Malcolm Lowenstein, Robert Fox, the maid (Carrie), Bessie Wiesenfeld Cohen, Marie Lowenstein Rothschild, Sarah Wiesenfeld (slightly back), Moses Wiesenfeld, Bernard Wiesenfeld, Moses Rosenfeld, Jesse Rosenfeld, and Joseph Wiesenfeld; (fourth row, standing) Goodie Rosenfeld, Morton Fox, Blanch Wiesenfeld, Bernice Wiesenfeld, Rose Rosenfeld, Marie W. Lowenstein, Flora Eiserman, Elsie Gutman, Helen Rosenfeld, Lee Eiseman, and Minnie Wiesenfeld. The picture was taken in 1918. (Jewish Museum of Maryland.)

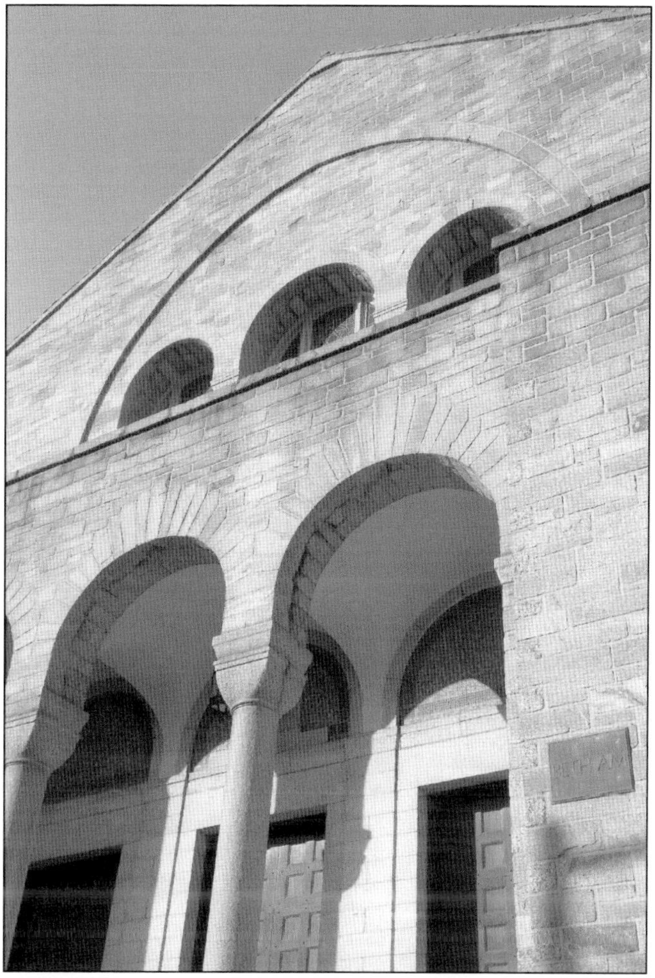

The advent of Beth Am Synagogue allowed for the building on Eutaw Place to remain in continuous use as a Jewish congregation—one that remains influential within the city and an active participant in the community. During the first half of the 20th century, the Reservoir Hill area was predominantly Jewish. Many of Baltimore's largest synagogues were once located in and around the Reservoir Hill area. Today, Beth Am is leading the way connecting the Jewish population to its neighbors in Reservoir Hill and the surrounding area. Jewish families have moved back, and Beth Am's most recent spiritual leaders, Rabbis Daniel Burg and Jon Konheim, have purchased homes in the neighborhood. Pictured at right is a recent exterior view, and shown below is an interfaith meeting in the lower-level community room. (Right, author's collection, below, Howard P. Fink.)

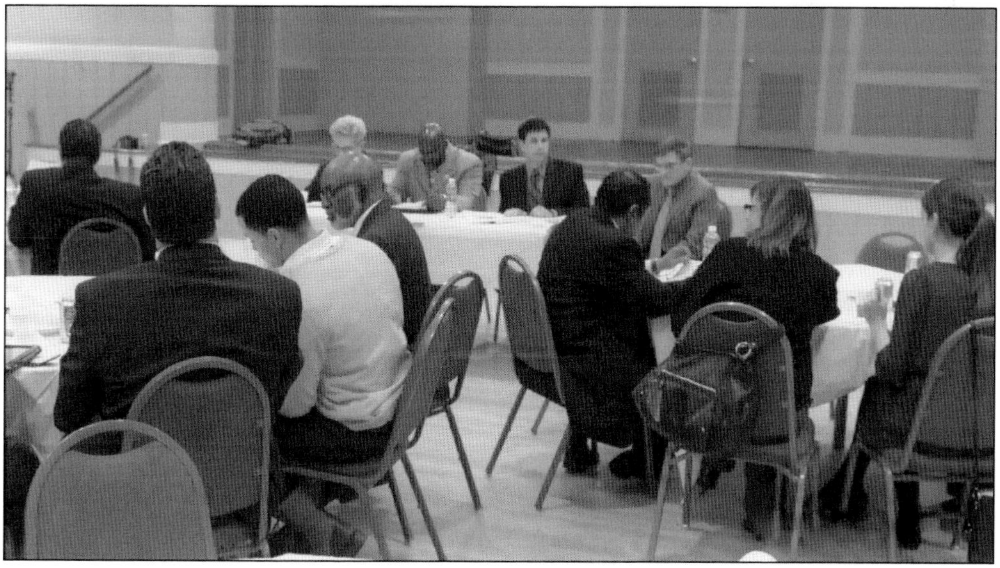

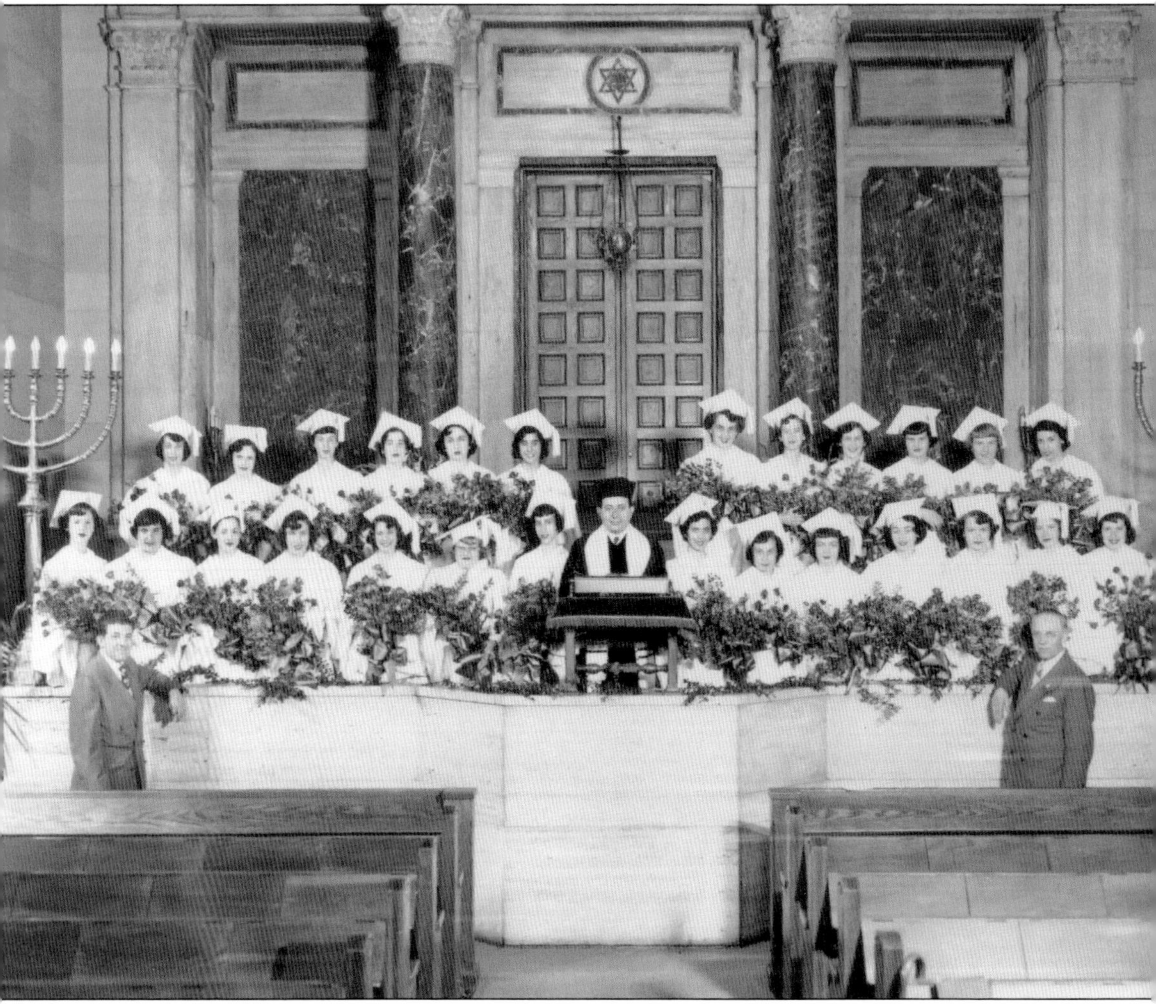

This is the girls' confirmation class in the interior of Chizuk Amuno Synagogue at Eutaw Place and Chauncey Avenue. From left to right, Rabbi Israel Goldman, Cantor Weisgal, and Hymen Saye also are depicted on the bimah. (Jewish Museum of Maryland.)

This photograph, taken on Linden Avenue near Whitelock in 1908, is of Moses Wisenfeld. Note the streetcar lines in the road. In an era before cars, seeing someone on horseback was not uncommon. In fact, many homes in Reservoir Hill have garages in their backyard that were originally carriage houses. (Jewish Museum of Maryland.)

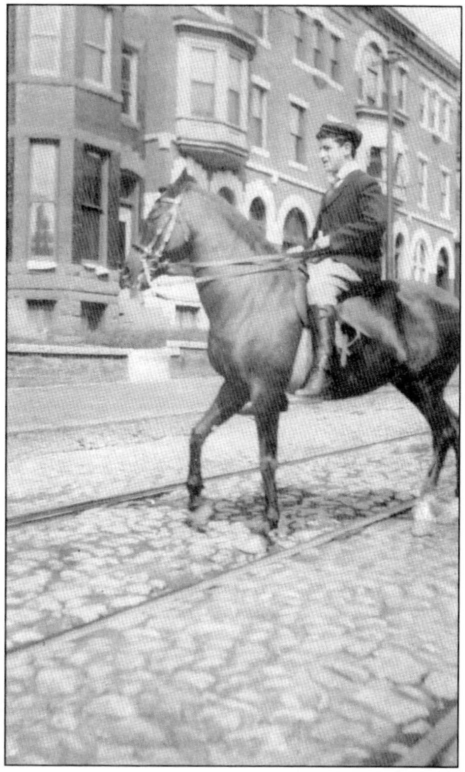

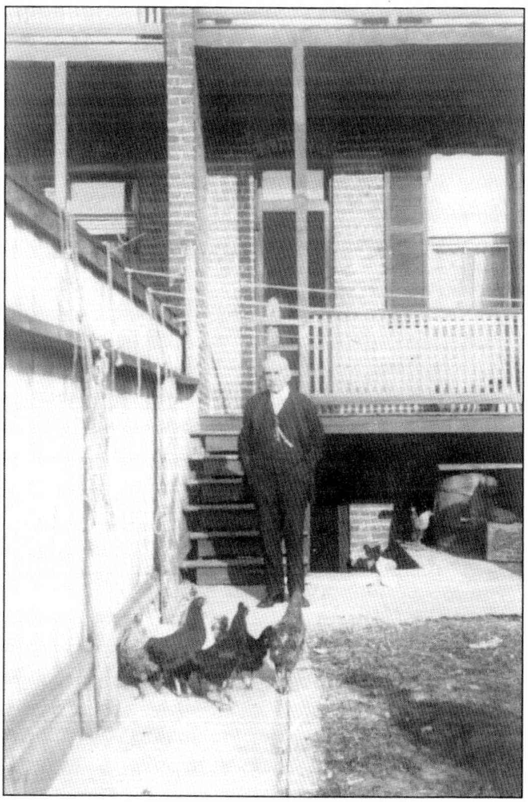

Pictured here is Aaron Summerfield at 2430 Lakeview Avenue. Note the chickens in the backyard, something that has not been allowed in the city for decades. At the time of this picture, Reservoir Hill would have still been on the outskirts of the city. (Jewish Museum of Maryland.)

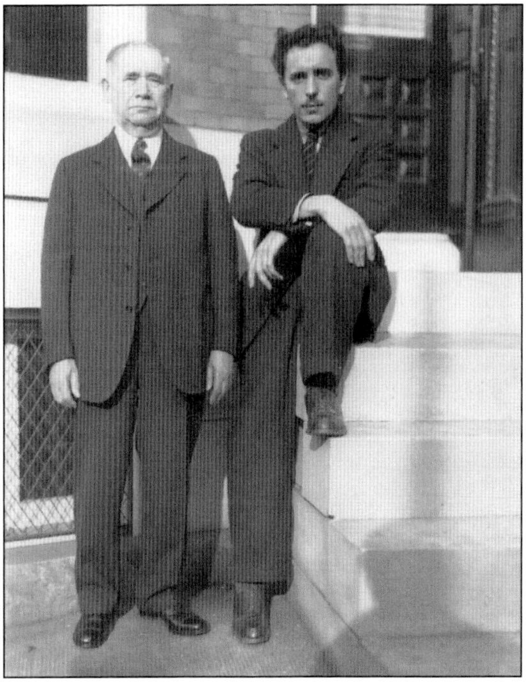

This is a 1939 photograph of Reuben Kramer and his father on the steps of 2323 Linden Avenue. The Kramers are both in suits, which was common for that era. Women would also look nice in dresses and hats. Considering it gets fairly hot in Baltimore during the summer, their clothing formality must have made for a miserable summer walk. (Jewish Museum of Maryland.)

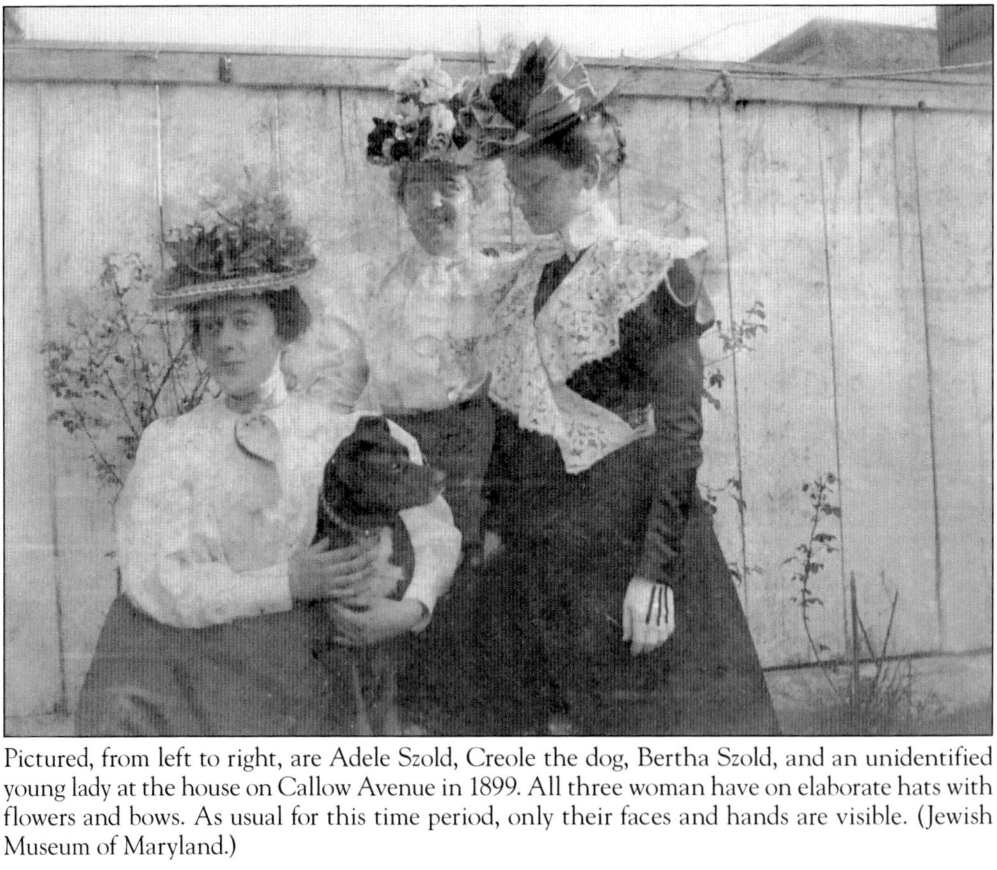

Pictured, from left to right, are Adele Szold, Creole the dog, Bertha Szold, and an unidentified young lady at the house on Callow Avenue in 1899. All three woman have on elaborate hats with flowers and bows. As usual for this time period, only their faces and hands are visible. (Jewish Museum of Maryland.)

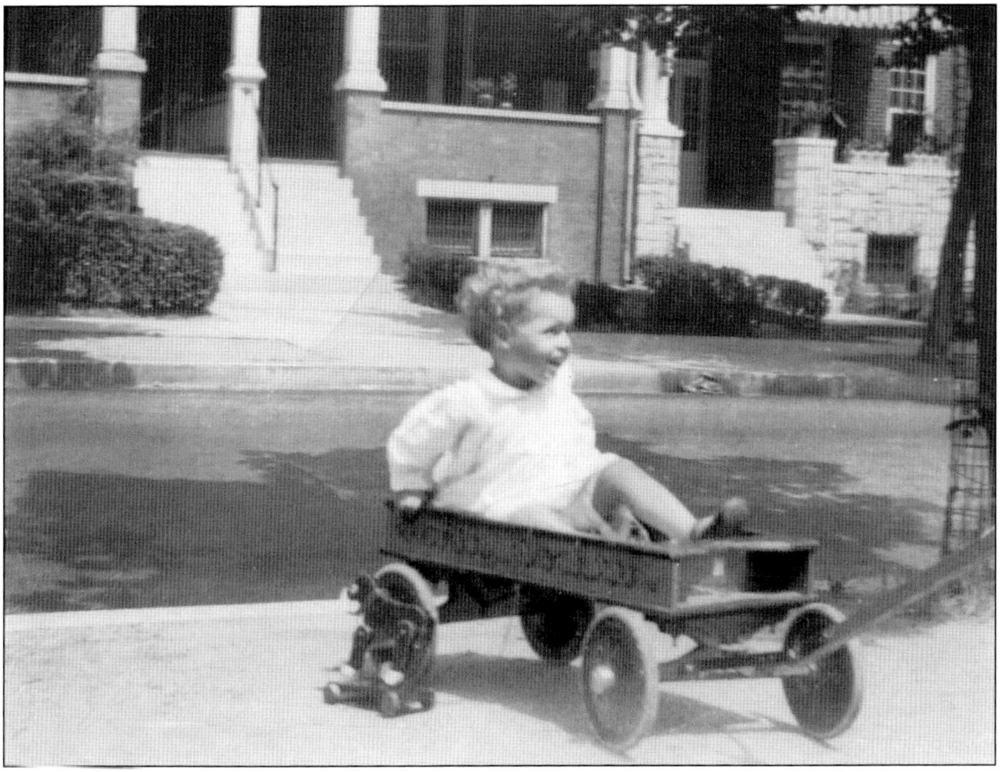

Robert L. Weinberg is pictured above at two years old sitting inside a wagon. The picture was taken at 943 Brooks Lane. Children often filled the streets and sidewalks playing games, a sight still common today. (Jewish Museum of Maryland.)

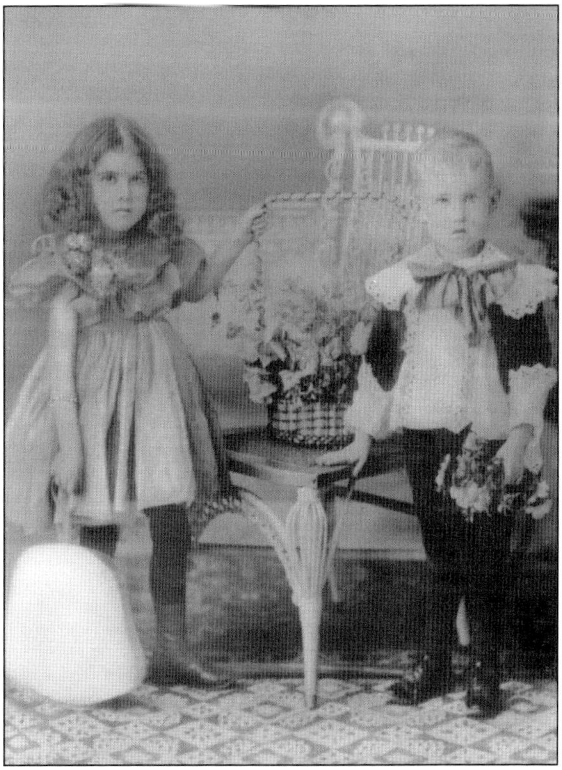

Edward Rosenfeld was born in Baltimore in 1900. He had two brothers and two sisters and never married. His father had a shoemaker shop on Baltimore Street. Eddie had an early job as sign painter's apprentice and went to the Maryland Institute College of Art for about one semester. During the war, he had a job in Washington, DC, framing pictures. Pictured are Edward Rosenfeld and his sister. (Jewish Museum of Maryland.)

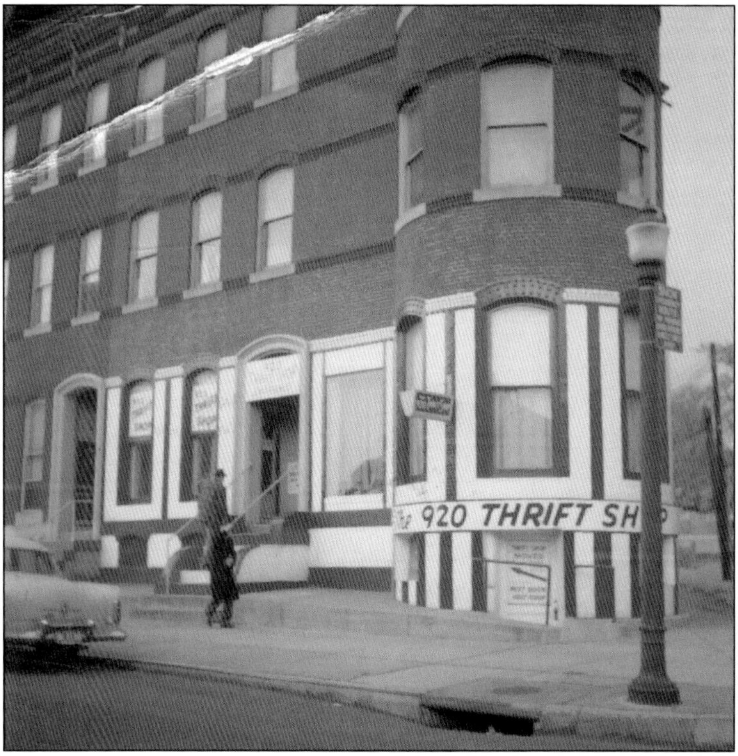

Pictured here is the exterior of the National Council of Jewish Women (NCJW) Council Thrift Shop at 920 West North Avenue in Baltimore, which was between Eutaw Place and Linden Avenue. The store was widely used by the Reservoir Hill residents and was known for great bargains. (Jewish Museum of Maryland.)

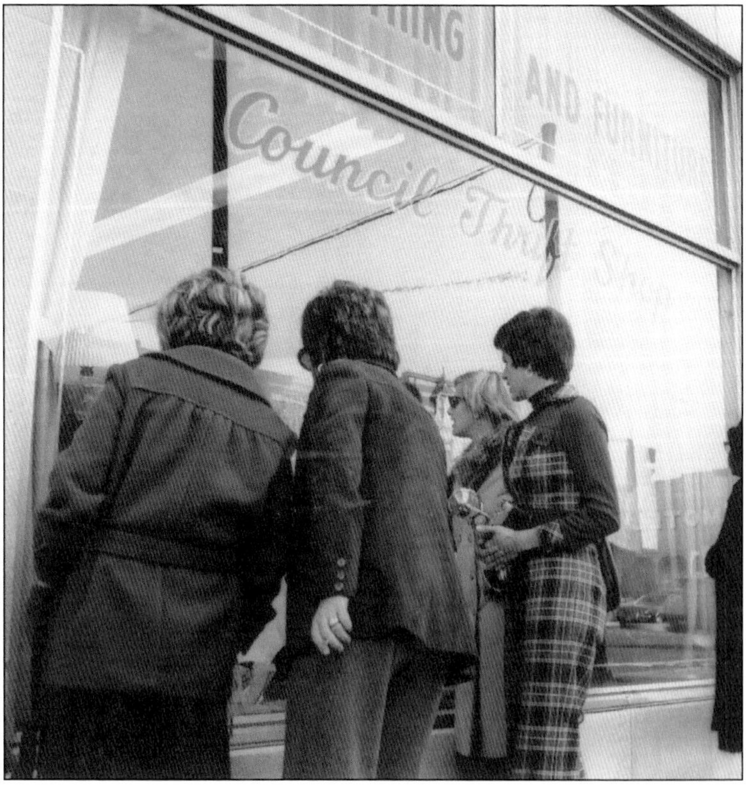

Pictured here are four women window-shopping outside the NCJW Council Thrift Shop on North Avenue between Eutaw Place and Linden Avenue. NCJW is a nondenominational national social service organization that has had a chapter in Baltimore since 1893. (Jewish Museum of Maryland.)

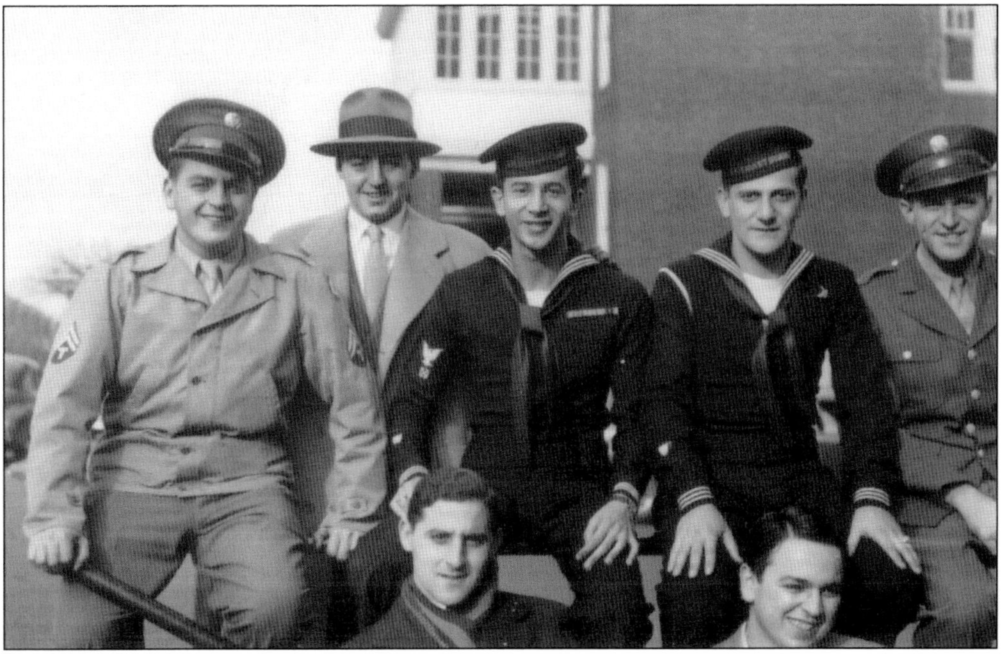

Standing on the corner of Whitelock Street and Callow Avenue in 1943 are seven neighborhood guys in the service. They are (first row) Jimmy Waranch and N. Peppy Gitomer; (second row) Jacob Gitomer (Army), Alvin Lavenstein, Coleman Weiss (Coast Guard), Elliott Robinson (Coast Guard), and Leonard Grossman (Army). (Jewish Museum of Maryland.)

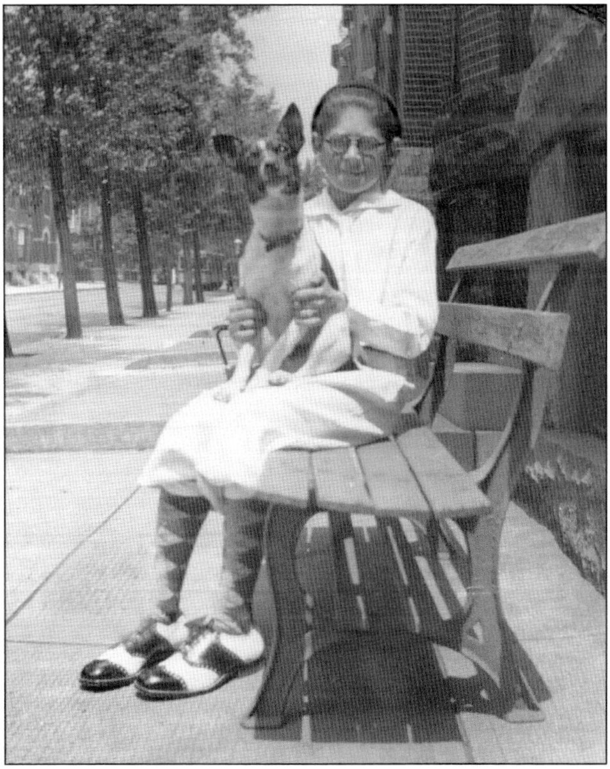

Daniel and Teresa Klotzman lived at 2103 Linden Avenue. Shown in front of their home is their son Melvin Klotzman, around age 12, with his pet dog. Note that in the top left corner a streetcar is seen entering the neighborhood. (Theoda Klotzman.)

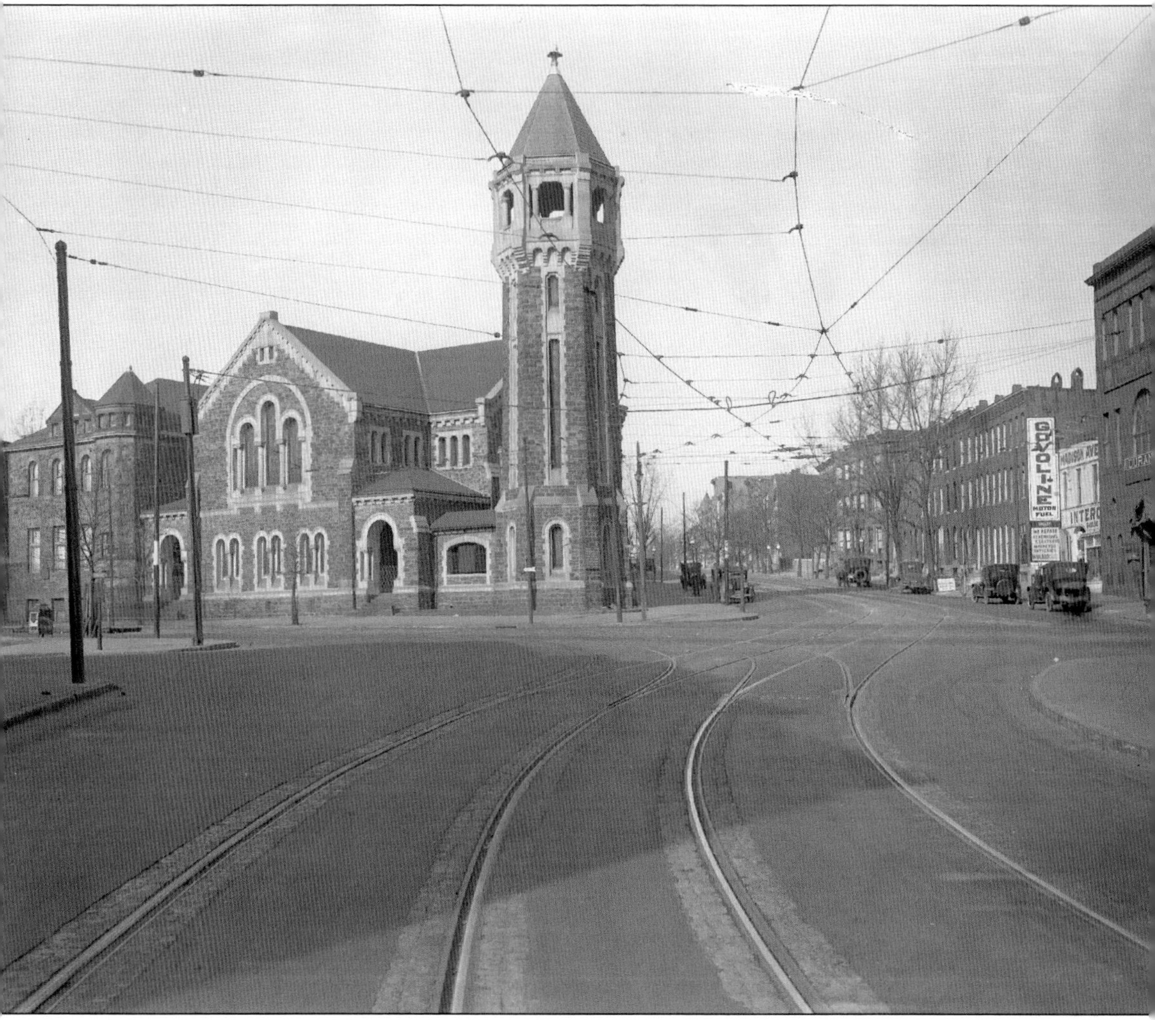

Originally home to Babcock Memorial Presbyterian Church, the building was complete on May 30, 1893. The church was named after Maltbie Davenport Babcock, the pastor of Brown Memorial Presbyterian Church located on Park Avenue in Bolton Hill. On October 18, 1953, the building was sold to Union Temple Baptist Church, which is still a thriving congregation today. The Rev. Gabriel P. Churn Jr. is the current pastor of Union Temple Church. (MDHS.)

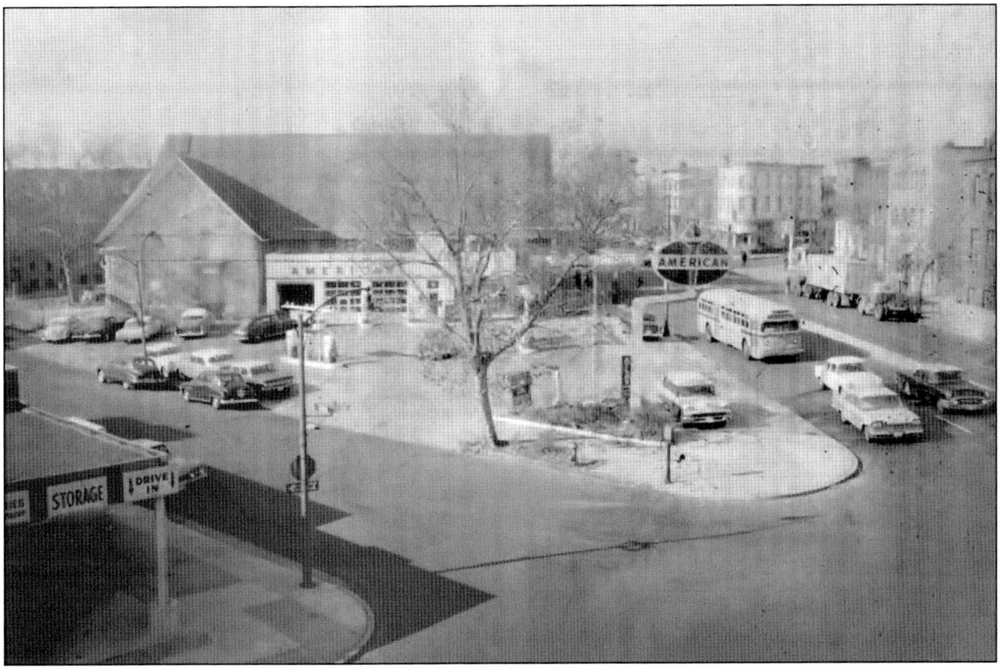

St. Bartholomew's Protestant Episcopal Church was located at North and Madison Avenues. It was built in 1856, and its last service was held on July 30, 1928. The congregation combined with Trinity Episcopal and moved to Edmonson Avenue. The building was sold to a gasoline filling station and turned into a maintenance shop. The building has been demolished, but the site is still a gas station. (BCPL.)

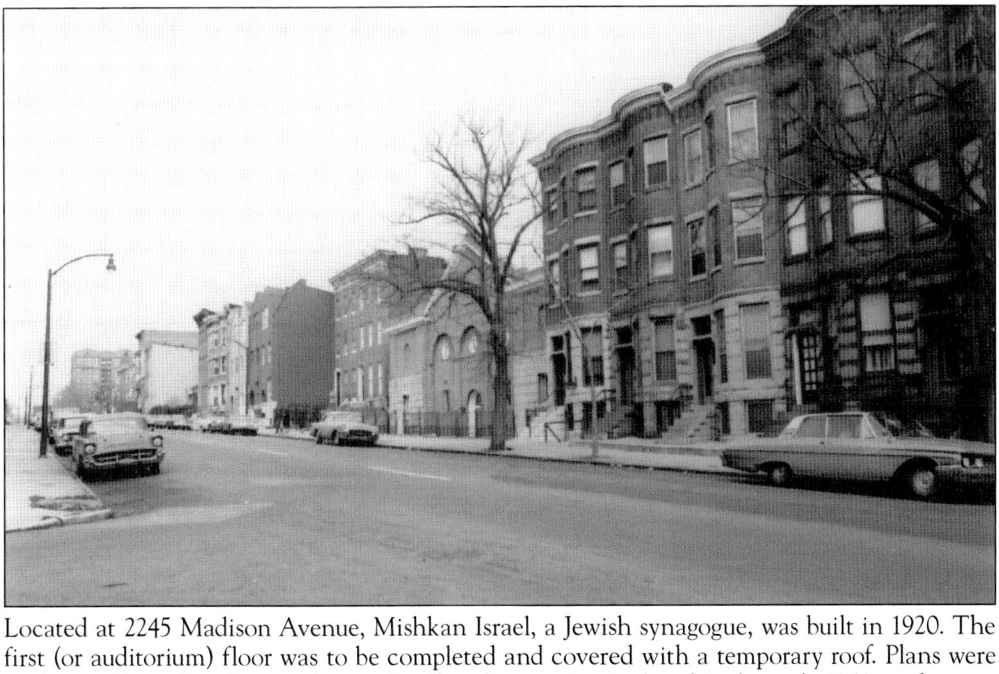

Located at 2245 Madison Avenue, Mishkan Israel, a Jewish synagogue, was built in 1920. The first (or auditorium) floor was to be completed and covered with a temporary roof. Plans were made to add another floor and more detail to the exterior. It closed in the early 1960s and is now home to a Christian Seventh Day Adventist congregation. (CHAP.)

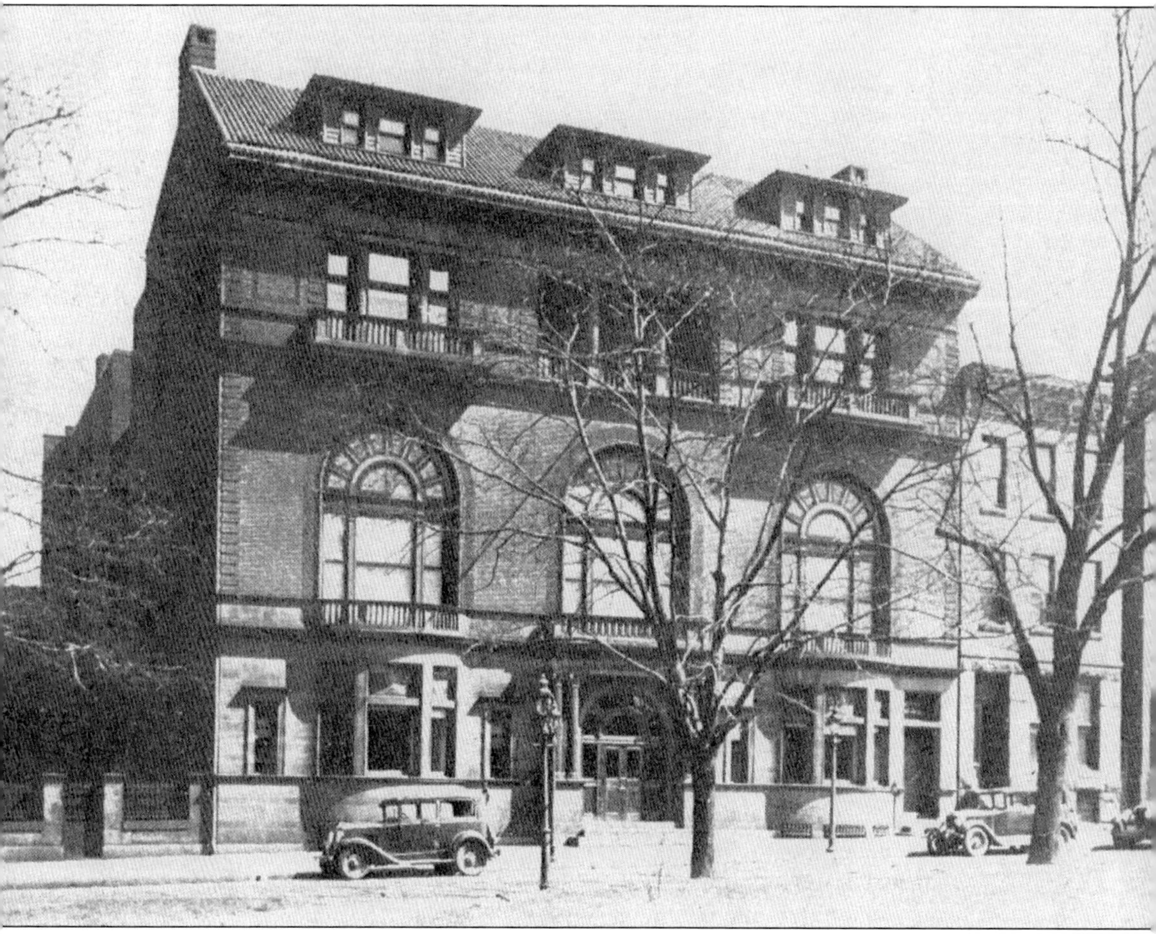

The Phoenix Club was the most prominent of all Jewish social clubs in Baltimore, though many other clubs were established in the surrounding area. Located at the 1500 block of Eutaw Place, it was a gathering place for prominent Jewish men and women. Built in Italian Renaissance style, it was three stories tall and made of brownstone and red brick. Inside were two grand ballrooms that had balconies overlooking Eutaw Place. Marble inside was imported from St. Baum, France. The Phoenix Club opened on Eutaw Place on November 16, 1891, and closed in 1956. (Dale Dusman collection.)

Seen to the right inside their home at 2444 Eutaw Place are Rabbi Israel Goldman; Mildred Goldman, his wife; and their two daughters, Anna and Toby. Rabbi Goldman served as rabbi of Chizuk Amuno Congregation both at the Eutaw Place synagogue (1948–1960) and at its present Stevenson Road location (1960–1976). He died in 1979. The interiors were typical for a home on Eutaw Place including elaborate mantels and decorative wallpaper. Working fireplaces in several rooms were commonplace. The Goldman family still comes back to visit Eutaw Place and Reservoir Hill. (Tom Hall.)

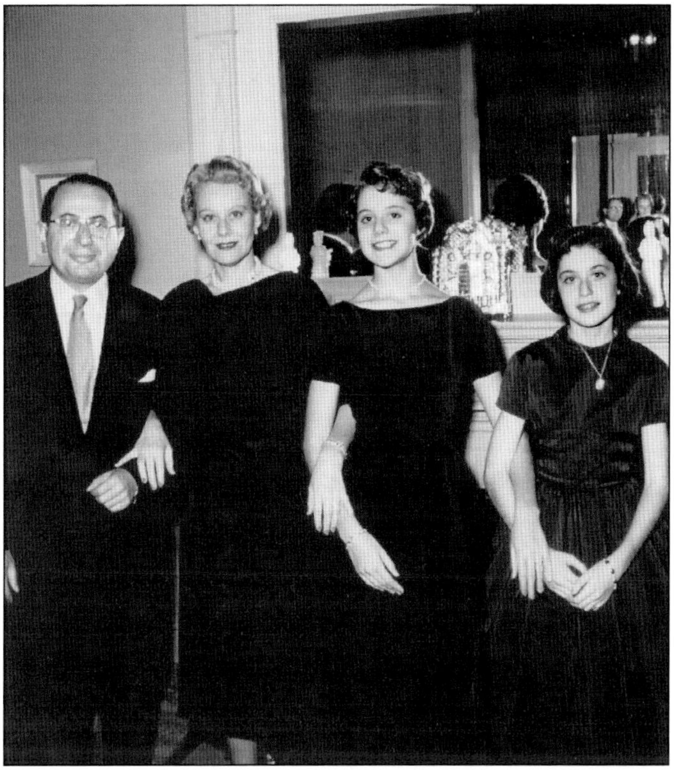

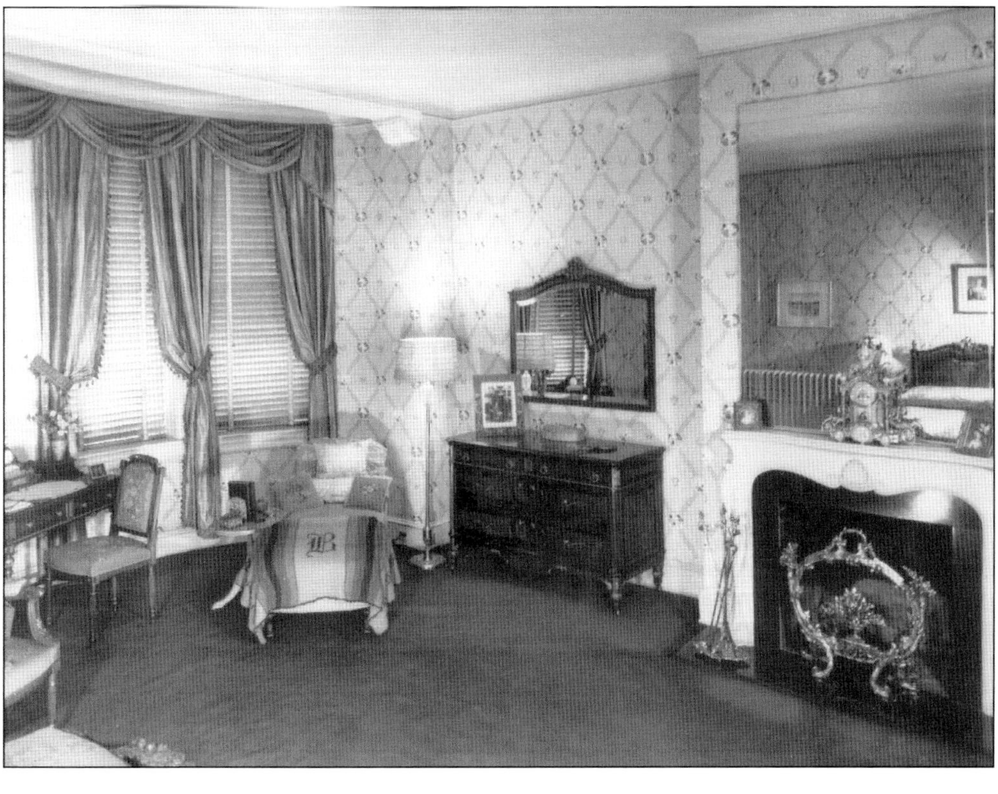

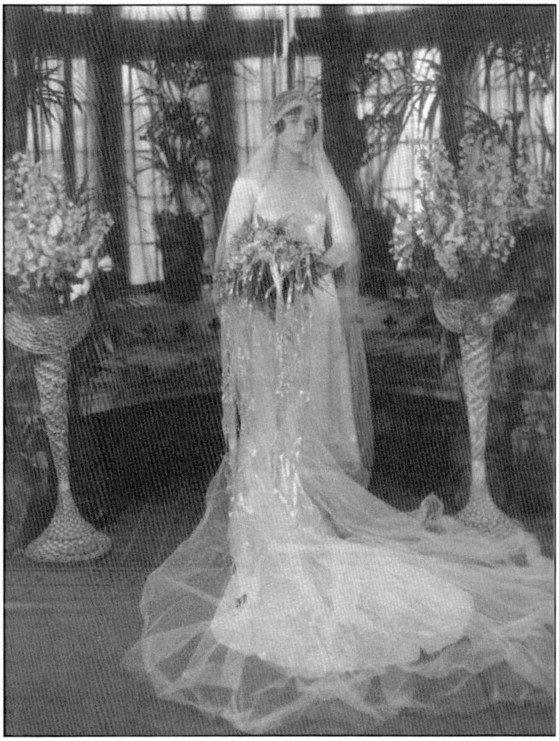

Pictured below is 907 Lake Drive, which is still standing directly across from the Druid Lake on Lake Drive. Morris Schapiro purchased it in 1922 from Eli Oppenheim. The Schapiro family owned the house for many decades. To the left is a photograph of the bride, Doris Schapiro, inside the home. Doris was Morris's daughter. She was married in the house in 1928. Mr. Schapiro gave the house to the American Red Cross, which in turn gave it to the city. The residence at 907 Lake Drive is now called the William Donald Schaefer House and is a home for young men going through substance abuse treatment. (Barbara Katz.)

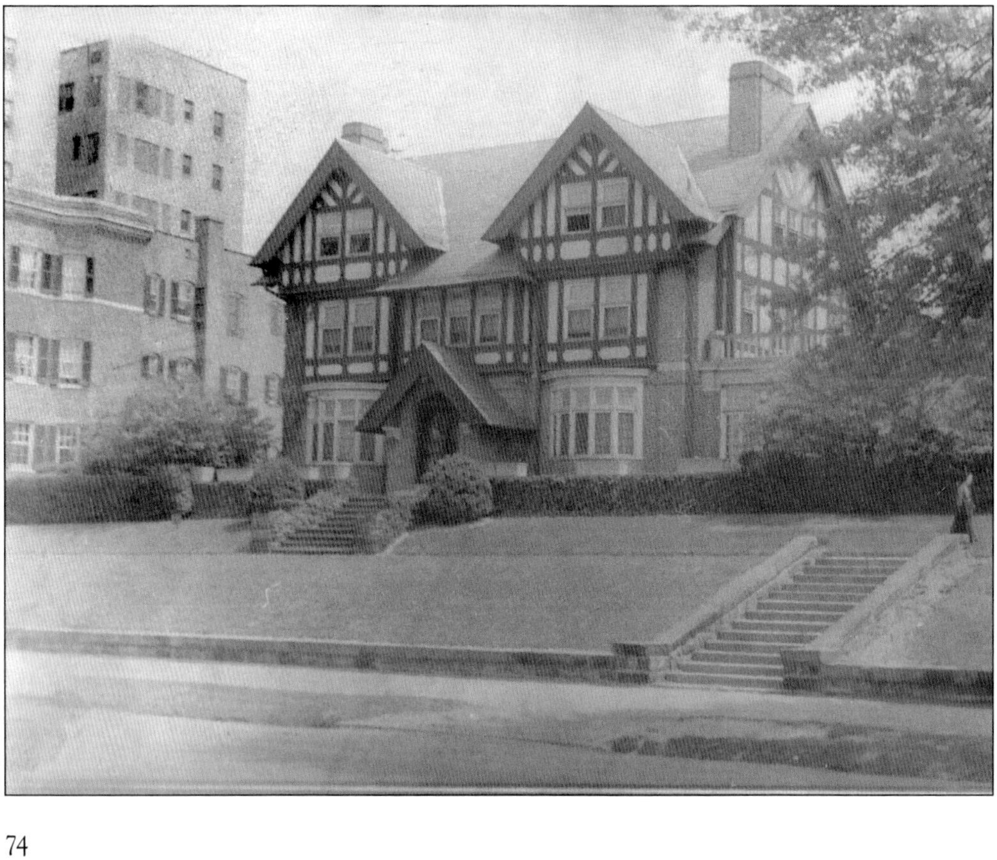

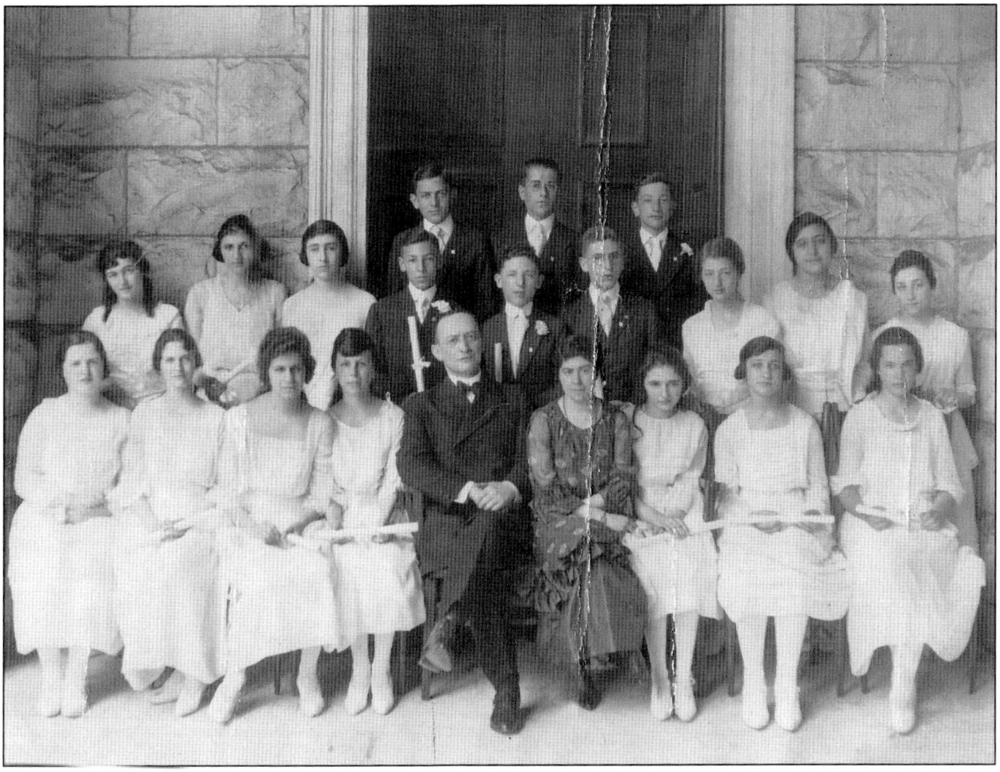

Seen here is a confirmation class of Oheb Shalom, found at 1307 Eutaw Place. Located within walking distance of Reservoir Hill, many residents were members of the congregation. Oheb Shalom is now a Reformed Jewish Congregation located in Baltimore County. (Susan Adler.)

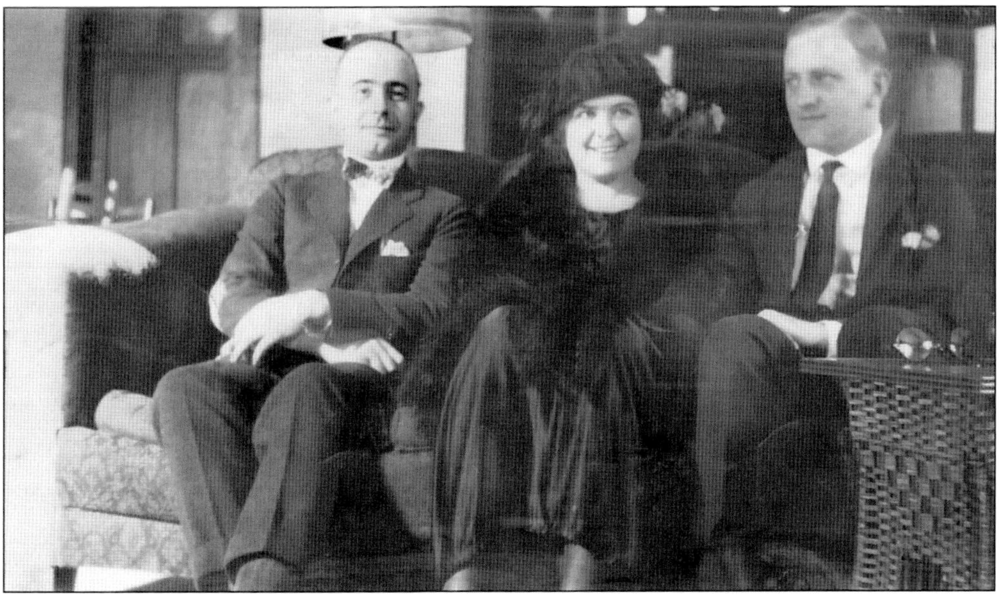

Pictured are unidentified relatives on the Adler family on Linden Avenue. Linden Avenue was a busy street that once went through both Reservoir Hill and Bolton Hill neighborhoods. During urban renewal, most of Linden Avenue was removed below North Avenue. (Susan Adler.)

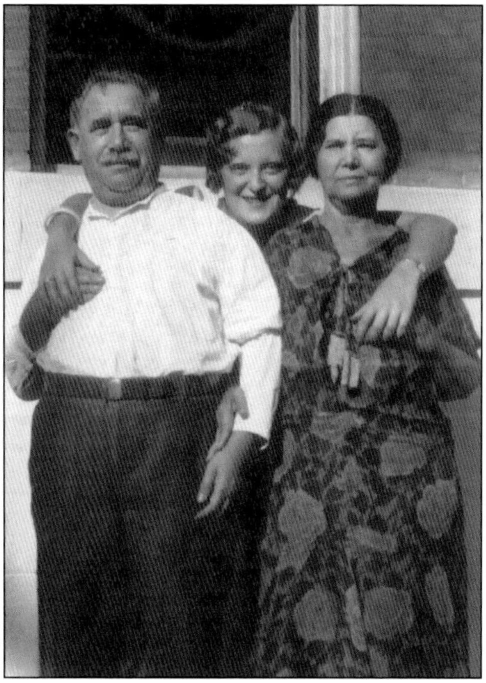

Pictured at left are Reuben Kramer's father, mother, and sister Jeannette in 1924. They lived at 2323 Linden Avenue, a street that once ran through downtown all the way through Reservoir Hill to Druid Hill Park. Linden Avenue is named for the Linden trees that used to flank both sides of the street. (Jewish Museum of Maryland.)

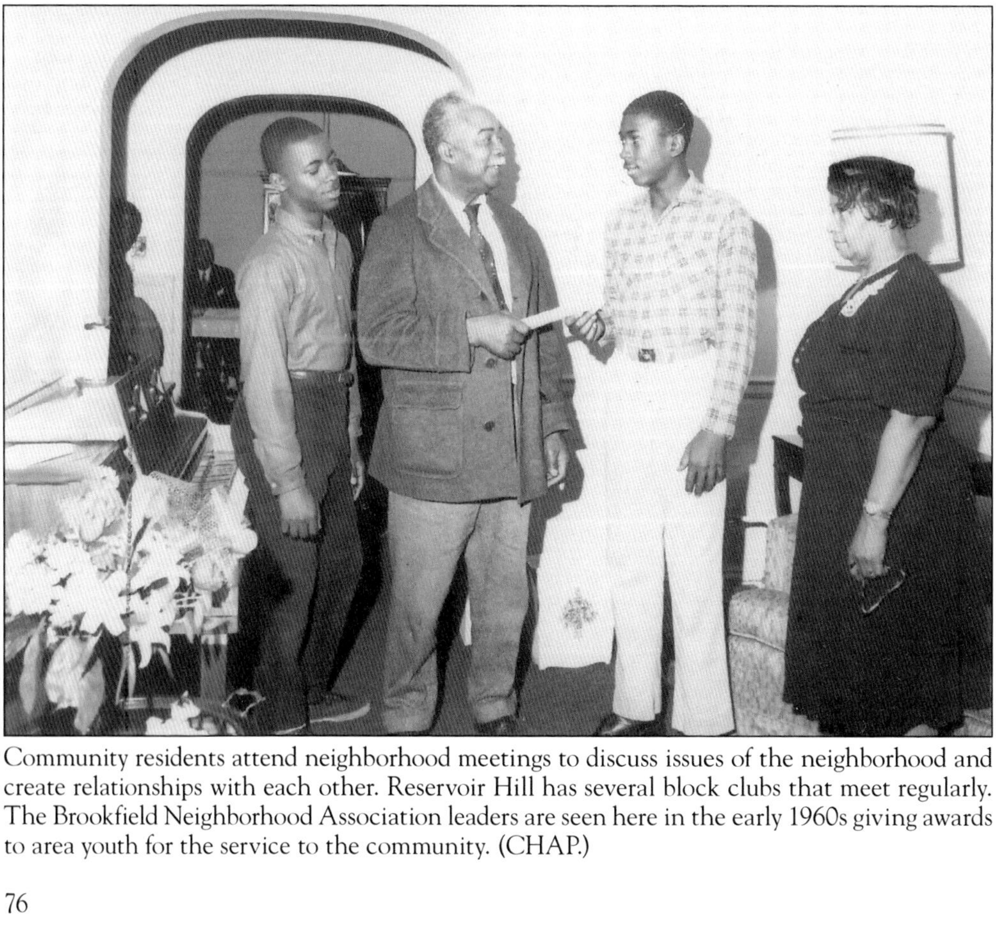

Community residents attend neighborhood meetings to discuss issues of the neighborhood and create relationships with each other. Reservoir Hill has several block clubs that meet regularly. The Brookfield Neighborhood Association leaders are seen here in the early 1960s giving awards to area youth for the service to the community. (CHAP.)

Pictured are members of the Brookfield Neighborhood Association meeting together to discuss issues of the day in the early 1960s. With 13 block clubs in Reservoir Hill, the neighborhood has been known for its community members participating and being engaged, ready to challenge city and state leaders to continue improvement of the neighborhood. (CHAP.)

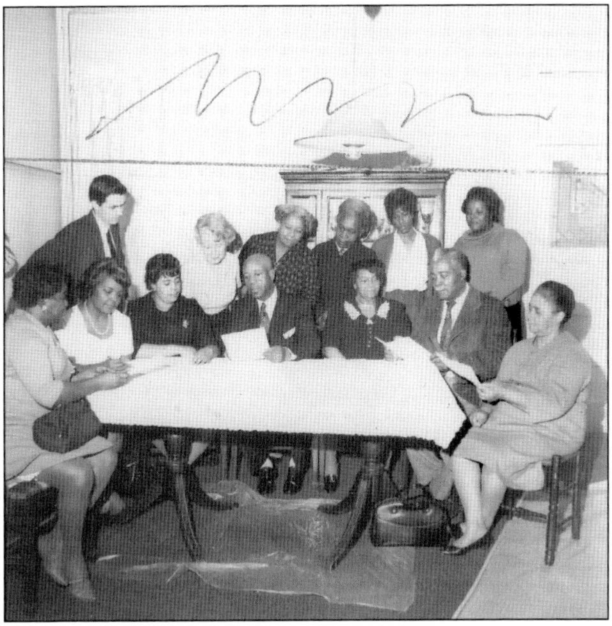

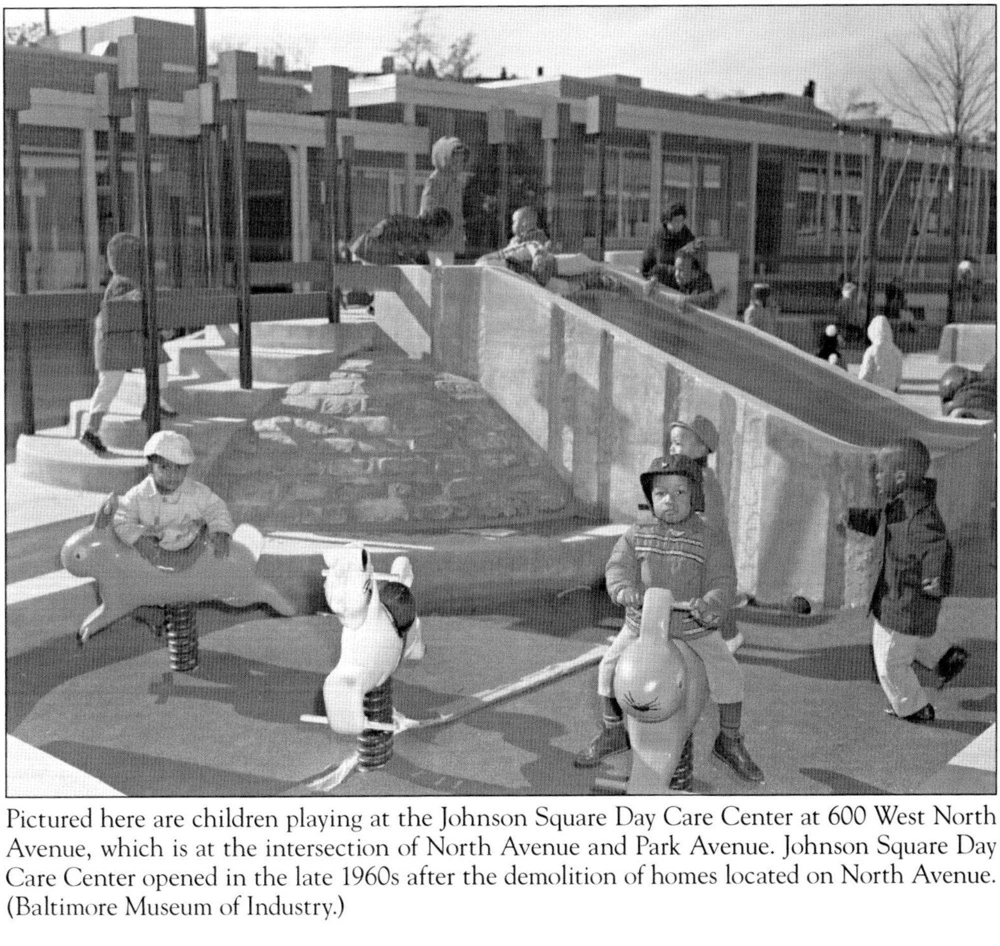

Pictured here are children playing at the Johnson Square Day Care Center at 600 West North Avenue, which is at the intersection of North Avenue and Park Avenue. Johnson Square Day Care Center opened in the late 1960s after the demolition of homes located on North Avenue. (Baltimore Museum of Industry.)

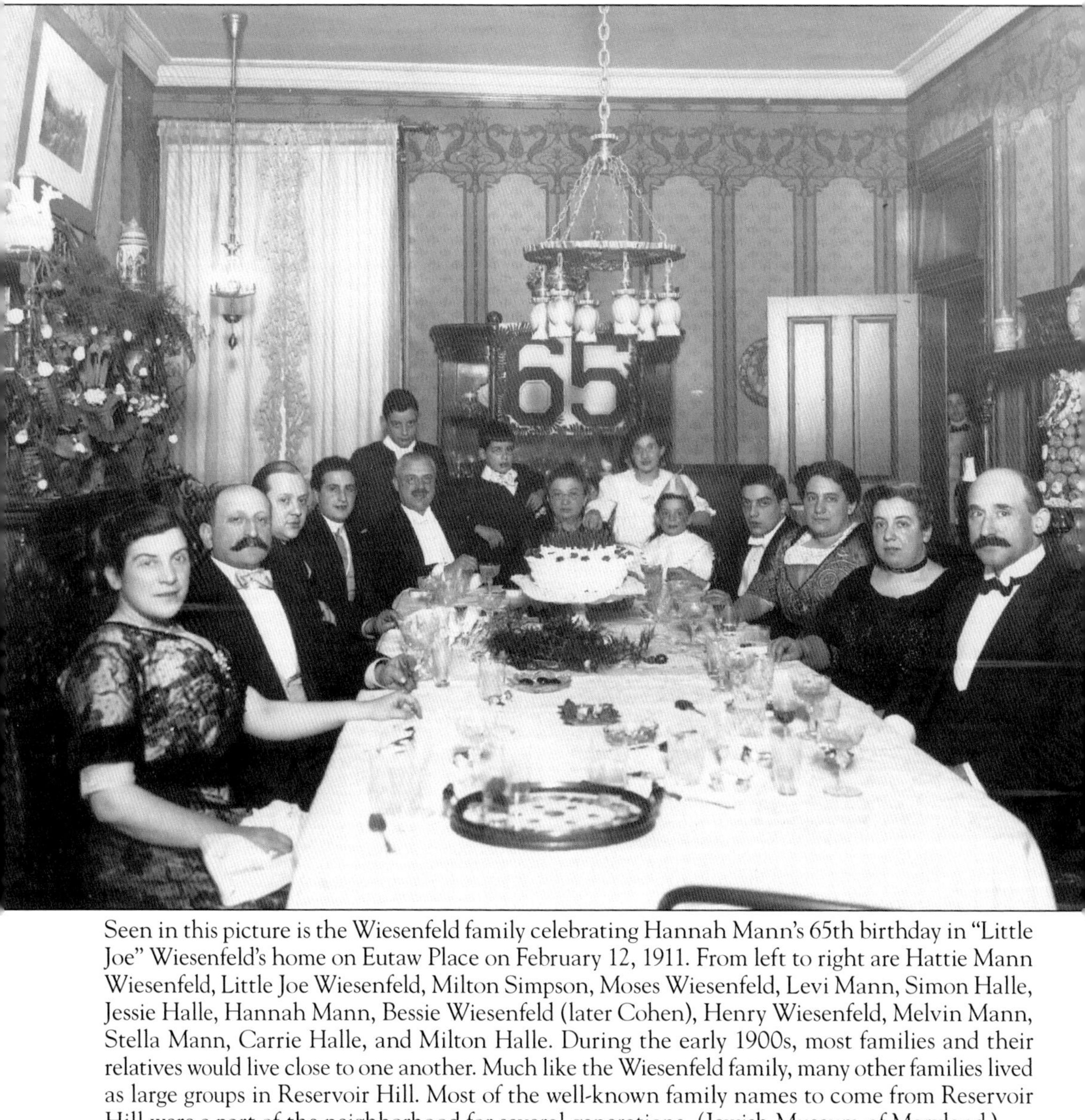

Seen in this picture is the Wiesenfeld family celebrating Hannah Mann's 65th birthday in "Little Joe" Wiesenfeld's home on Eutaw Place on February 12, 1911. From left to right are Hattie Mann Wiesenfeld, Little Joe Wiesenfeld, Milton Simpson, Moses Wiesenfeld, Levi Mann, Simon Halle, Jessie Halle, Hannah Mann, Bessie Wiesenfeld (later Cohen), Henry Wiesenfeld, Melvin Mann, Stella Mann, Carrie Halle, and Milton Halle. During the early 1900s, most families and their relatives would live close to one another. Much like the Wiesenfeld family, many other families lived as large groups in Reservoir Hill. Most of the well-known family names to come from Reservoir Hill were a part of the neighborhood for several generations. (Jewish Museum of Maryland.)

Six

Notable Residents

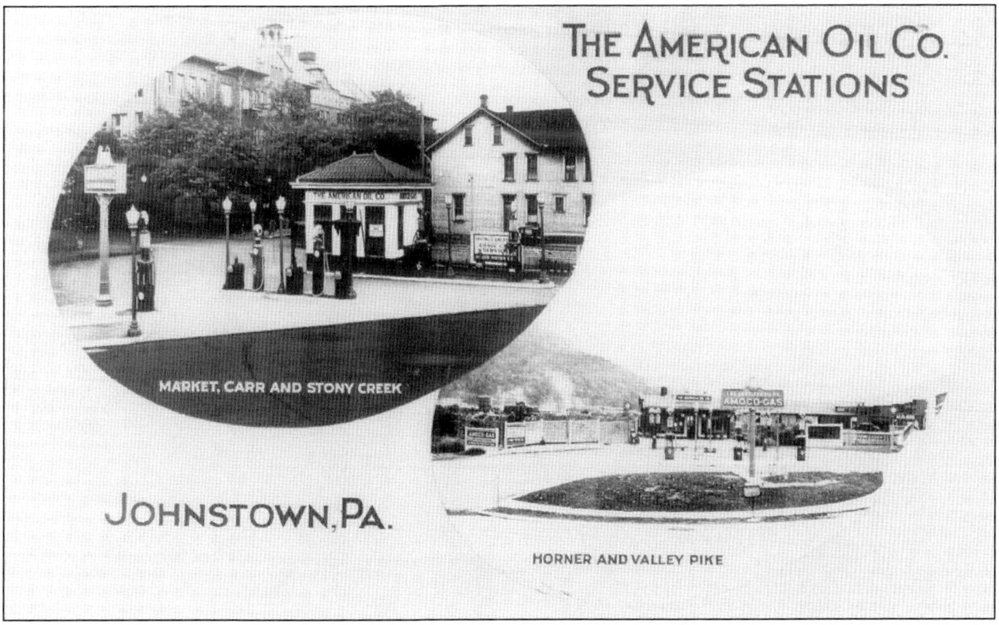

Louis Blaustein was founder and president of American Oil Company (AMOCO). By 1910, he began selling gasoline through the streets of the city by horse and wagon. Subsequently, he opened the first gasoline filling station in America. Eventually, Pan American and American Oil became an integrated enterprise. Blaustein became president of Pan American and chairman of the board at American Oil. Memorial services were held at his residence in the Emersonian Apartments on July 29, 1937. (Mr. Tigues Antiques and Collectibles.)

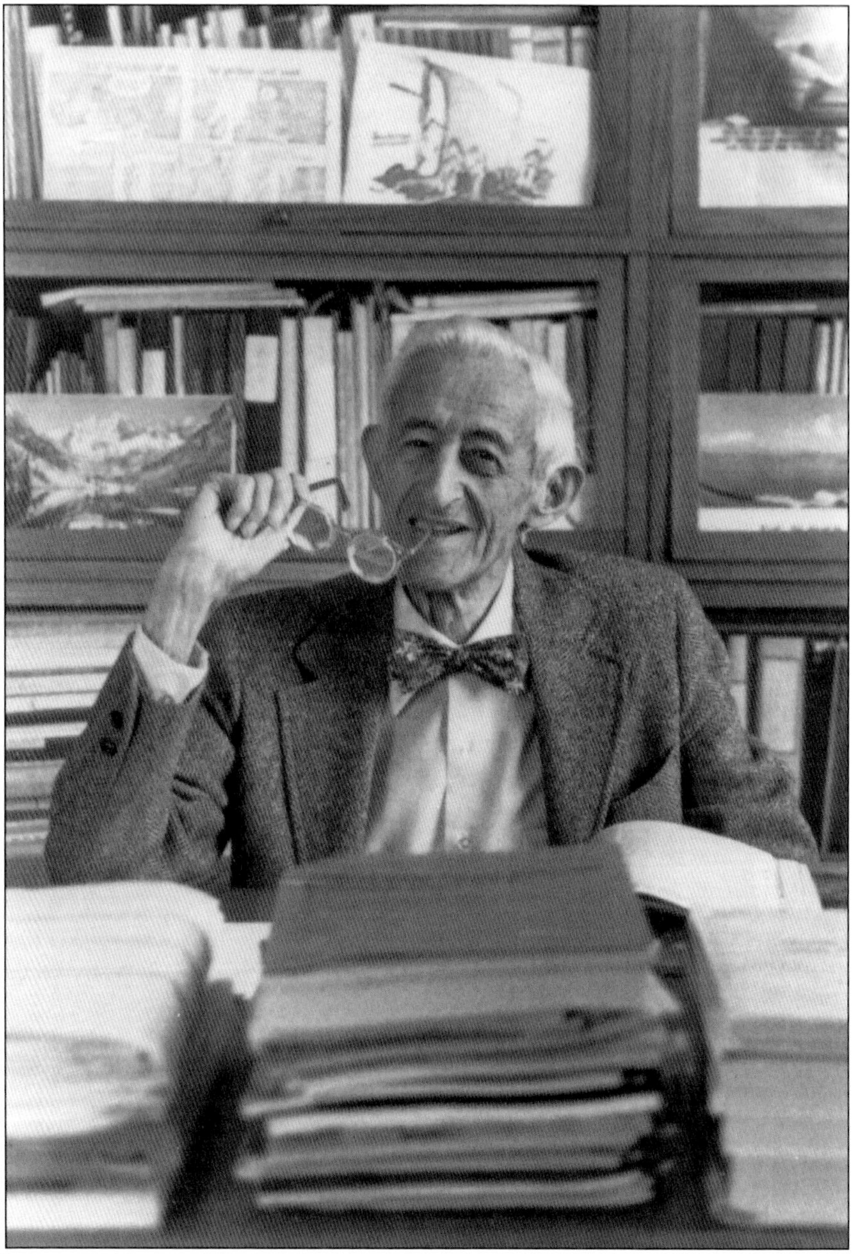

It has been said that Abel Wolman enhanced the lives of people around the globe more than any other Baltimorean. Wolman graduated from Johns Hopkins in 1913 and between 1922 and 1939, he was chief of the Maryland Bureau of Sanitary Engineering. During that time, he developed a chlorination-controlled method for purifying water that was adopted by practically every major municipal and industrial water-supply system in the country. In 1986, the City of Baltimore renamed the Public Works Building in honor of Abel Wolman. The Wolman Building still stands today and is where city residents pay their property tax, parking fines and water bills. Wolman passed away on February 22, 1989, at 96 years of age. For many years, Wolman and his family lived in a row house at the intersection of Eutaw Place and Whitelock Street. (Jewish Museum of Maryland.)

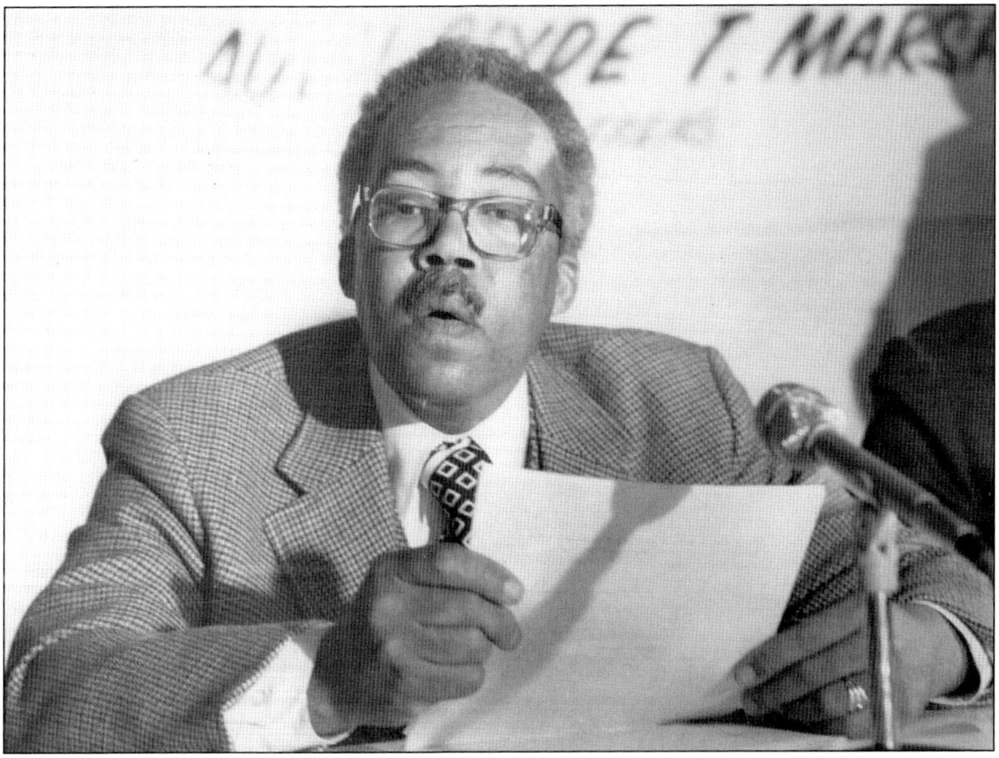

The Reverend Marion Bascom was a civil rights leader and pastor of Douglass Memorial Community Church for 46 years. He marched with Dr. Martin Luther King Jr. in Alabama and was involved in speeches King gave at the Masonic Temple on Eutaw Place. He was one of the founders of Associated Black Charities and was named Baltimore's first black fire commissioner. Pastor Bascom lived on Park Avenue until his death in 2012. (Tribune Photo Archives.)

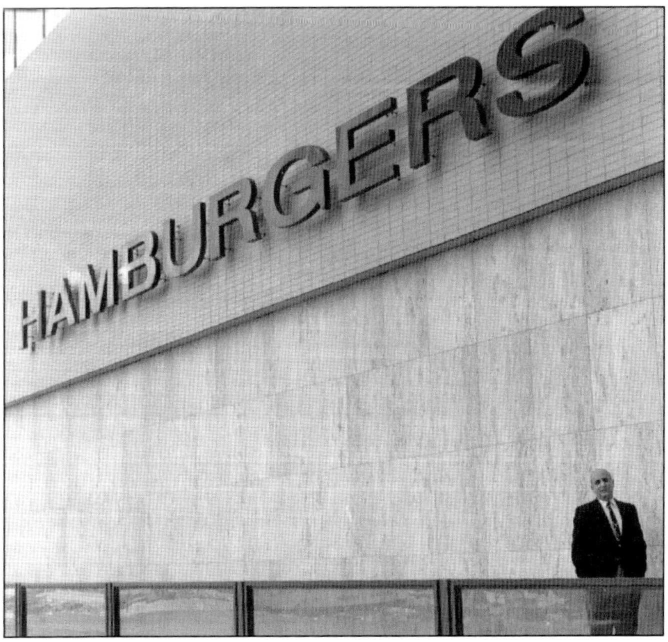

Hamburgers opened this location in 1962 at One Charles Center, the skyscraper in downtown Baltimore built as a part of urban renewal. Until the 1980s, most downtown department stores had been located close to the intersection of Howard and Lexington Streets. Moving into One Charles Center marked a change in the retail pattern downtown. Many department stores, including Hamburgers, were also opening suburban branches in the 1960s. (Jewish Museum of Maryland.)

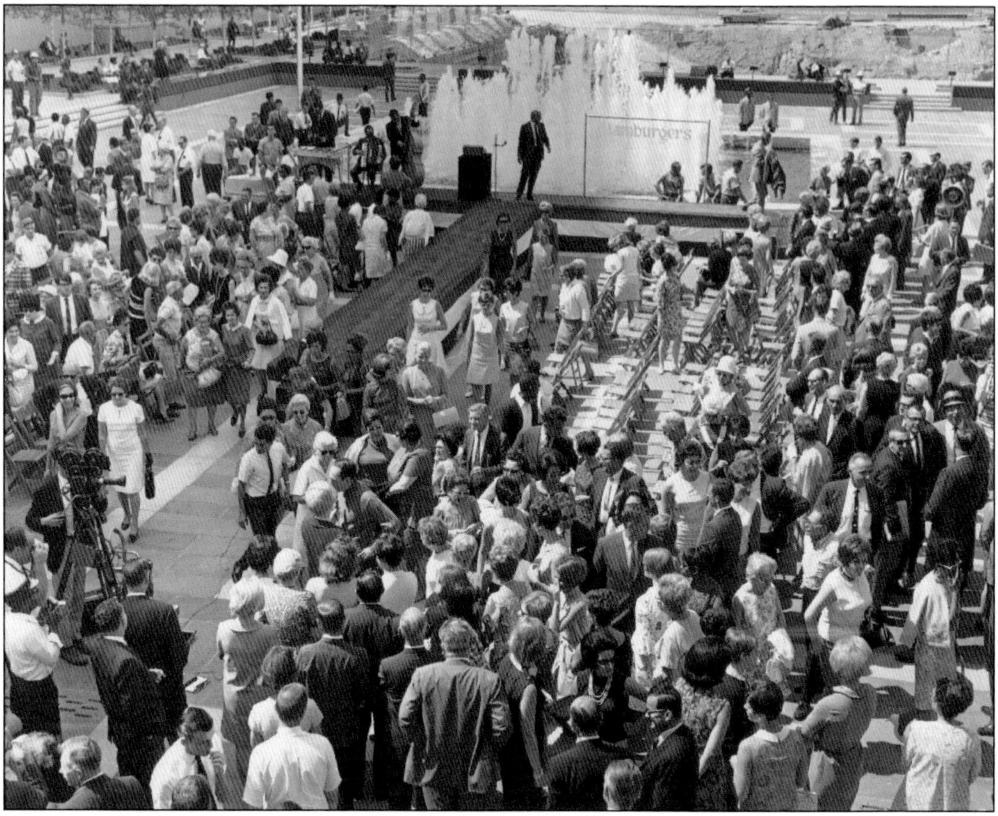

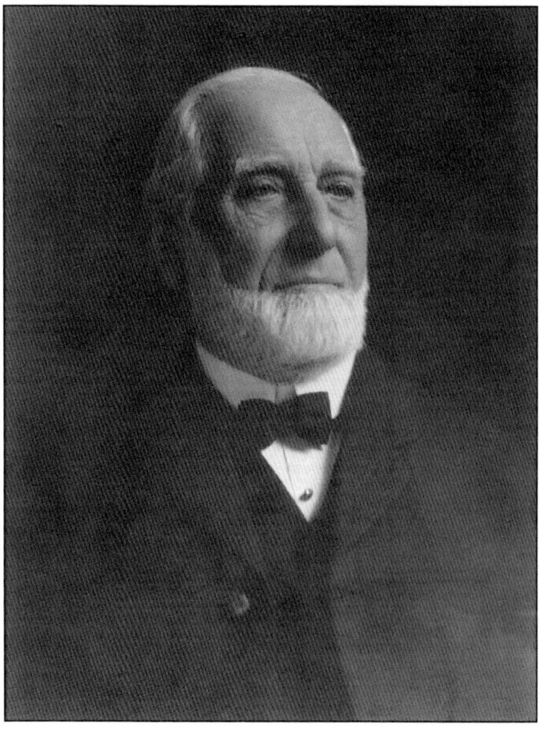

Manes Isaac Hamburger was the president of Isaac Hamburger and Sons Clothing store and president of the Hamburger Building Company. Isaac Hamburger and Sons Clothing was one of the largest and oldest department stores in Baltimore. At its peak, there were 10 stores in Maryland; three in Wilmington, Delaware; and 11 in Boston, Massachusetts. The first store opened in 1850, and by 1989, it was owned and operated by Hugo Boss, which shut down the remaining stores in 1992. Manes Isaac, who resided at the Esplanade Apartments, died on June 20, 1940. His brother and co-owner of Hamburgers, Henry, lived at 2245 Eutaw Place. (Both, Jewish Museum of Maryland.)

Known as "the Pants King," Jacob Schoeneman was one of the largest slacks producers in the country. His business was located at Eutaw Street and Paca Street downtown. He died on December 23, 1910, at his home at 2202 Linden Avenue. (Jewish Museum of Maryland.)

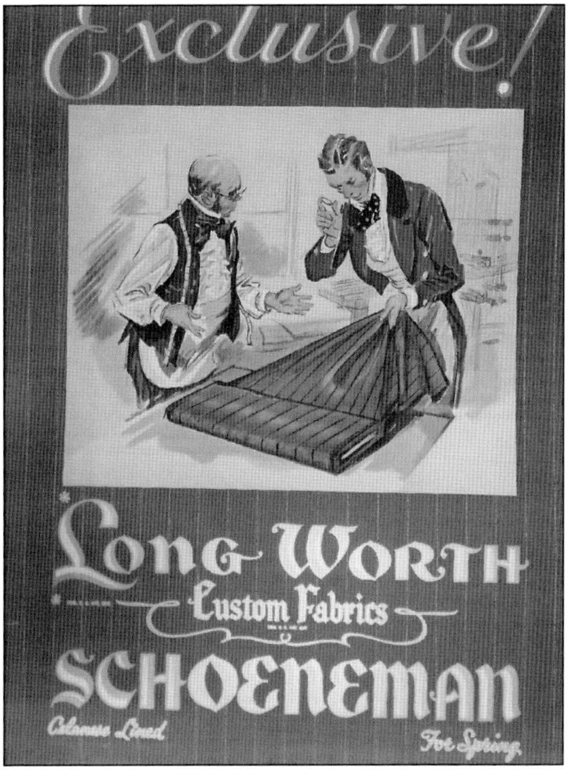

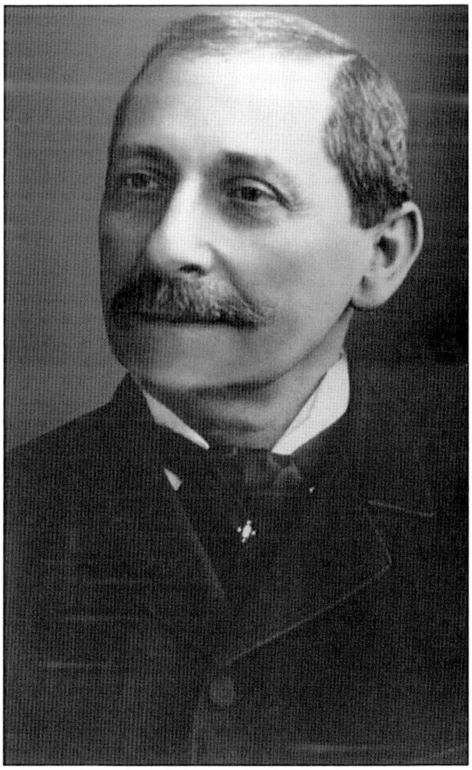

Max Greif was the founder of the wholesale clothing firm L. Greif and Bros. He died at home in the Rivera Apartments on October 7, 1921. L. Greif and Bros. was at one point the second-largest clothing manufacturer in the United States. L. Greif and Bros., famous for its Griffin brand clothing, was sold to a conglomerate in 1957. (Jewish Museum of Maryland.)

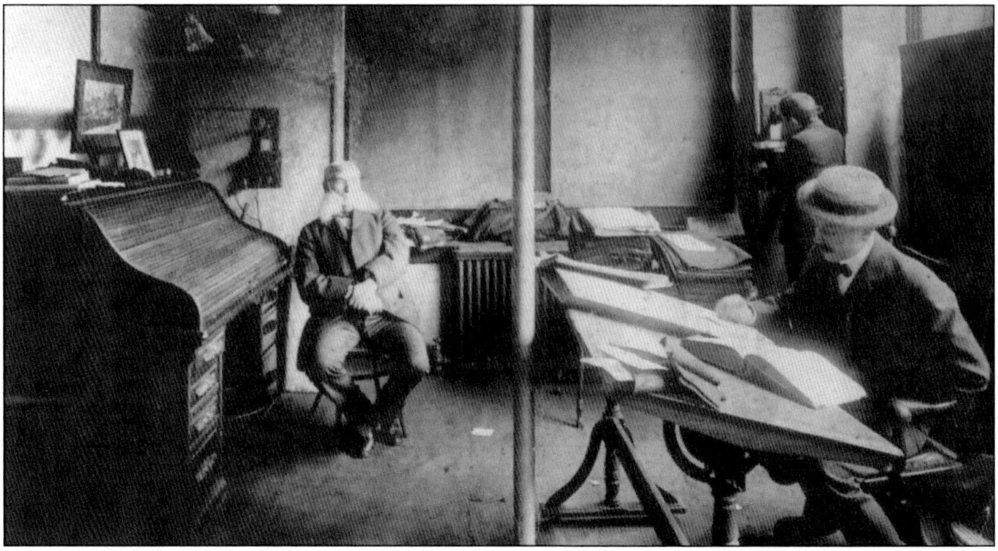

Henry Sonneborn was the founder of Henry Sonneborn & Co. Sigmund Sonneborn was president of the company when it became one of the pioneer employers to begin collective bargaining with its employees. At one point, the company was making 3,000 suits a day. Sigmund Sonneborn and his wife, Auguste, lived at 2420 Eutaw Place. He died on December 26, 1917. Sonneborn & Co. ceased operation in 1931 following the Great Depression. Henry Sonneborn is seated at left, Sigmund Sonneborn is seated at right, and an unidentified man is standing in the background. Their office was located at the corner of Eutaw and German Streets. Below is a photograph of descendants of the Hutzler, Hamburger, and Sonneborn families. (Jewish Museum of Maryland.)

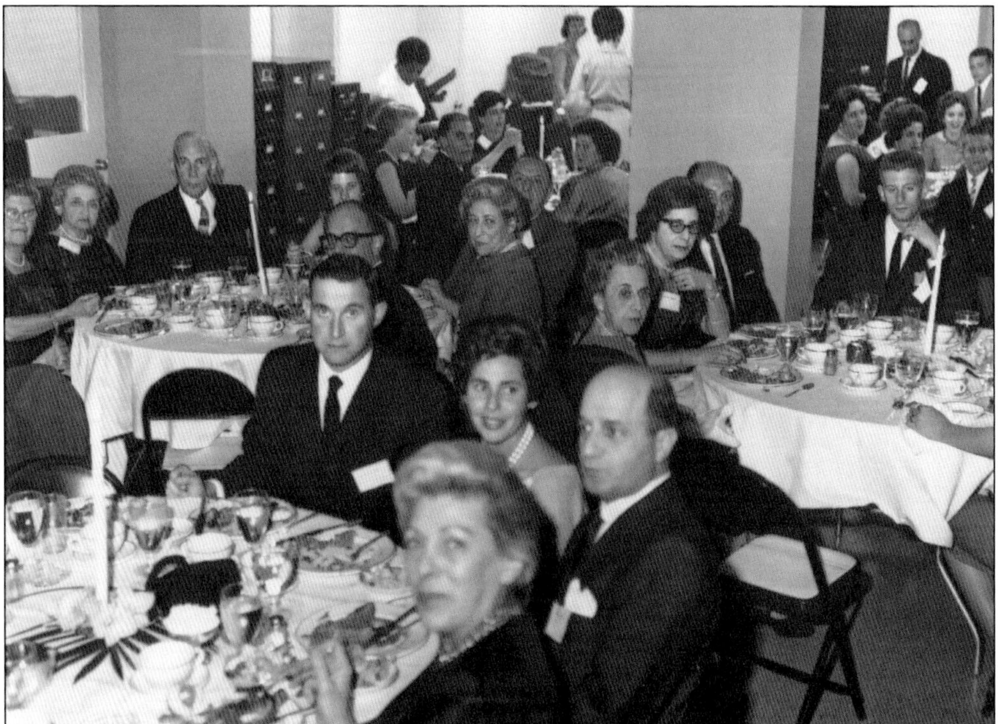

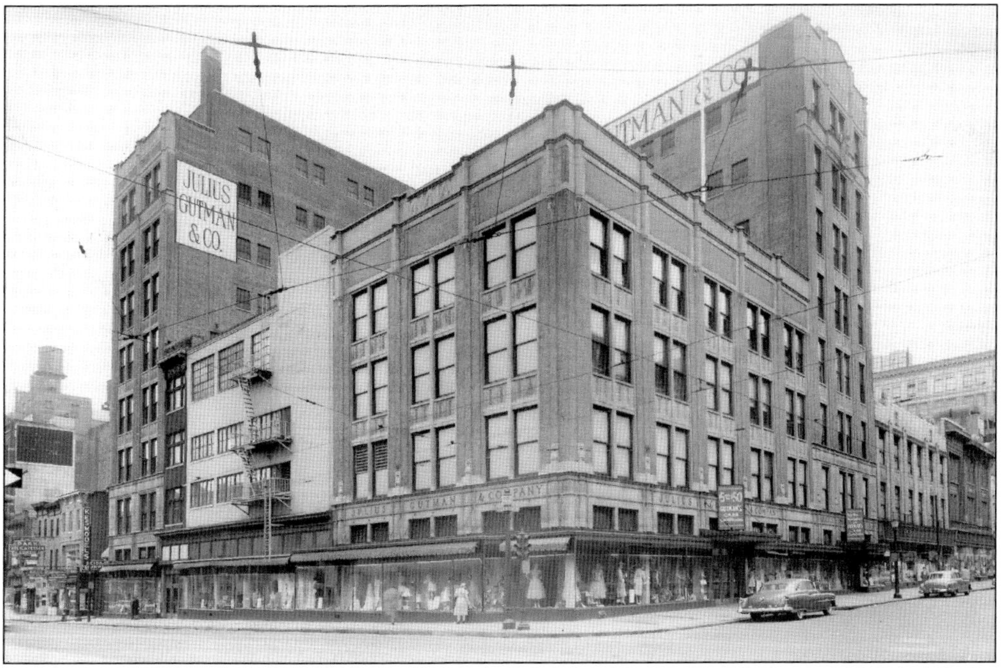

Julius Gutman founded Julius Gutman and Company in 1871. In 1959, the store merged with the Brager department store, forming Brager-Gutman's. Decades later, the store pictured above closed and was sold to Epsteins Department Store, which made the former Brager-Gutman's location its flagship store. It was located the entire time at Park and Lexington Avenues. By 1960, it had six locations in and around the Baltimore area. Brager-Gutman's was considered to have the lowest prices on life's necessities and little luxuries for the budget conscious. Julius Gutman died on April 26, 1921, at his home in the Emersonian Apartments. (Both, BCPL.)

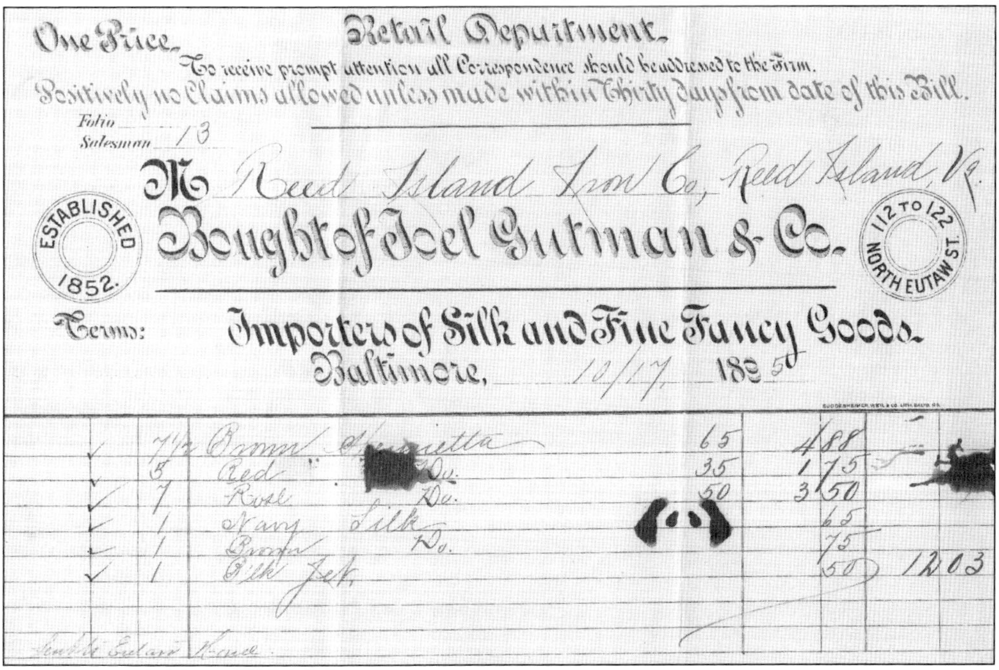
One Price. Retail Department.
To receive prompt attention all Correspondence should be addressed to the Firm.
Positively no Claims allowed unless made within Thirty days from date of this Bill.
Folio
Salesman 13
M Reed Island Iron Co, Reed Island, Va.
ESTABLISHED 1852.
Bought of Joel Gutman & Co.
112 TO 122 NORTH EUTAW ST.
Terms: Importers of Silk and Fine Fancy Goods.
Baltimore, 10/17, 1895

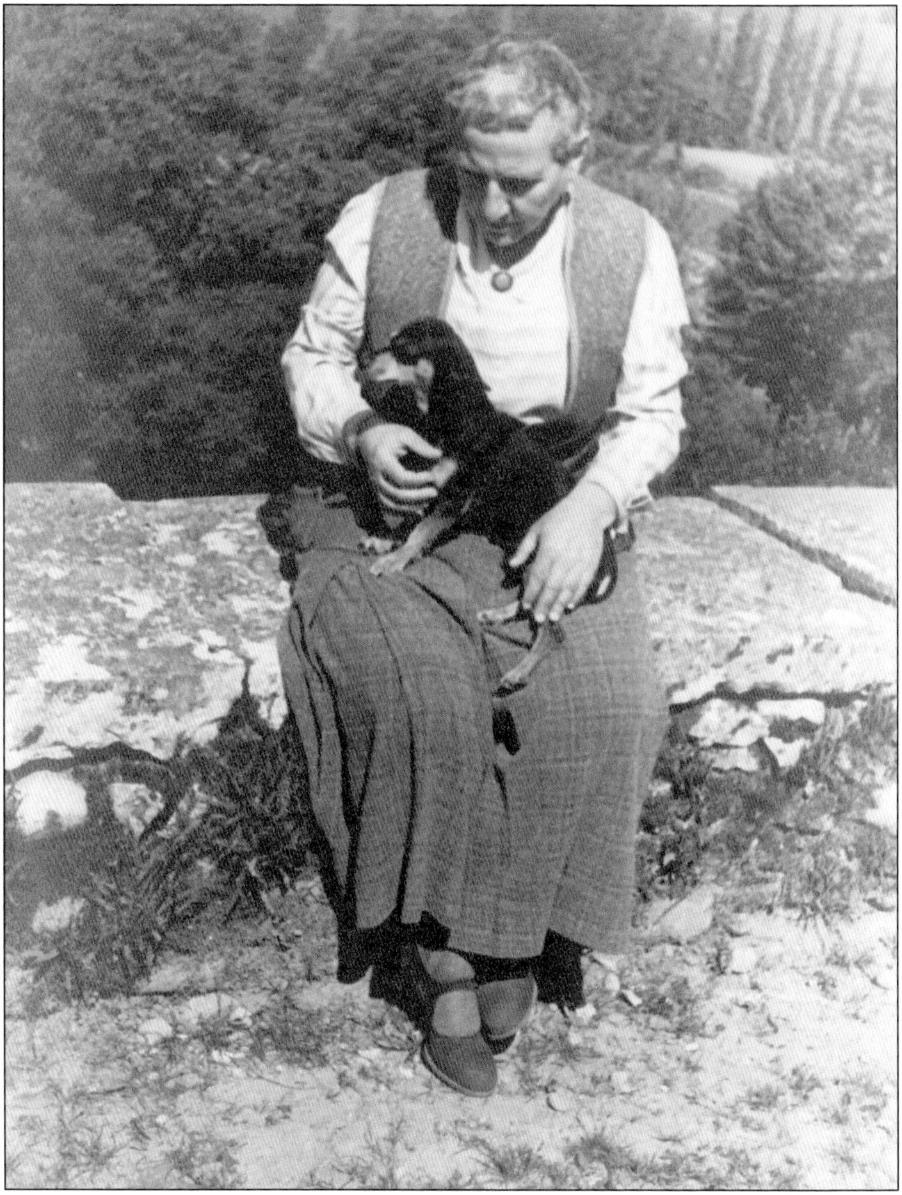

Gertrude Stein was a famous author and major promoter of modern art. While Baltimore cannot claim Gertrude Stein as a native child, she moved to Baltimore after the death of her parents and lived with her mother's family. She resided at 2408 Linden Avenue for a few years with her uncle David Bachrach. When she returned to Baltimore to attend classes at Johns Hopkins Medical School after studying psychology at Radcliffe, she met Claribel and Etta Cone, wealthy Baltimore socialites and art collectors. Stein attended the Cone sisters' "Saturday evening salons" with many local artists and writers and later brought that tradition with her to France, where she spent most of her life. Written in 1903 but not published until after her death, Stein's *Q.E.D. (Quod Erat Demonstrandum)* reflects her years of challenges at Hopkins and is one of the earliest coming-out stories. She is probably best known for her memoirs of her time in Paris, published as *The Autobiography of Alice B. Toklas* in 1933. Stein mentored Ernest Hemingway and was godmother to his son. She died in France at the age of 72 on July 27, 1946. (Library of Congress.)

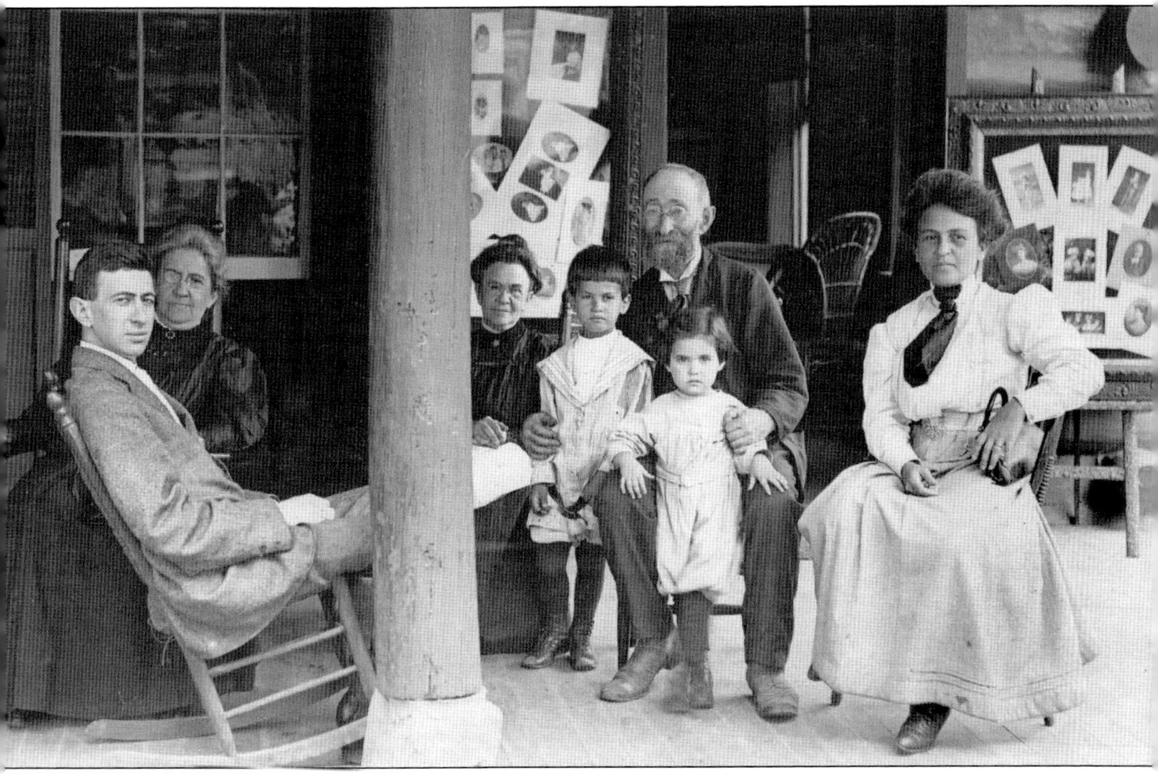

David Bachrach, seated second from the right, was a commercial photographer and founder of Bachrach, Inc. As a young man, he photographed Abraham Lincoln giving the Gettysburg Address and worked for *Harper's Weekly* during the Civil War. He was the dean of the portrait photographers, and Bachrach, Inc., has done photography for every modern US president. Bachrach died on December 10, 1921. His residence was 2408 Linden Avenue. Pictured are Bachrach and his family. (Jewish Museum of Maryland.)

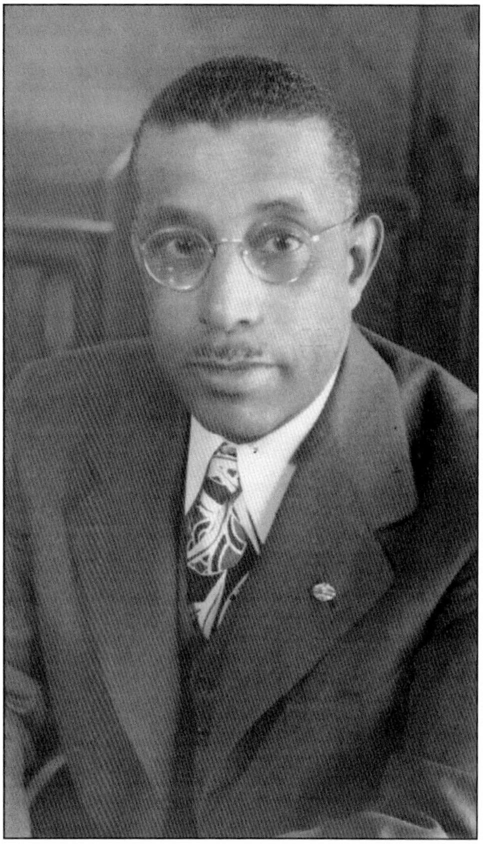

Carl Murphy was born in Baltimore and was a journalist, civil rights leader, and educator. In 1922, he assumed control of the *Afro-American* after the death of his father and solidified its place as a major African American newspaper over the next four decades. At its peak, the *Afro-American* published more than a dozen editions in Baltimore; Washington, DC; Richmond, Virginia; and Newark, New Jersey. Over this time frame, Dr. Murphy increased circulations by 93 percent and employed more than 200 workers. In addition to his work as a journalist, he was active in the Baltimore branch of the NAACP and was influential in challenging the racial segregation at the University of Maryland. One of his greatest contributions to the Baltimore African American cause came in 1935 when he brought about the election of Lillie Carroll Jackson to the presidency of the local NAACP branch, a tireless worker who served the NAACP for 35 years. Murphy met his wife, Vashti Turley, when they were both students at Howard University. She and 21 other young women founded the Delta Sigma Theta Sorority, Inc., which is today the largest African American Greek sorority. (Both, *Afro-American*.)

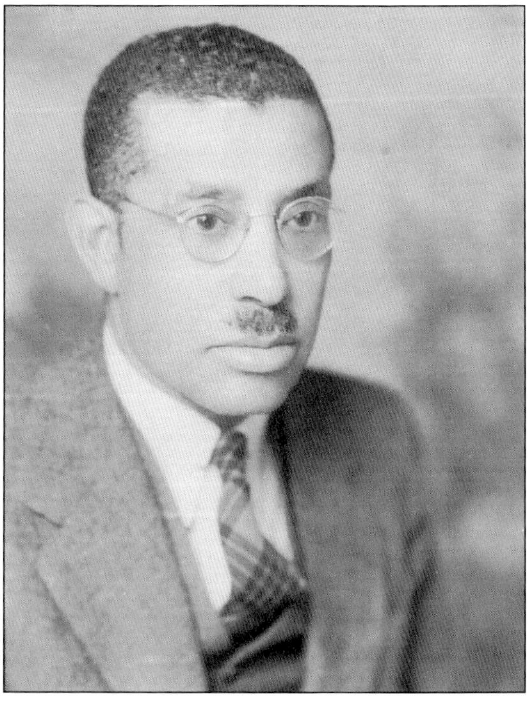

Karl Shapiro won a Pulitzer Prize for Poetry in 1945 for his work *V-Letter and Other Poems*. The first Jewish American to win a Pulitzer Prize, he was also editor of a magazine called *Poetry* (1950–1955). Shapiro was known for his outspoken opinions and was still active until the late 1990s. He lived at 930 Brooks Lane and died in 2000. (Jewish Museum of Maryland.)

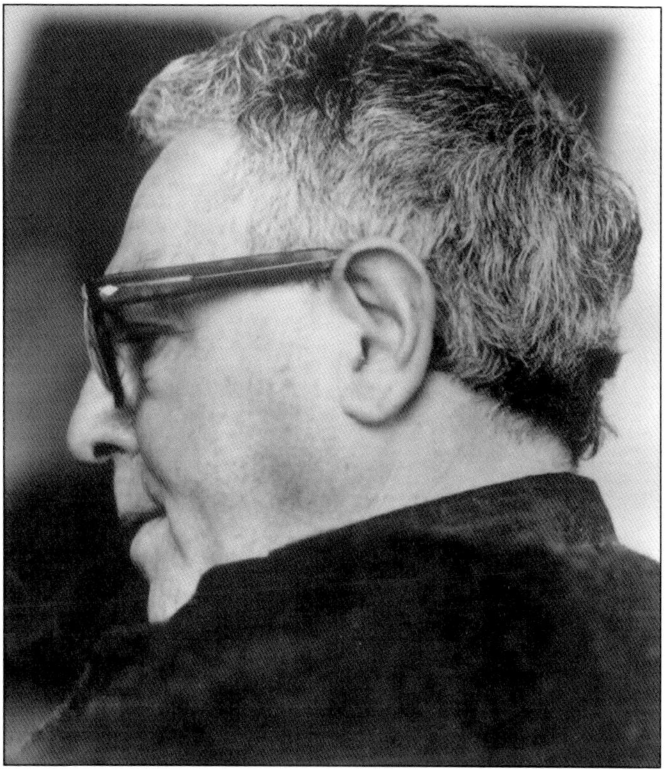

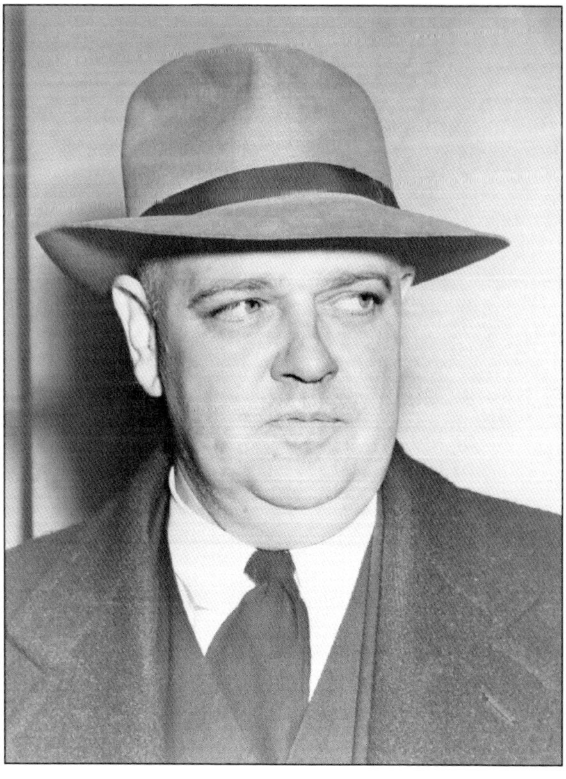

Whittaker Chambers was the key witness before Congressman Richard Nixon at the beginning of Sen. Joseph McCarthy's Cold War hunt for subversives. He was the accuser of Alger Hiss, who ironically lived close by on the 1400 block of Linden Avenue. He defected from the Communist Party while living at his address at 2124 Mount Royal Terrace. Chambers died in 1961. (Library of Congress.)

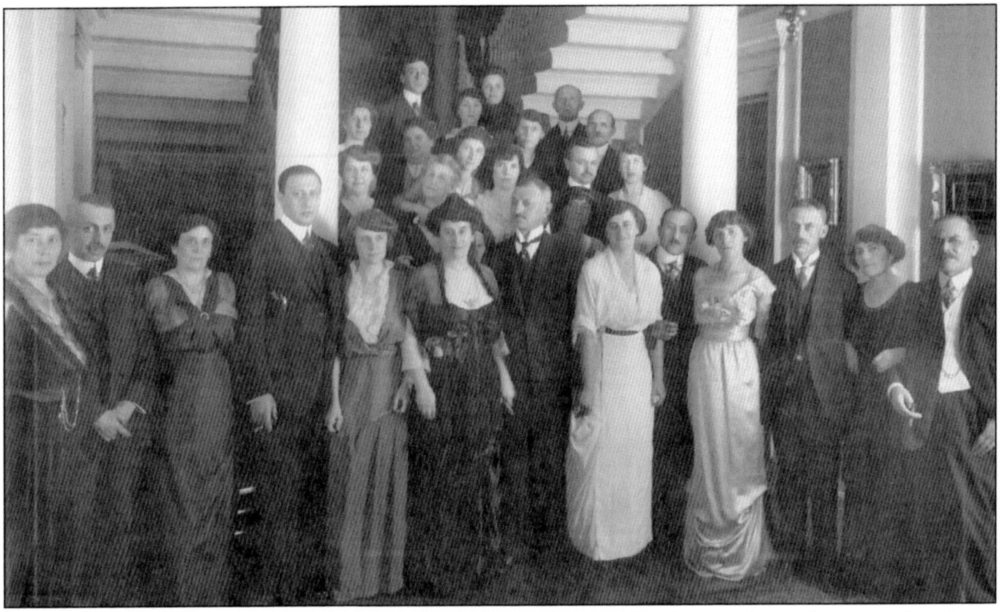

Jacob Epstein was an innovative wholesale clothier who was the first in the industry to do a large portion of his business in the South. Additionally, he was the inaugurator of matching grants in philanthropy. He was the donor of many works to the Baltimore Museum of Art. Shown here is the Epstein mansion, now demolished, overlooking Druid Lake at the top of Eutaw Place. Epstein, seventh from the left in the first row, is pictured along with family and friends. He died in 1942. (Jewish Museum of Maryland.)

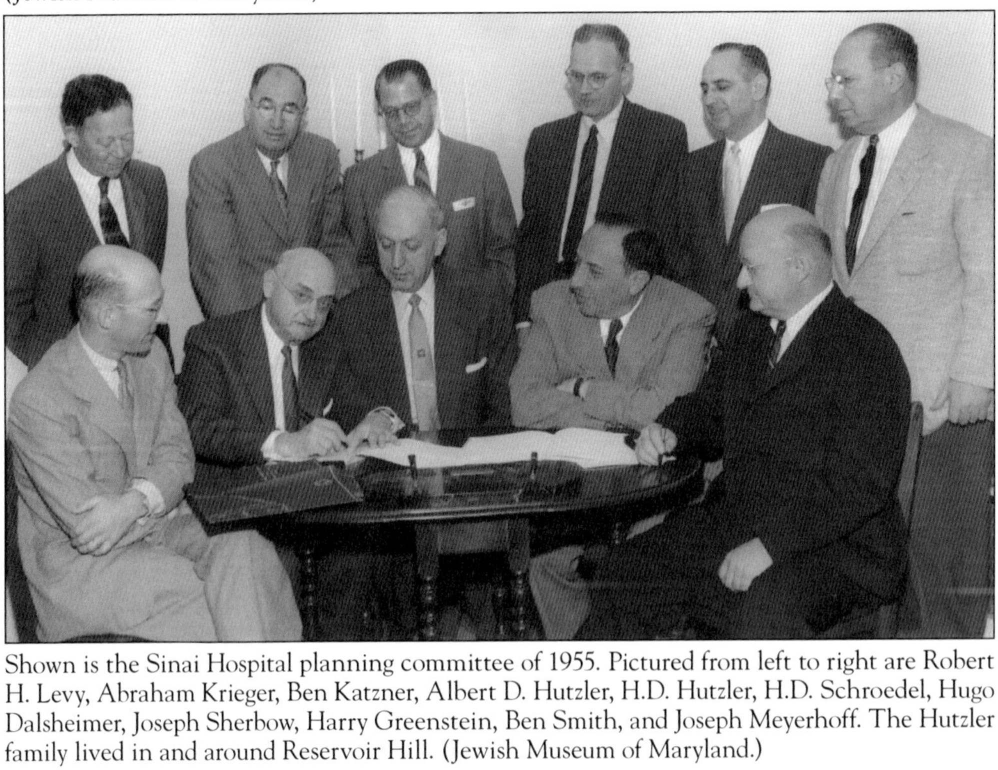

Shown is the Sinai Hospital planning committee of 1955. Pictured from left to right are Robert H. Levy, Abraham Krieger, Ben Katzner, Albert D. Hutzler, H.D. Hutzler, H.D. Schroedel, Hugo Dalsheimer, Joseph Sherbow, Harry Greenstein, Ben Smith, and Joseph Meyerhoff. The Hutzler family lived in and around Reservoir Hill. (Jewish Museum of Maryland.)

Albert Hutzler was one of the owners and president of Hutzler Brothers Department Store, arguably the best and nicest department store in Baltimore. The Hutzler name remains recognizable and evokes many pleasant memories for Baltimoreans. Hutzler Brothers Department Store had its start at Howard and Lexington Streets downtown and was the last of the giant department stores to leave downtown in the 1990s. There were multiple locations in and around Baltimore, including the Towson Hutzler store, which was the last to close. Hutzler Brothers Department Store was known for its charge accounts and direct home-delivery service. Hutzler had a mansion built at 1801 Eutaw Place and later lived in the Esplanade Apartments up the street. He died in 1964. To the right is the entrance to Hutzler's in the White Marsh Mall, and below is the original Hutzler's in downtown Baltimore. (BCPL.)

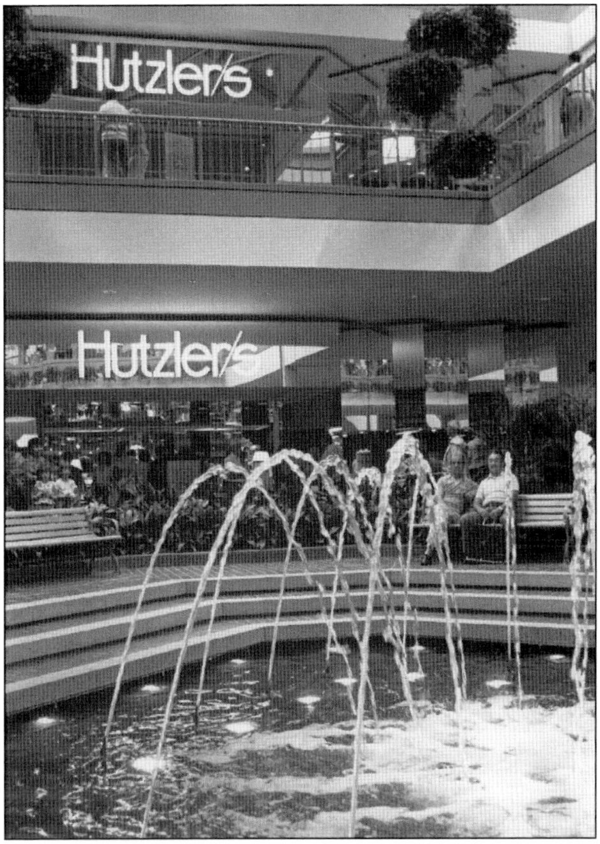

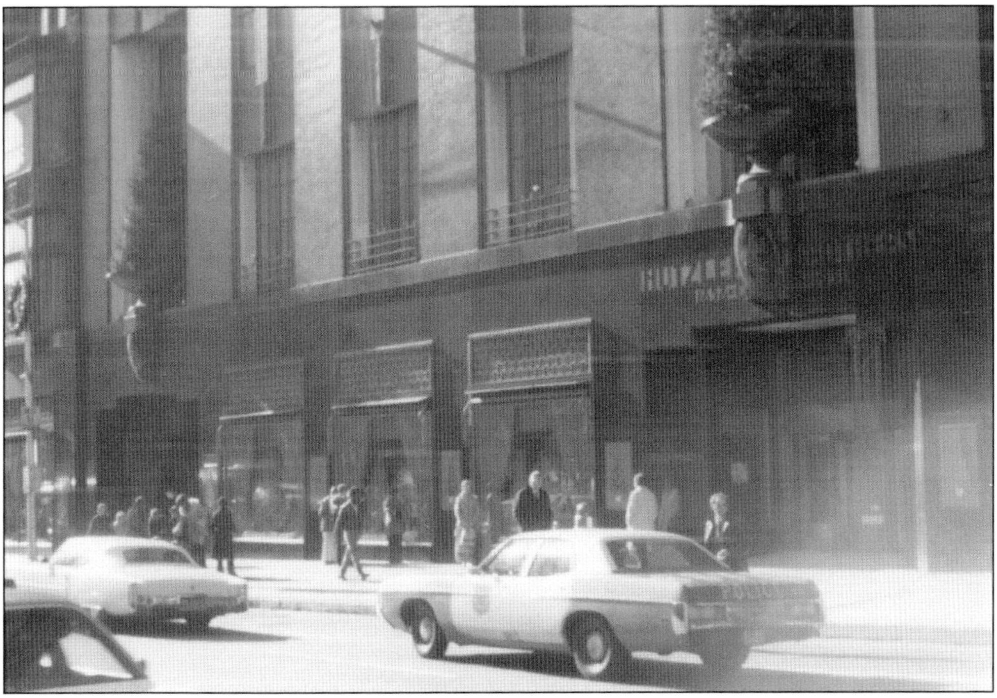

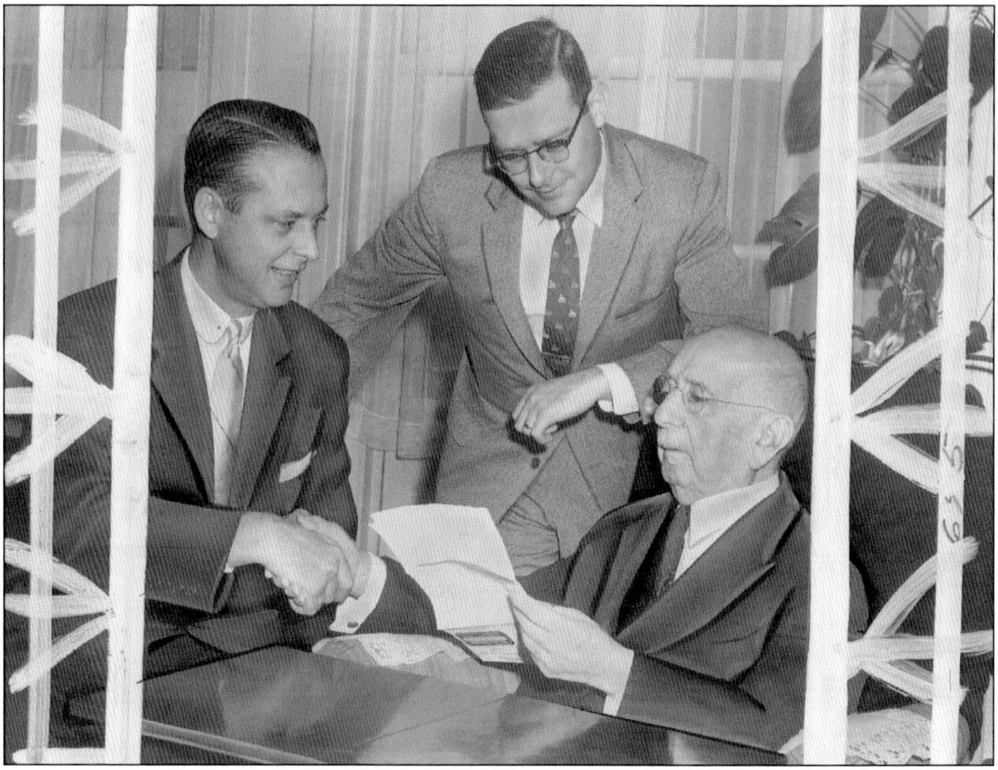

Max Hochschild was the owner and president of Hochschild-Kohn's, a Baltimore-based department store chain that prospered under his leadership. The store was started in 1897 as a partnership between Max Hochschild, Benno Kohn, and his brother Louis B. Kohn. Its largest location was the downtown store at Howard and Lexington Streets. As the suburbs flourished, the stores spread to other locations throughout the region, including the first suburban location at Edmonson Village. Hochschild's remained at Lexington and Howard until 1977, when it became the first of the Baltimore department stores to abandon its downtown flagship. During the civil rights upheaval in the 1960s, Hochschild's continued its series of "firsts" when it integrated and changed its strict policies of not allowing African-Americans to try on or return clothing. The chain went out of business in 1983. Hochschild lived in the Emersonian Apartments. He kept an office in the downtown store from his retirement in 1925 until shortly before his death on June 1, 1957, just before his 102 birthday. (Above, Tribune Company; below, BCPL.)

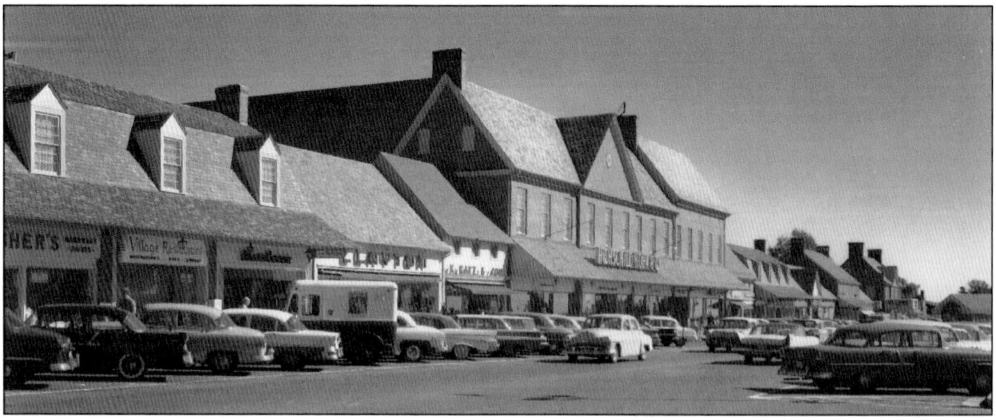

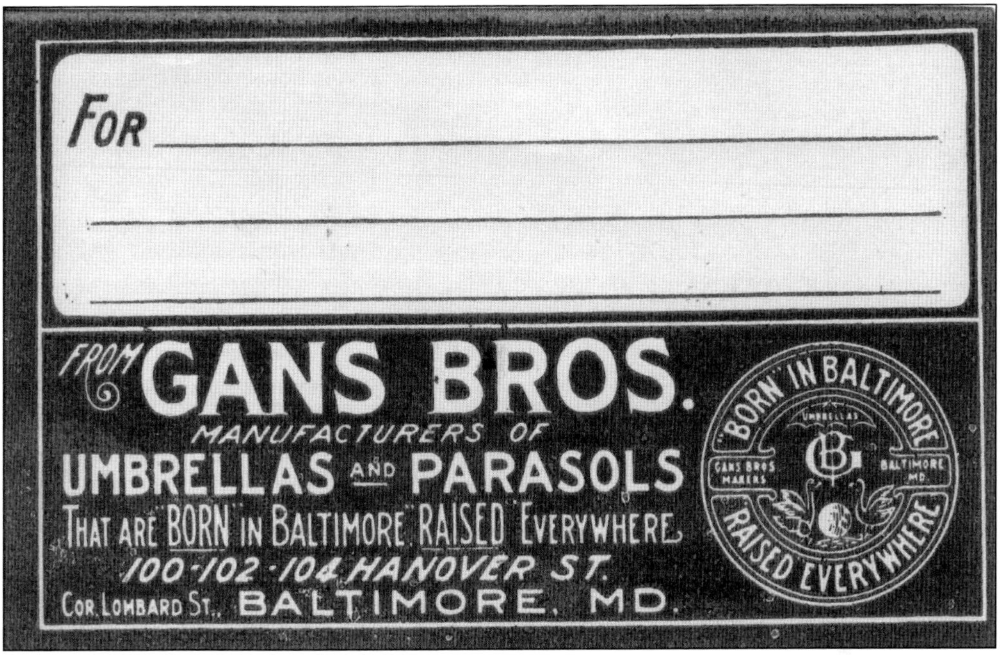

The first umbrella supposedly to be made in America was in Baltimore in 1772. Gans Brothers was the pioneer of the umbrella industry, which was producing more than two million umbrellas per year by 1922. Gans Brothers umbrellas and parasols were popular throughout the United States, Canada, and the West Indies. Thomas Gans lived at 2222 Eutaw Place. (Jewish Museum of Maryland.)

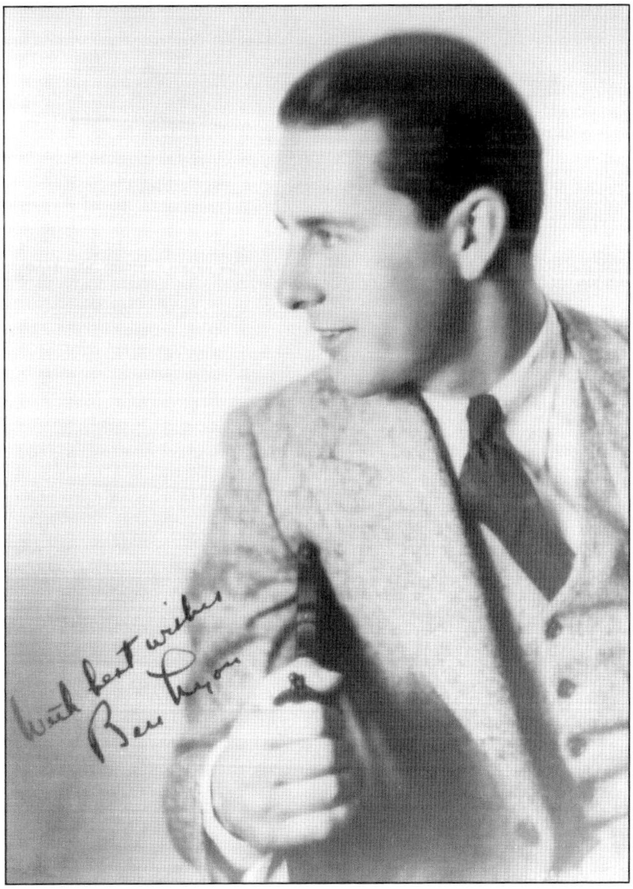

Ben Lyon was a leading man in Hollywood. He was an actor who appeared opposite many famous actresses, like Jean Harlow in *Hell's Angels*, and he was a producer. He was responsible for the discovery of Marilyn Monroe and securing her first contract. He lived at 2400 Callow Avenue. (silentsaregolden.com.)

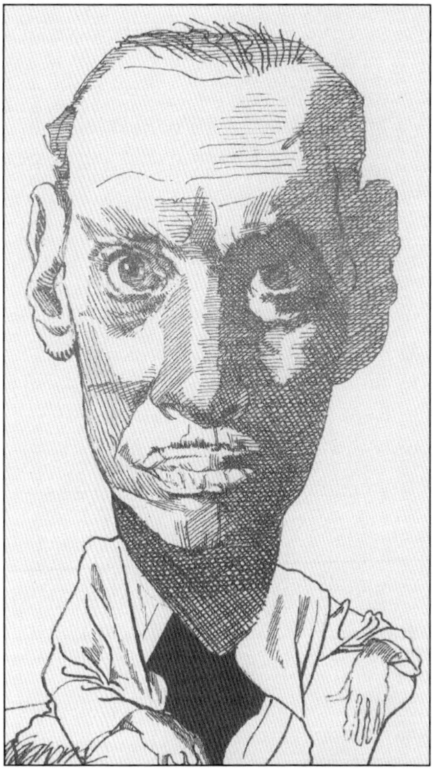

Born and raised in the Baltimore area, John Waters spent a portion of his young-adult life living in the Temple Gardens Apartments at the top of Madison Avenue, overlooking Druid Hill Park. Waters has a career spanning from the mid-1960s until present, which includes directing, acting, and writing. He has appeared in many television shows show, such as *My Name is Earl* and *Saturday Night Live*. His most famous movie has been *Hairspray*, which was based in Baltimore. It went on to become a Broadway musical in 2002 with much success and was then adapted to be released as a movie in 2007, grossing $202 million worldwide. (Both, Tribune Photo Archives.)

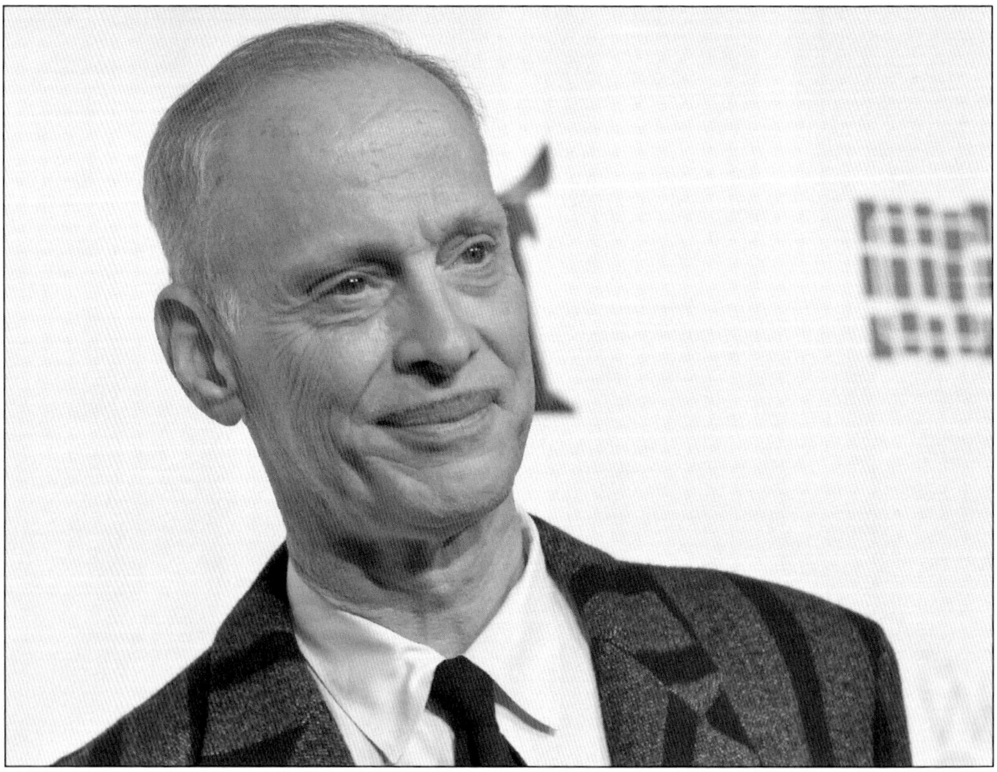

Felix Morley was a Pulitzer Prize–winning journalist who lived at 2026 Park Avenue. He was editor of the *Washington Post* when the paper's first Pulitzer Prize was won. Later, he became president of Haverford College after having battled with Pres. Franklin D. Roosevelt on his New Deal programs. He later supported the liberal Republican presidential candidate Wendell Willkie, who lost to Roosevelt in 1940. Morley died in 1982. (Triceratops Repository at Haverford College.)

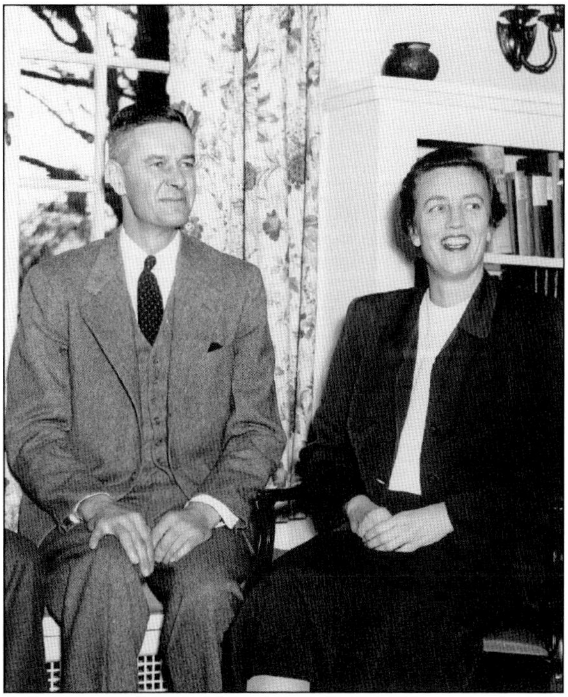

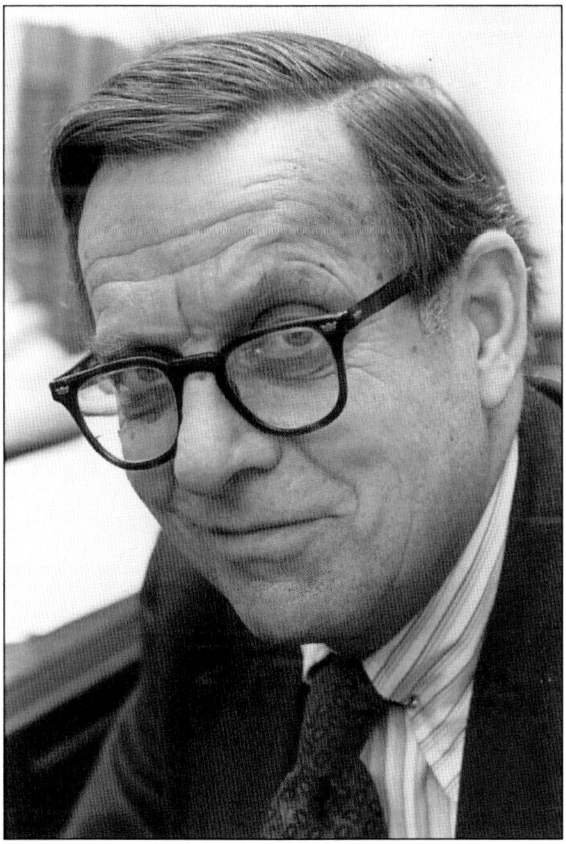

Dr. Lewis Thomas was a physician, poet, etymologist, essayist, administrator, educator, policy advisor, and researcher. He bridged the gap between science and literature through his insightful essays. Dr. Thomas lived at 1819 Park Avenue while attending Johns Hopkins to practice pediatrics and conduct research on rheumatic fever. He later became the dean of Yale Medical School and New York University School of Medicine. In 1973 he became the president of Memorial Sloan-Kettering Institute and led it to its eminence in cancer research and treatment. A collection of his monthly essays titled "Notes of a Biology Watcher," were published as "The Lives of Cells" and won the National Book Award in 1975. He died in 1993. (Yale Medical Historical Library)

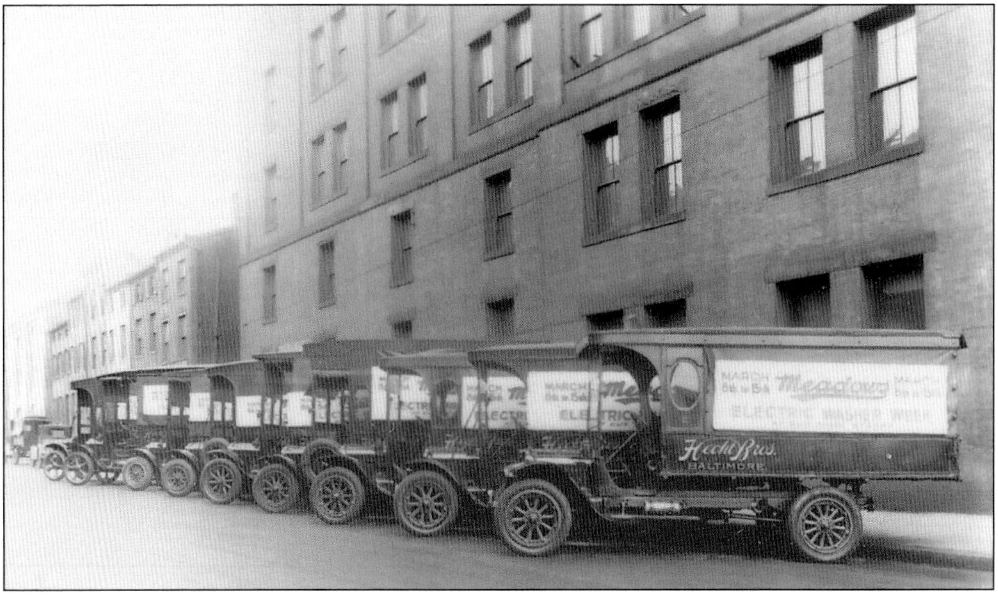

Alexander Hecht was president and vice chairman of the board for Hecht's department store. He died on February 4, 1949, in his home at the Emersonian Apartments. In 2005, Hecht's operated 81 stores in 19 markets in Maryland; Washington, DC; Virginia; North Carolina; Tennessee; Delaware; New Jersey; and Pennsylvania. Hecht's opened in 1857 and was sold to Macy's Department Stores in 2006. It was the last of the local Baltimore-based department stores to close. Above is a photograph of Hecht's delivery trucks, and below is a Hecht's sign shortly before being replaced for a Macy's sign. (Above, BCPL; below, author's collection.)

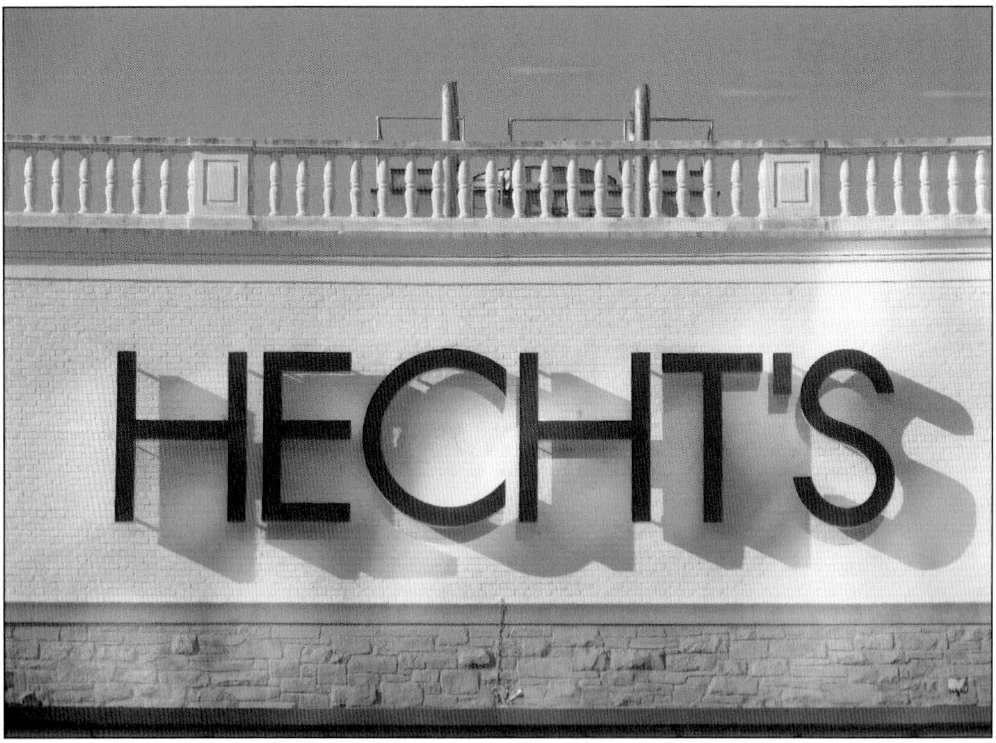

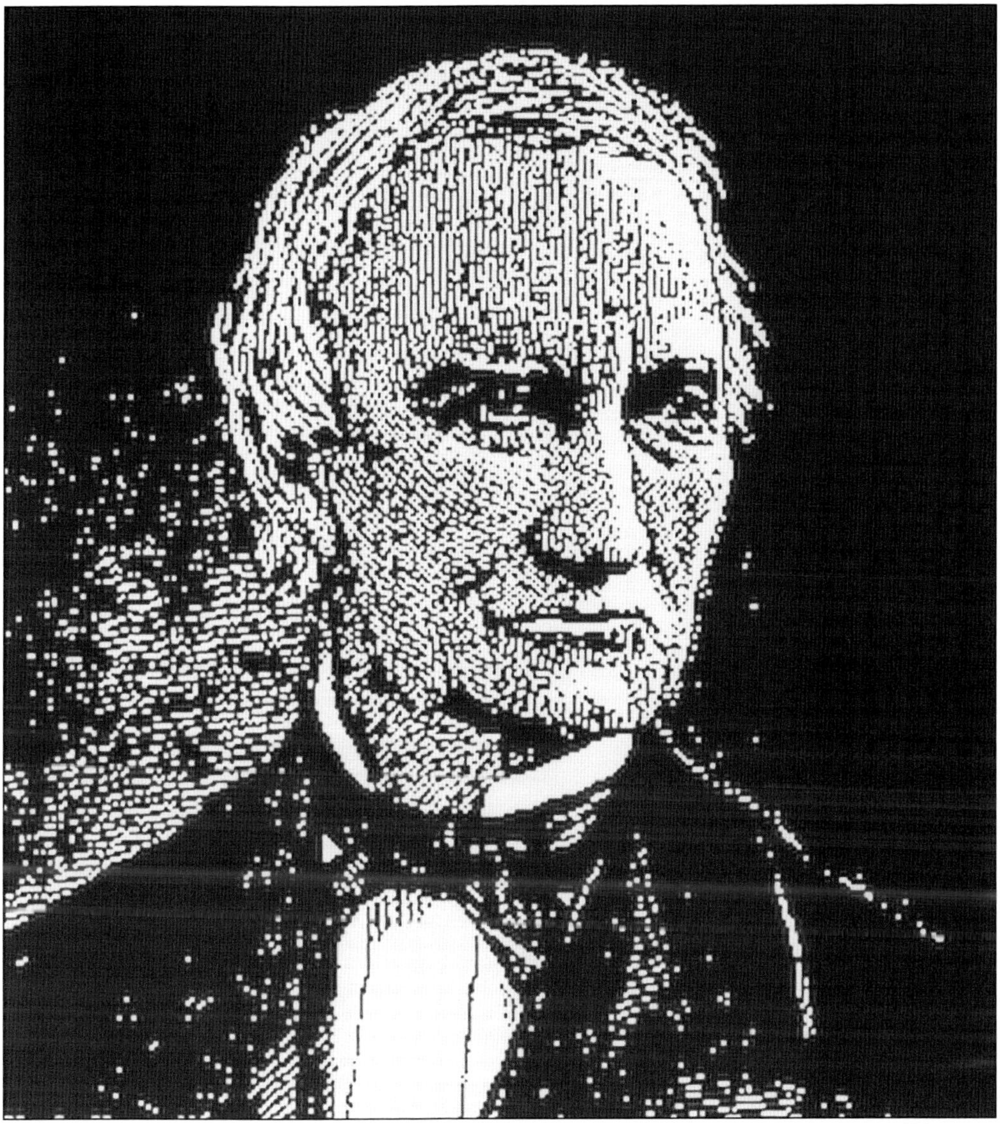

Chauncey Brooks was the president of the B&O Railroad. He is one of the most well-known persons in Baltimore history and was one of the early leaders of the city. Brooks came to Baltimore after the War of 1812 and is credited for stopping the B&O Railroad strike of 1857, something that two companies of soldiers and a governor could not successfully complete. He started a number of well-known businesses in his career and was the original director of the Peabody Institute and Western National Bank. He was the owner to the Cloverdale estate at Eutaw Place and Druid Hill Park. He died on May 18, 1880. (Tribune Photo Archives.)

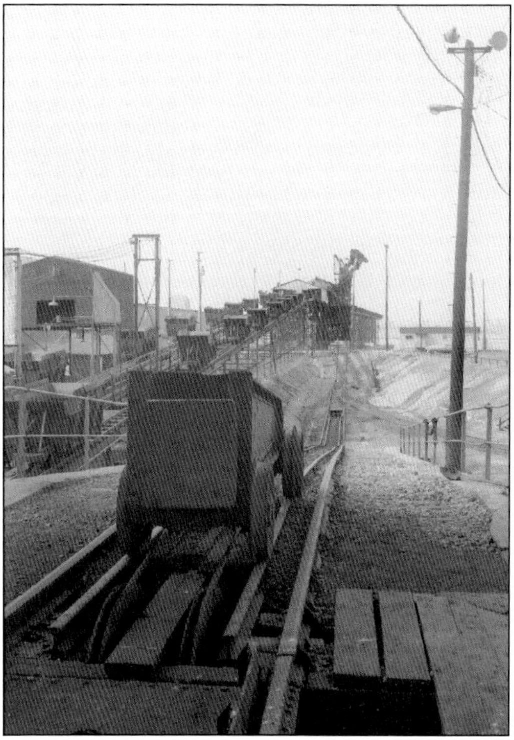

Pictured at left is the Canton Company coal pier. Walter B. Brooks, son of Chauncey Brooks, was president of the Canton Company, which was the developer of the land and owner of the railroad and piers that now include the well-known Baltimore neighborhood of Canton. He was the unsuccessful Republican candidate for governor in 1887. Brooks died January 17, 1896, at his home on Lake Drive. (Library of Congress.)

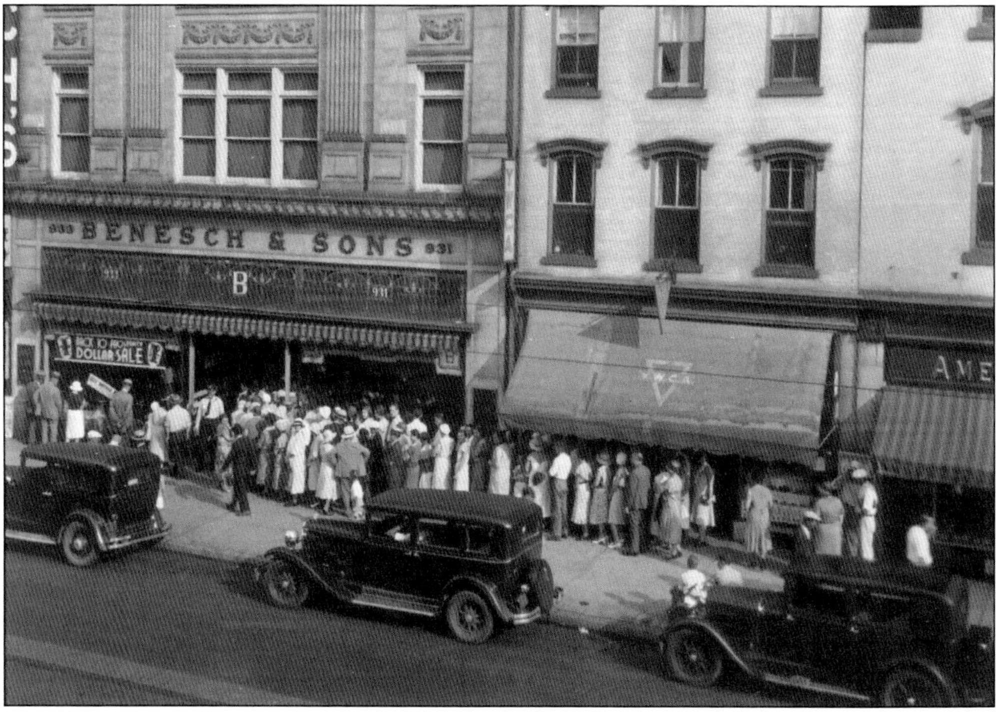

Isaac Benesch was the founder and president of Isaac Benesch and Sons department store. It had locations in Baltimore and Annapolis, Wilkes-Barre, Pennsylvania, and Pottsville, Pennsylvania. He died on January 4, 1910, at his home at 2438 Eutaw Place. (Jewish Museum of Maryland.)

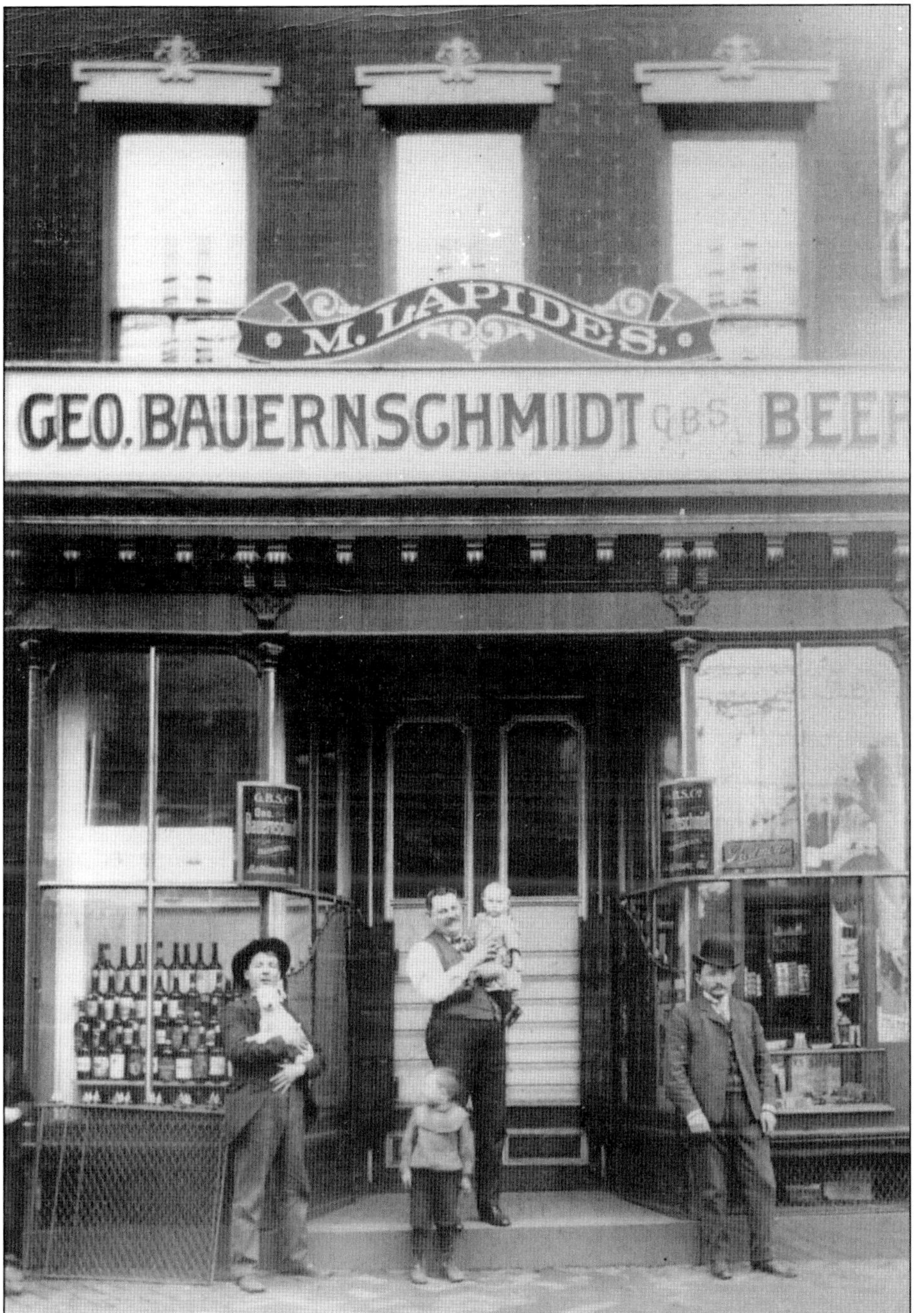

Frederick Bauernschmidt was owner and president of Frederick Bauernschmidt American Brewing Company. Throughout his life he gave millions of dollars to area hospitals, including the donation for the Bauernschmidt Wing of Union Memorial Hospital. The company closed not long after the Volstead Act was enacted and Prohibition began. During the late 1800s, it was the largest brewery in Baltimore, producing more than 60,000 barrels per year. Bauernschmidt died on March 8, 1933. He lived at 2450 Eutaw Place. Bauernschmidt's father, George, lived at North Avenue and Broadway at a mansion that is now part of the Great Blacks in Wax Museum. (Jewish Museum of Maryland.)

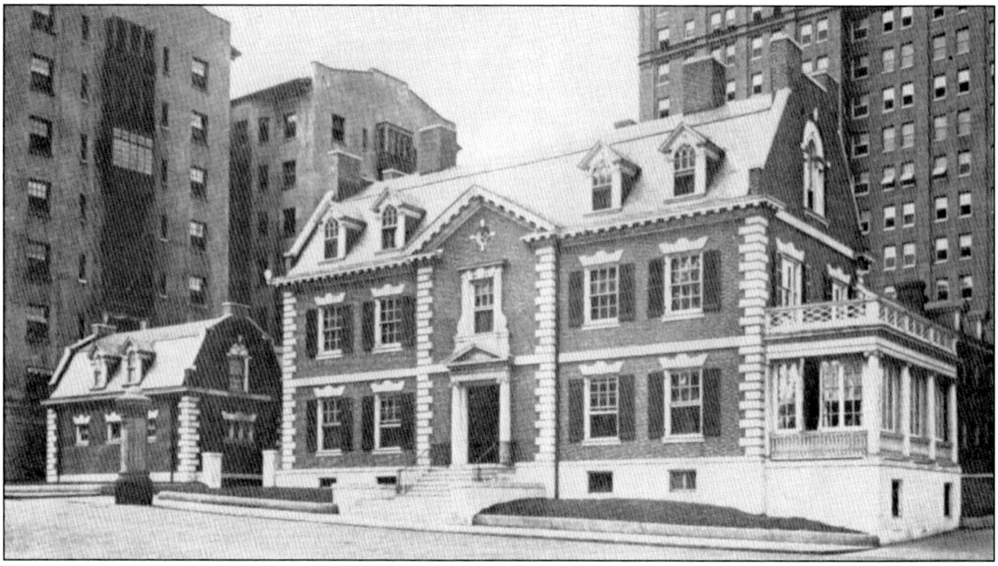

Gen. Alfred E. Booth, along with his brother, owned and operated Booth & Co., a fish- and oyster-packing and transportation company. In 1902, it was thought to be the largest fish-packing firm in the world. At its peak, 85 branches of the company operated in the United States and Canada. Booth died on May 10, 1914, at his home at Eutaw Place and Lake Drive. (Dale Dusman.)

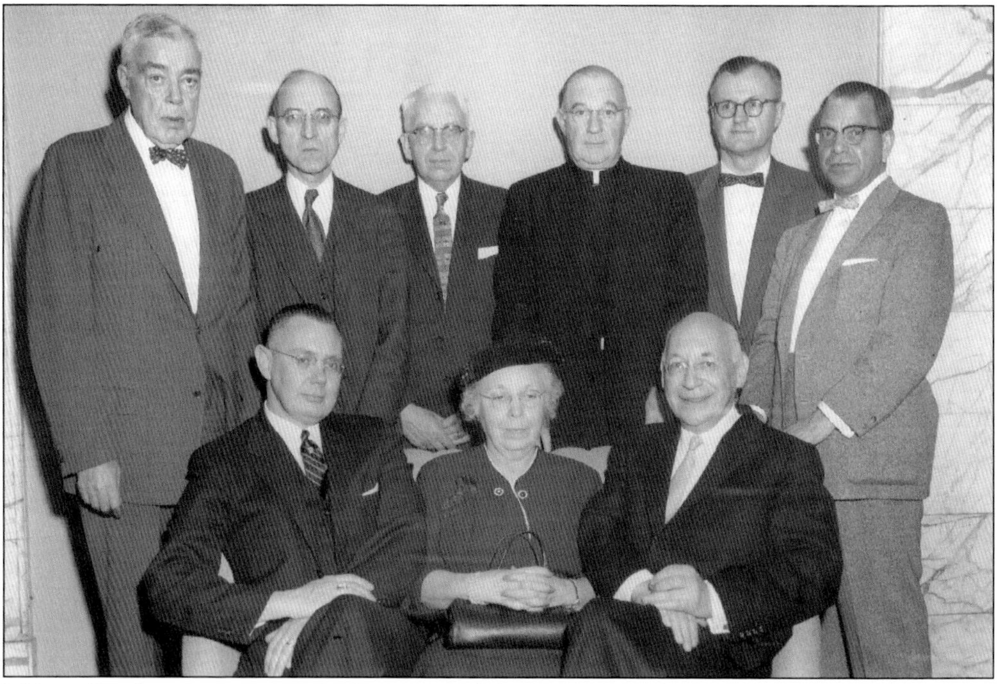

J. Kemp Bartlett, a pioneer in the formation of the Mount Royal Protective Association, lawyer, and a leader in Republican state politics, lived at 2100 Mount Royal Terrace. Bartlett, along with John R. Bland, organized the US Fidelity and Guaranty Company (USF&G), which became one of the largest surety/casualty companies in the United States. USF&G remained on Fortune 500 list until its acquisition in 1998. Bartlett died on October 20, 1948. Pictured is Bartlett standing on the left. (Jewish Museum of Maryland.)

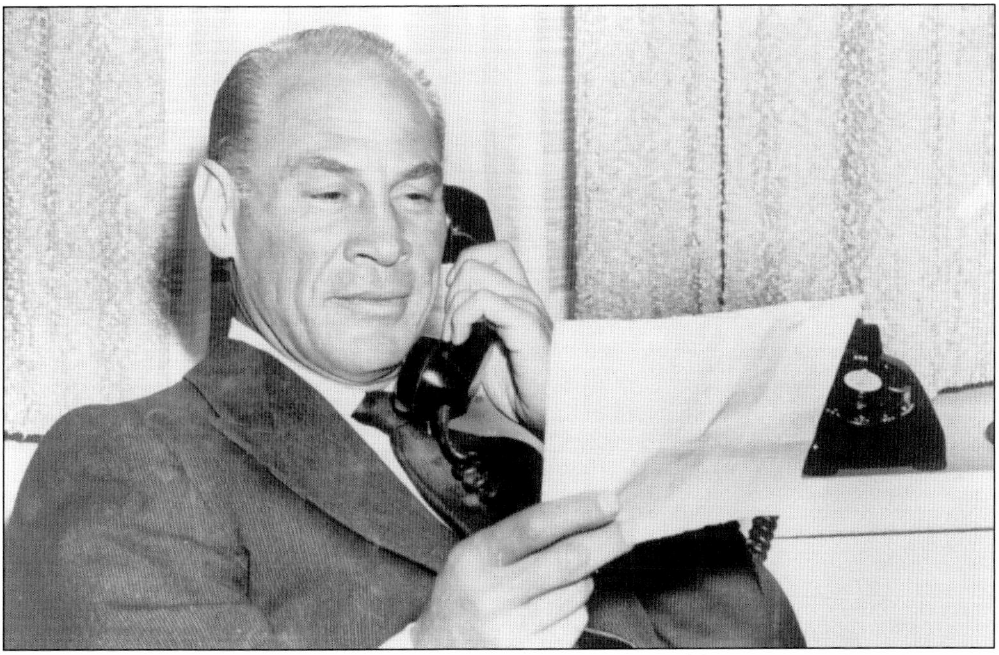

Carroll Rosenbloom was born in Baltimore on March 5, 1907, and became a modern American entrepreneur. He graduated from Baltimore City College and later played football at the University of Pennsylvania. As the owner of the Baltimore Colts (and later the Los Angeles Rams), he negotiated contracts for television which contributed to the profitability of professional football. During his tenure, the Baltimore Colts won the 1958 and 1959 NFL championships and the 1971 Super Bowl. Rosenbloom died on April 2, 1979, in Golden Beach, Florida. He lived in a mansion on Mount Royal Terrace, which was the last home on the block before entering Druid Hill Park. (Above, Tribune Photo Archives; below, Historic Images.)

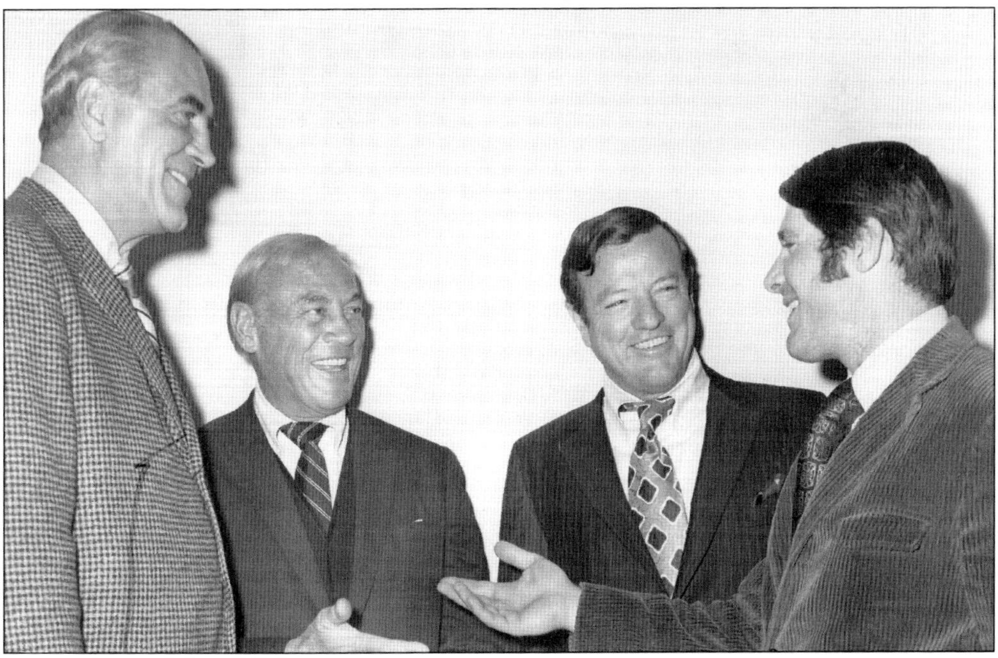

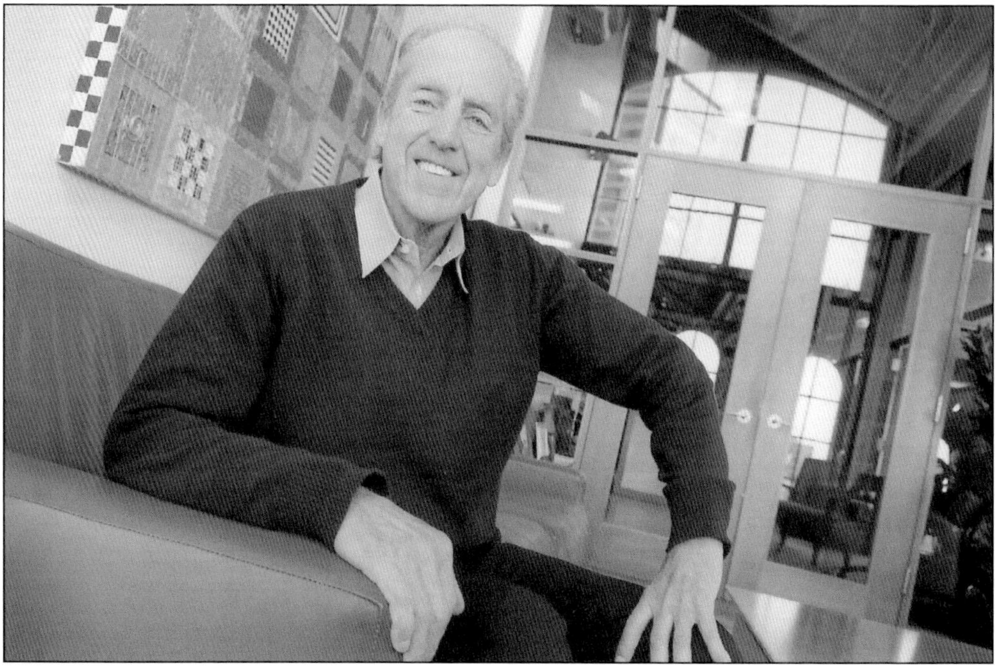

David Cordish is the president and chairman of the Cordish Company, a third-generation company headquartered in Baltimore and founded by his father, Paul Cordish. Today, it is well known for its real estate expertise and is the largest and most successful developer of entertainment districts and for revitalizing urban locations around the country. Prominent projects of the Cordish Company in Baltimore include the Baltimore Inner Harbor and Power Plant Live! seen below. David Cordish lived on the 900 block of Brooks Lane. (Both, *Maryland Daily Record*.)

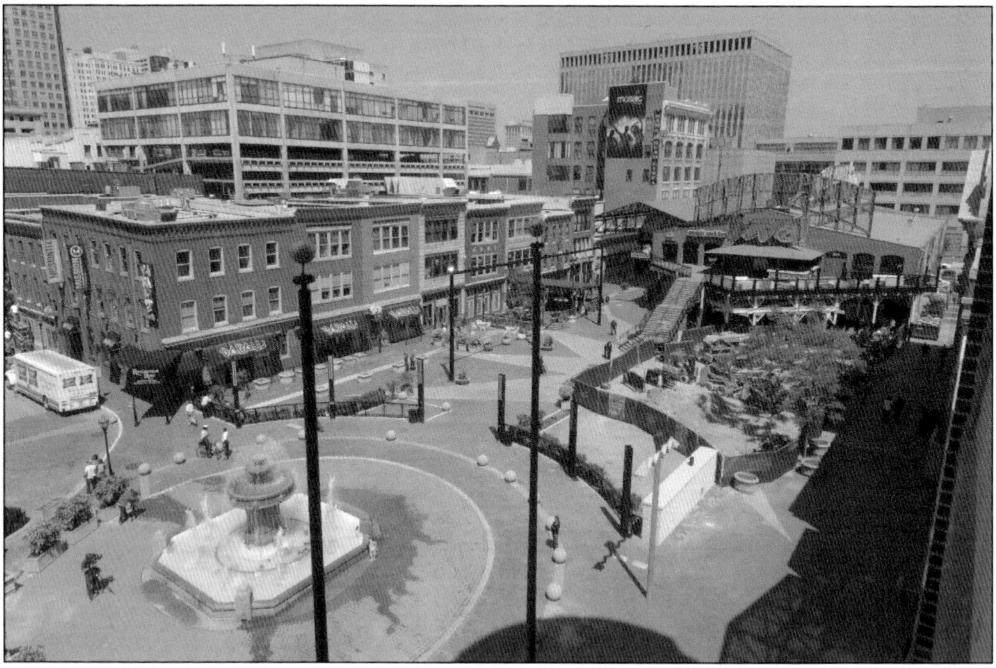

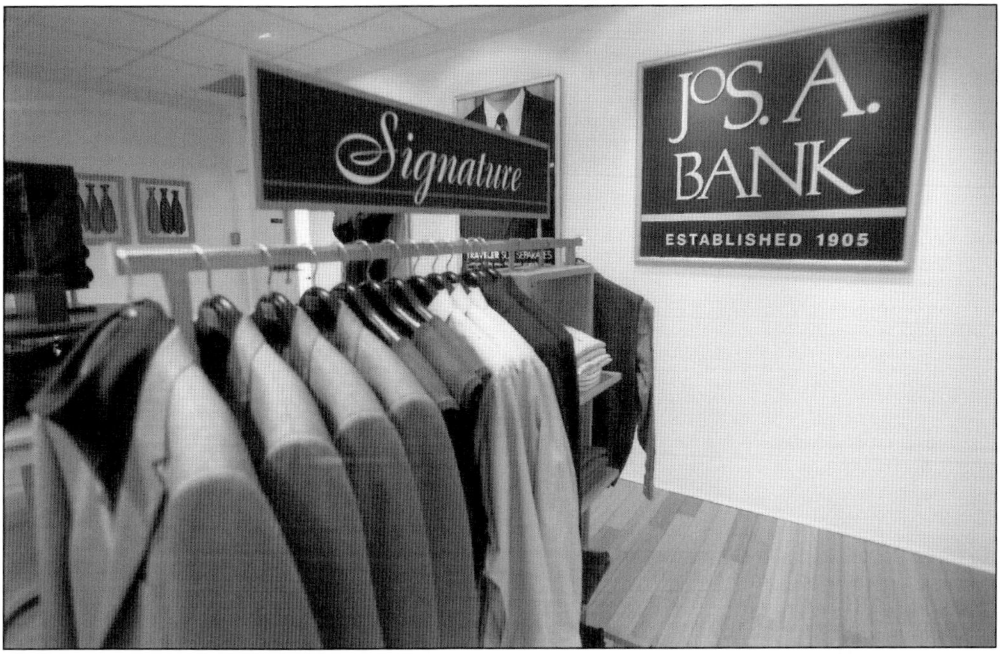

In 1903, Joseph A. Bank founded the Jos. A. Bank & Co. A publicly traded company on NASDAQ, Jos. A. Bank & Co. specializes in men's suits and clothing and has more than 500 locations nationwide. Bank merged his company with Hartz Clothing in 1922 and changed its name to Hartz and Bank. In 1945, Bank bought out the Hartz interest in the company and changed its name to Jos. A. Bank & Co. Bank, who died in 1954, lived at 2405 Linden Avenue. His home still stands and is now the location of the St. Francis Neighborhood Center. Below is the Jos. A Bank store in downtown Dallas, Texas. (Both, *Maryland Daily Record*.)

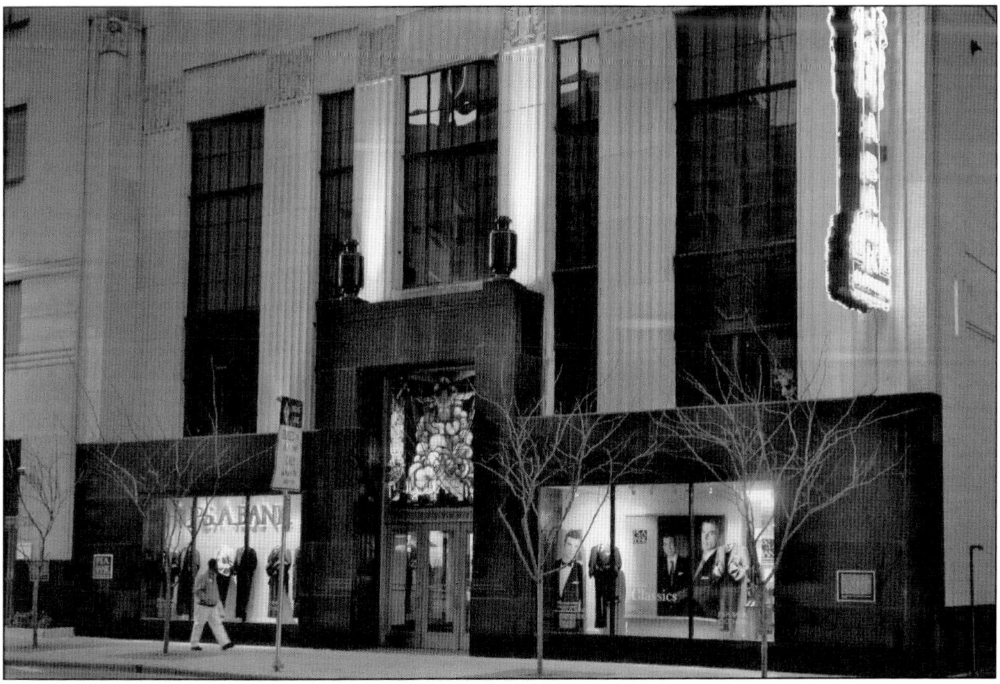

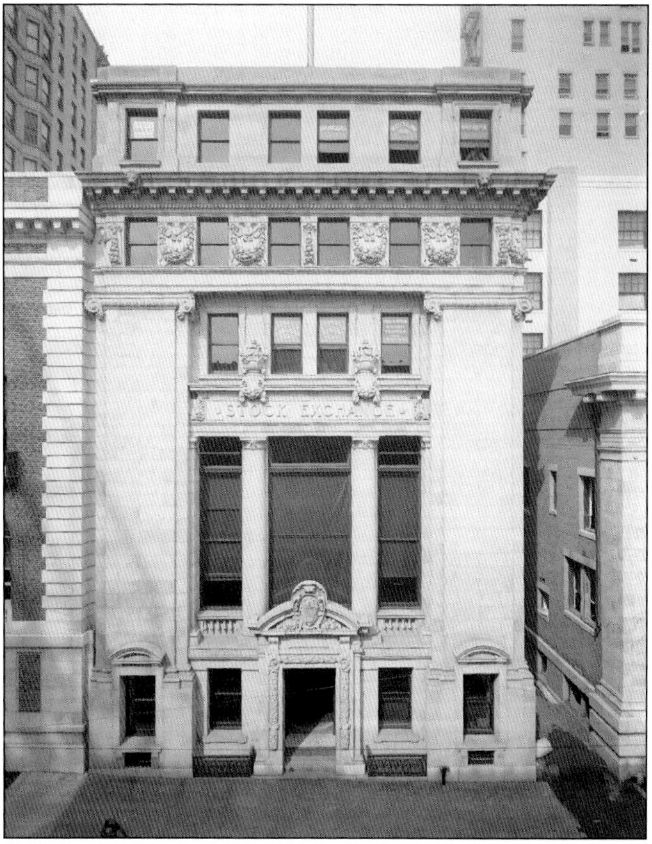

Derek Fahnestock was the owner and founder of the bank D. Fahnestock & Co. He was the president of the Baltimore Stock Exchange for 14 years. The Baltimore Stock Exchange merged with the Philadelphia Stock Exchange in 1949, which is the oldest stock exchange in the United States. Fahnestock died on May 11, 1903. He lived at 2503 Madison Avenue. Pictured is the original home of the Baltimore Stock Exchange. (Tribune Photo Archives.)

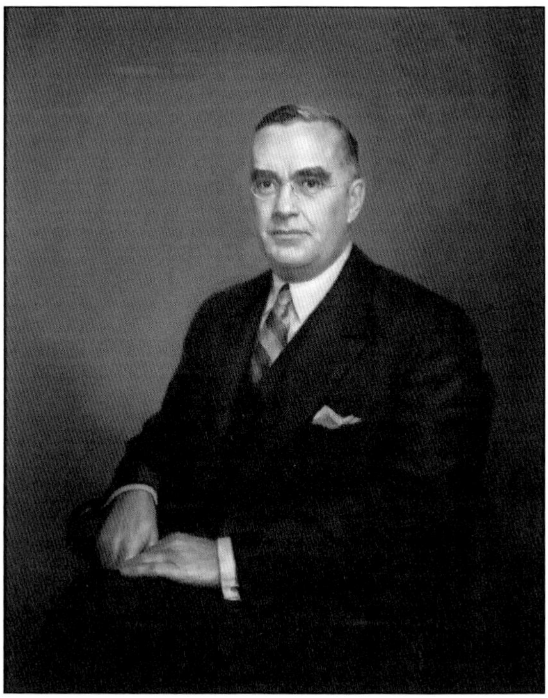

W. Wallace Lanahan was one of the more well-known philanthropists of Baltimore. He was president of the board of the Johns Hopkins Hospital and trustee of Johns Hopkins University. Professionally, he was the founder of W.W. Lanahan & Co., which merged with Alex Brown and Sons in 1942. He was also a member of the board of governors for the New York Stock Exchange. Lanahan died on August 30, 1948, at 2418 Eutaw Place. (Johns Hopkins Hospital Library.)

Dr. Randolph Winslow is best known for introducing antiseptic surgery to Maryland. He was a professor of surgery at the University of Maryland Medical School and the founder of Women's Medical College. Winslow died on February 27, 1937, after 61 years of service at the University of Maryland Medical School. He lived at 1900 Mount Royal Terrace for more than five decades. (Health Sciences and Human Services Library, University of Maryland.)

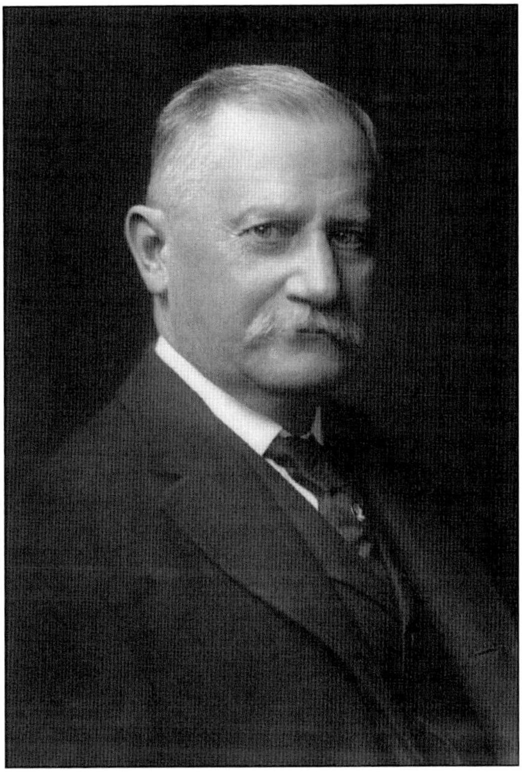

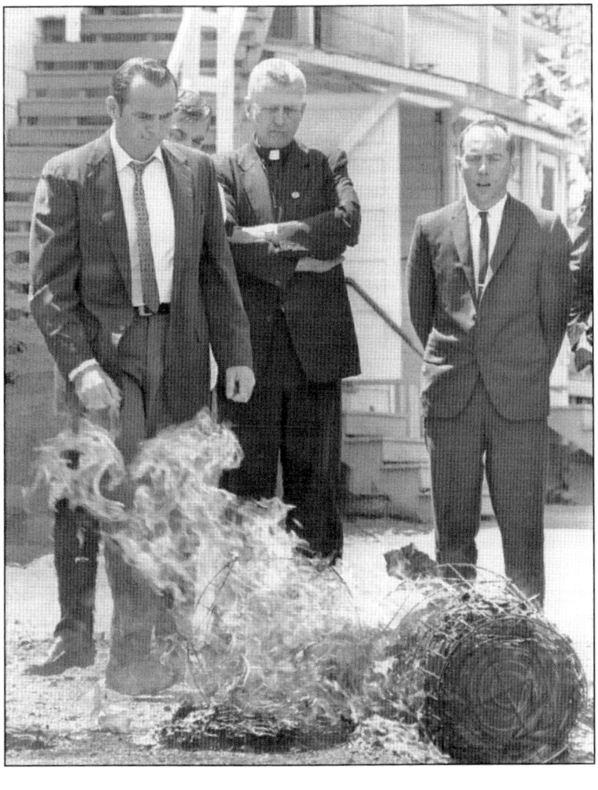

Philip Francis Berrigan (October 5, 1923–December 6, 2002) was an internationally renowned nonviolent, anti-war activist who was part of the Catonsville Nine, a group of Catholic priests who protested by burning draft records. For a time, he was on the FBI's Most Wanted List, along with his brother Daniel Berrigan, for this destruction of government property. He left the priesthood and married Elizabeth McAllister and together they founded the Jonah House in Baltimore to support the anti-war movement. Berrigan lived on the 1900 block of Park Avenue. (Tribune Photo Archives.)

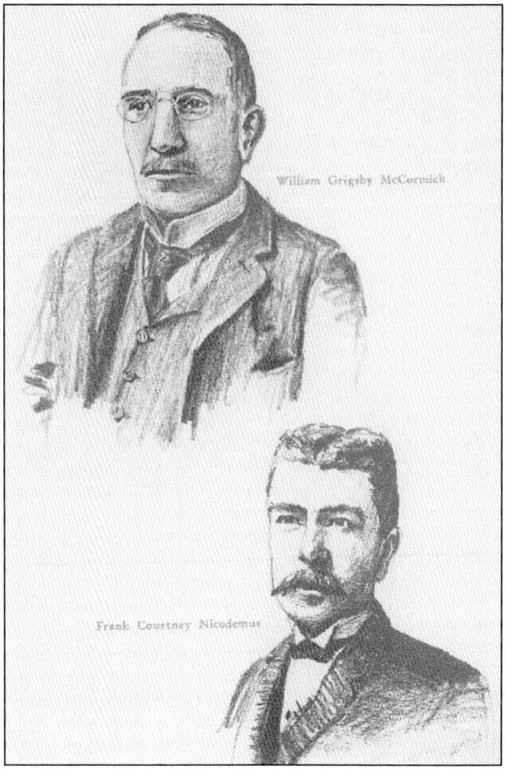

William Grigsby McCormick, pictured at the top of the photograph, was a Chicago businessman and politician who spent his later years living at the Cloverdale estate near present-day Brooks Lane. He married Eleanor Brooks, daughter of Walter Brooks. McCormick was the cofounder of the fraternity Kappa Sigma and was a city councilman in Chicago. His company was listed with the Chicago Board of Trade and the New York Stock Exchange. McCormick died on November 29, 1941, in Wheaton, Illinois. (Paul Walker collection.)

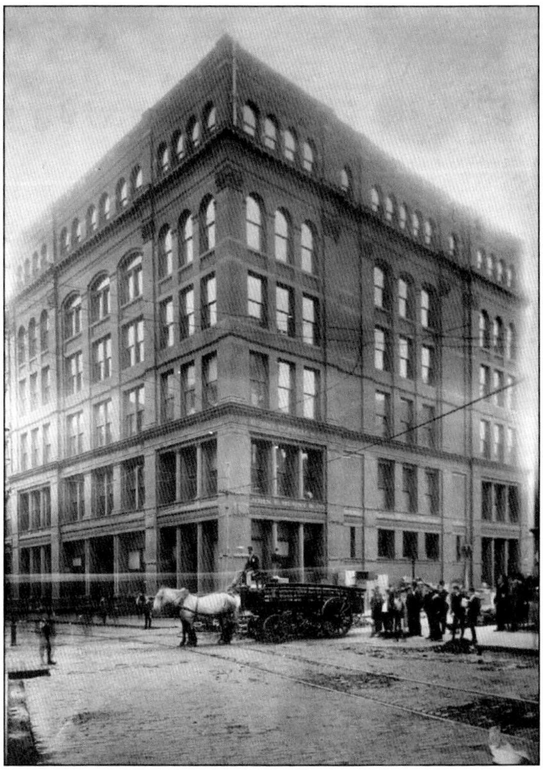

Millard F. Burgess, resident of 2233 Eutaw Place, was the head of John E. Hurst & Co., pictured at right. This building was the location of the start of the Great Baltimore Fire of 1904, which destroyed much of downtown Baltimore. He was active in Republican politics and was once considered as candidate for mayor. He died on April 24, 1926. (Fire Museum of Maryland.)

Frank O'Hara, raised at 2044 Linden Avenue, was one of the foremost poets of the New York School, which was an informal group of American poets, painters, dancers, and musicians. During his lifetime, Frank O'Hara worked as a curator for the Museum of Modern Art in New York, wrote for *Art News* as an art reviewer, and published seven books of poetry. He died on July 25, 1966. (Sensual World, Inc.)

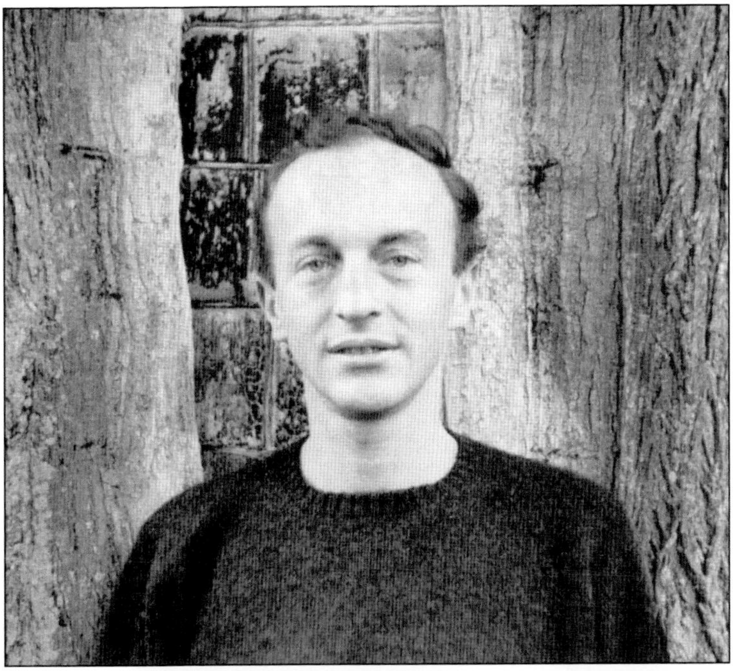

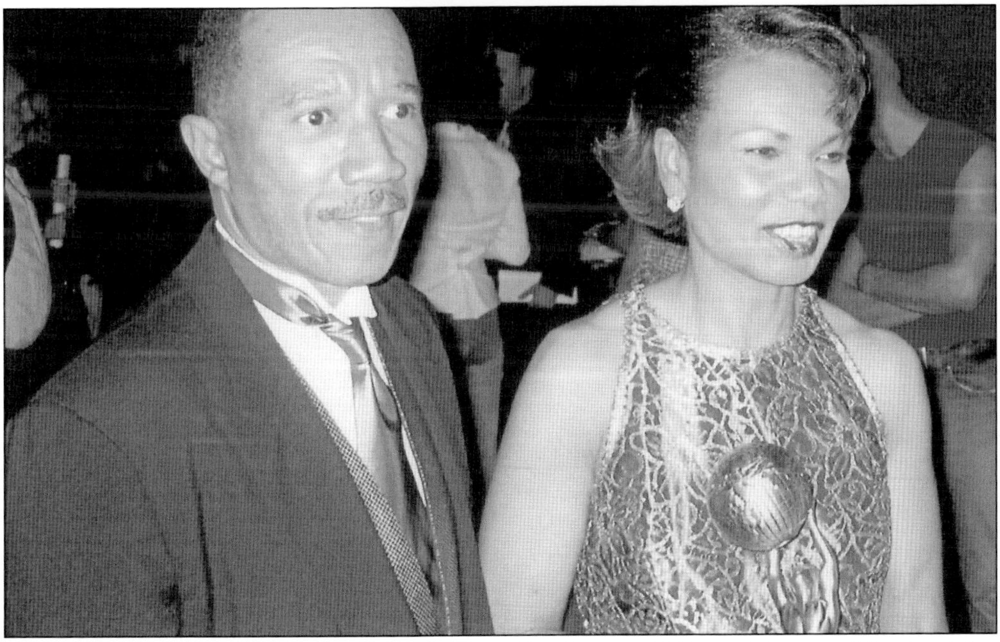

Kweisi Mfume was born Frizzell Gerald Gray on October 24, 1948, in Baltimore, Maryland. He struggled as a teen, dropping out of school at 16 but at the age of 23 he turned his life around, obtained his GED, and went on to graduate magna cum laude from Morgan State University. He left the Maryland House of Representatives after serving as a five-term Democratic congressman from Maryland's 7th congressional district to become the president/chief executive officer of the National Association for the Advancement of Colored People (NAACP). Mfume decided to run for the US Senate after Sen. Paul Sarbanes declared he would not run for reelection in 2006; he lost his primary campaign to Sen. Ben Cardin. (Bauer Griffin.)

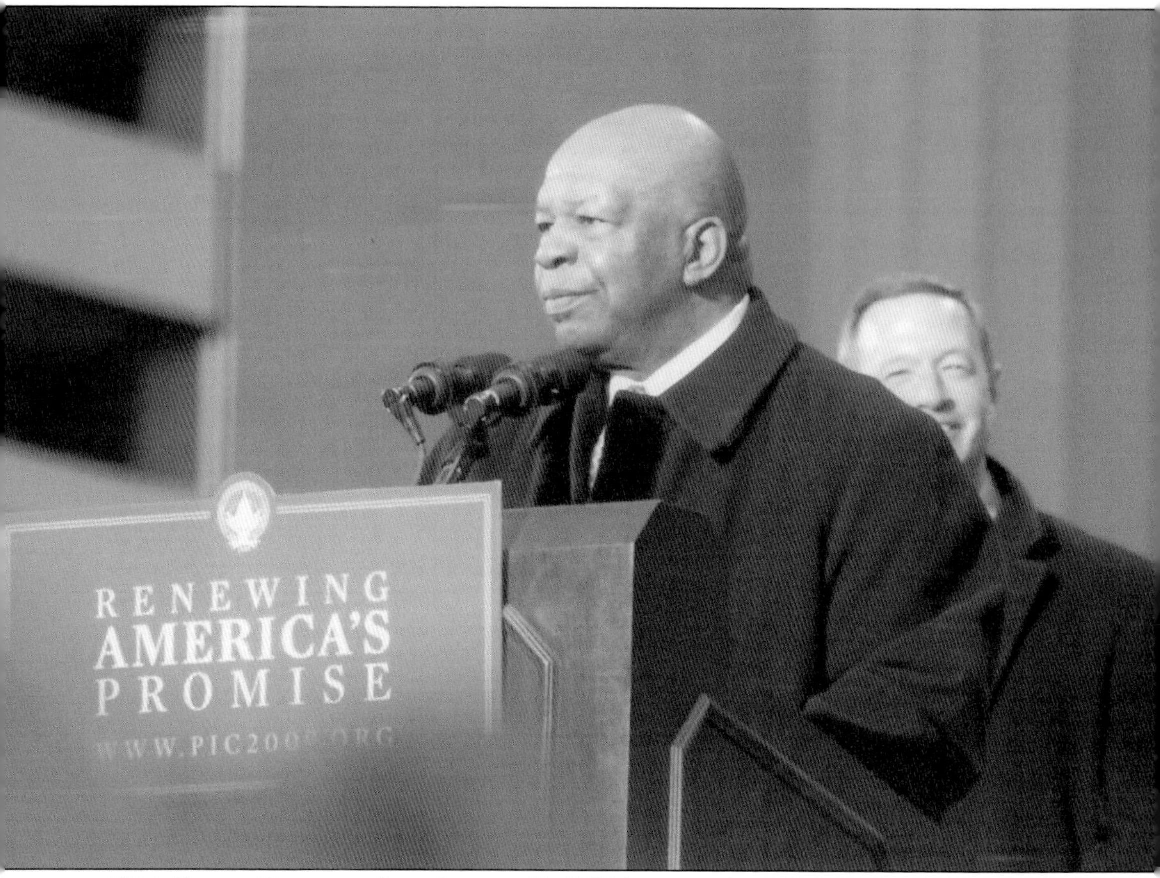

Elijah Eugene Cummings (born January 18, 1951) has served as a Democratic US representative for Maryland's 7th Congressional District since 1996. This district includes more than half of Baltimore City, as well as most of Howard County, Maryland. While serving in the Maryland General Assembly, he was the chairman of the Legislative Black Caucus of Maryland and the first African American in Maryland history to be named speaker pro tempore, the second-highest position in the House of Delegates. He is a board member for the Maryland Zoo and the Baltimore Area Council of the Boy Scouts of America among many of his community roles. He lives on Madison Avenue. (Choice Imagery.)

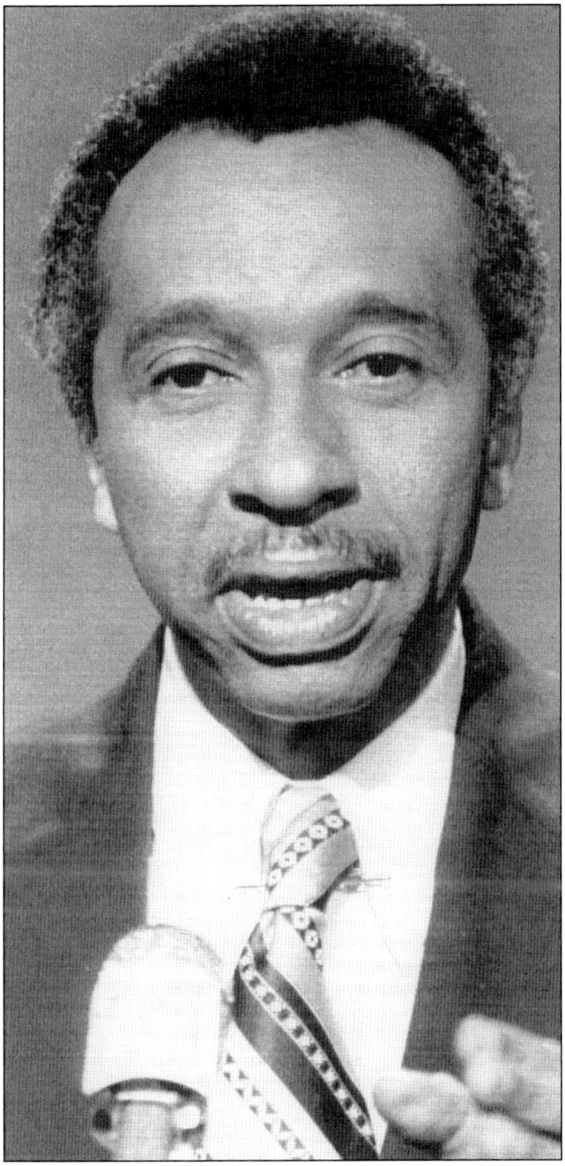

Parren James Mitchell was a US congressman who represented the 7th district from 1971 to 1987. He graduated from Frederick Douglass Senior High School in 1940 and obtained his bachelor's degree from Morgan State University. He was the first African American graduate student to complete his coursework on the campus of the University of Maryland, College Park and received his master of arts degree in sociology in 1952. Parren was one of the inaugural members of the university's alumni hall of fame, which is especially significant in light of the fact that he sued and won in order to be admitted to the University of Maryland Graduate School in 1950. He was one of the founding members of the Congressional Black Caucus and was an ardent supporter of affirmative action. Parren was the brother of Clarence Mitchell who was one of the chief advisors to Lyndon Johnson during the civil rights movement. When Parren died in 2007, Congressman Elijah Cummings delivered his eulogy and honored him with these words: "He earned the trust of people throughout the country and the world because he was constantly building bridges for others to cross, while tearing down the walls that had excluded them." (Tribune Photo Archives.)

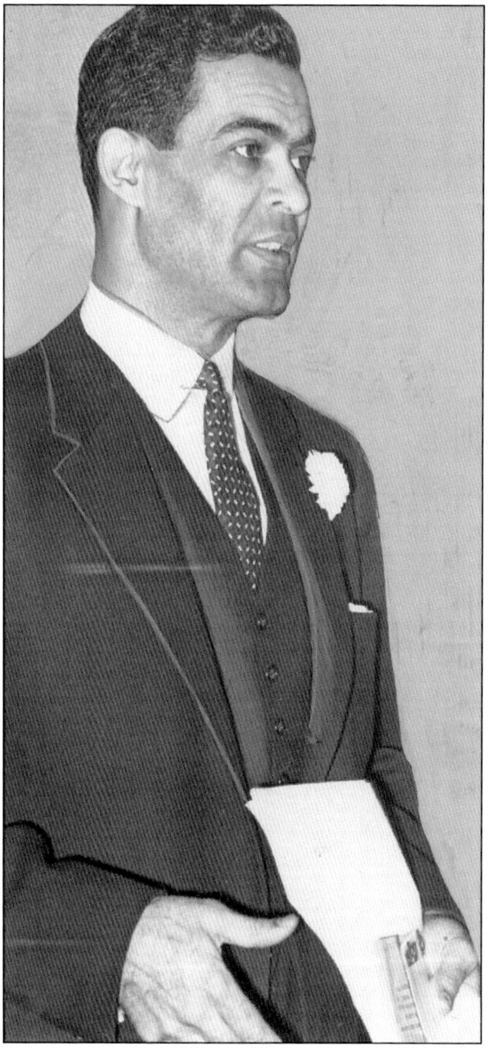

Henry Parks was a successful businessman, owner, and founder of Parks Sausage Co. The company started out as a small company with only two employees that eventually grew into a multimillion dollar enterprise with over 200 employees. Parks Sausage, one of the United States's leading food manufacturers, was the first black-owned business to be publicly traded in the United States. Parks lived on the 1900 block of Park Avenue and died on April 14, 1989. (Both, Library of Congress.)

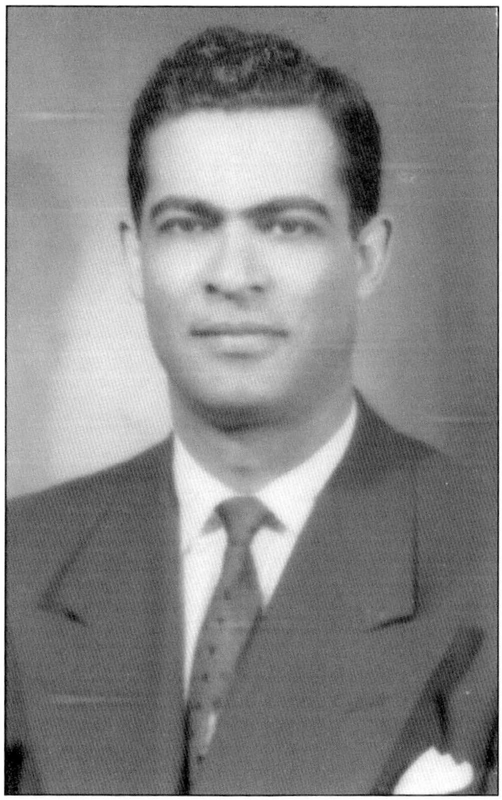

Isaac Emerson was founder of the Emerson Drug Company; Bromo-Seltzer, Inc.; Maryland Glass Corporation; and the Emerson Hotel. The Emersonian Apartments are named after him and sit between his former home at 2500 Eutaw Place and Druid Hill Park. Once the building was completed, his ex-wife, Ann McCormack, who had resided in the home after the divorce, could no longer see the park from their former home. Emerson died on January 24, 1931. (Library of Congress.)

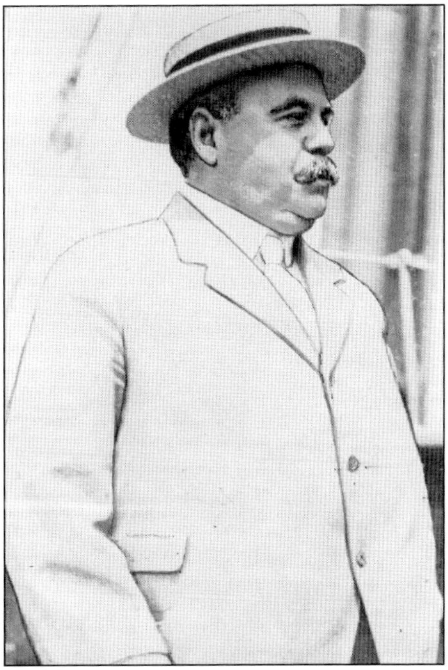

This is a portrait of the Hendler family in their living room at Lake Drive and Eutaw Place. Pictured in 1935 are, from left to right, (first row) Belle Hendler (mother of Manuel), Joann Kolodny, and Sophie Duke (mother of Rose); (second row) Manuel Hendler, Bernice Kolodny (mother of Joann and daughter of Rose and Manuel), and Rose Hendler (wife of Manuel). Jacob Udel took this photograph. (Jewish Museum of Maryland.)

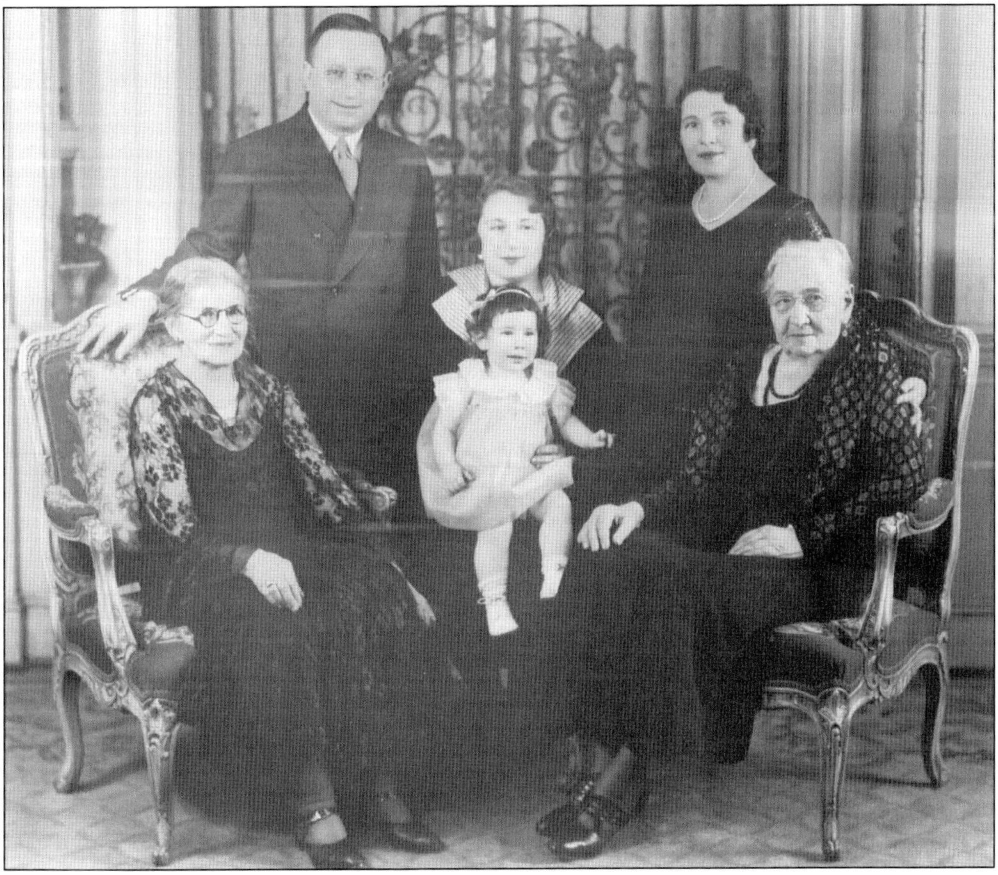

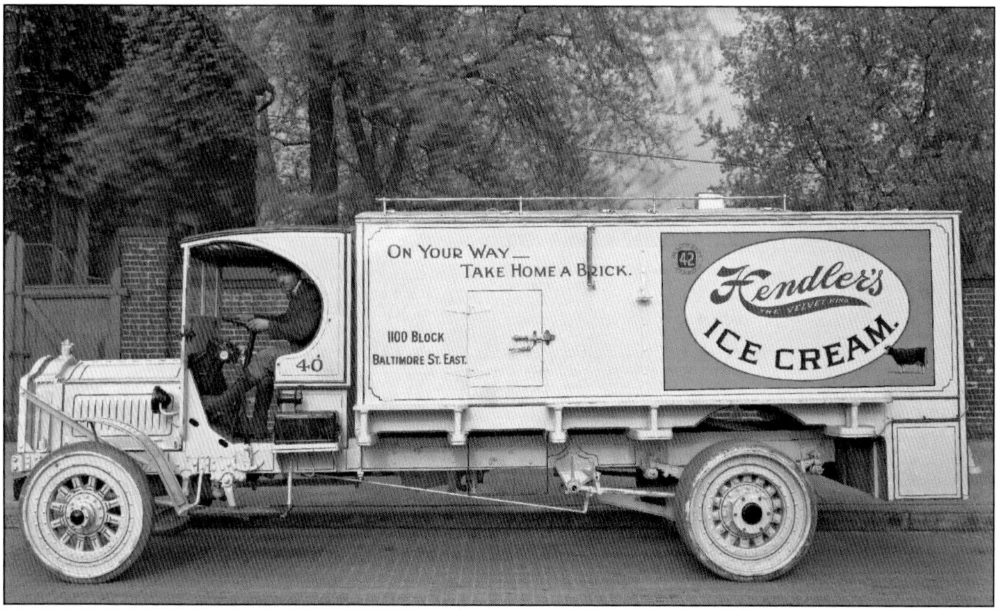

Manuel Hendler and his son Albert owned and operated Hendler Creamery Company from 1905 until 1965. As one of Baltimore's most popular ice creams, the company had 400 stores that were served by the company's fleet of 120 delivery trucks. The Hendler name could be found in drugstores, supermarkets, and neighborhood groceries. Perhaps the Hendler product whose loss is most lamented is the eggnog ice cream flavored with rum. According to the *Baltimore Sun*, "Hendler's was the only ice cream company in America to have a liquor license in order to blend liquor into ice cream." (Above, Jewish Museum of Maryland; below, Baltimore Museum of Industry, BGE Collection.)

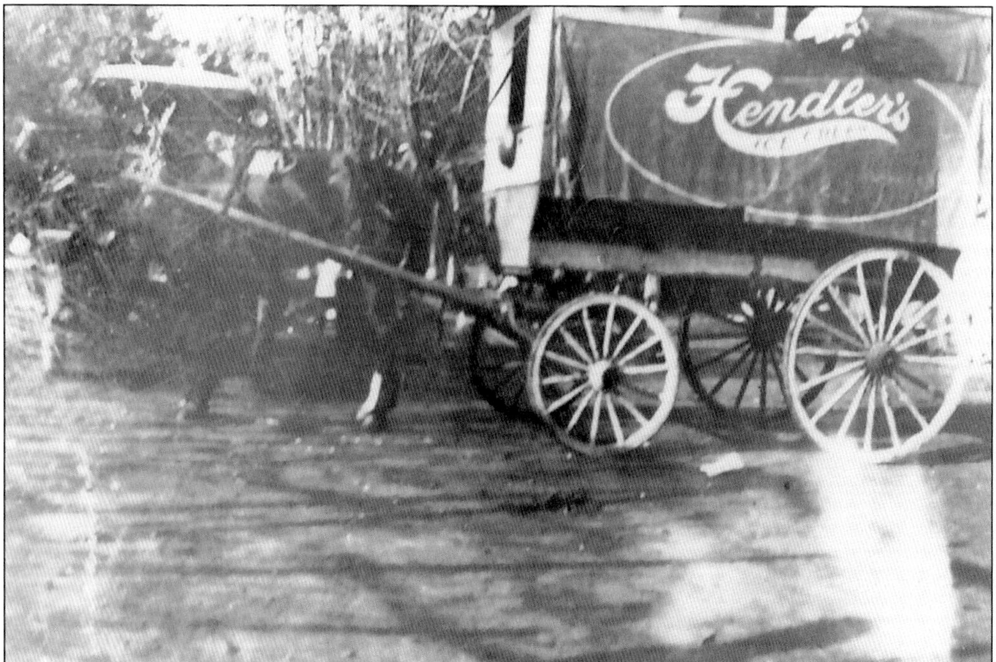

Seven

Business, Education, and Leisure

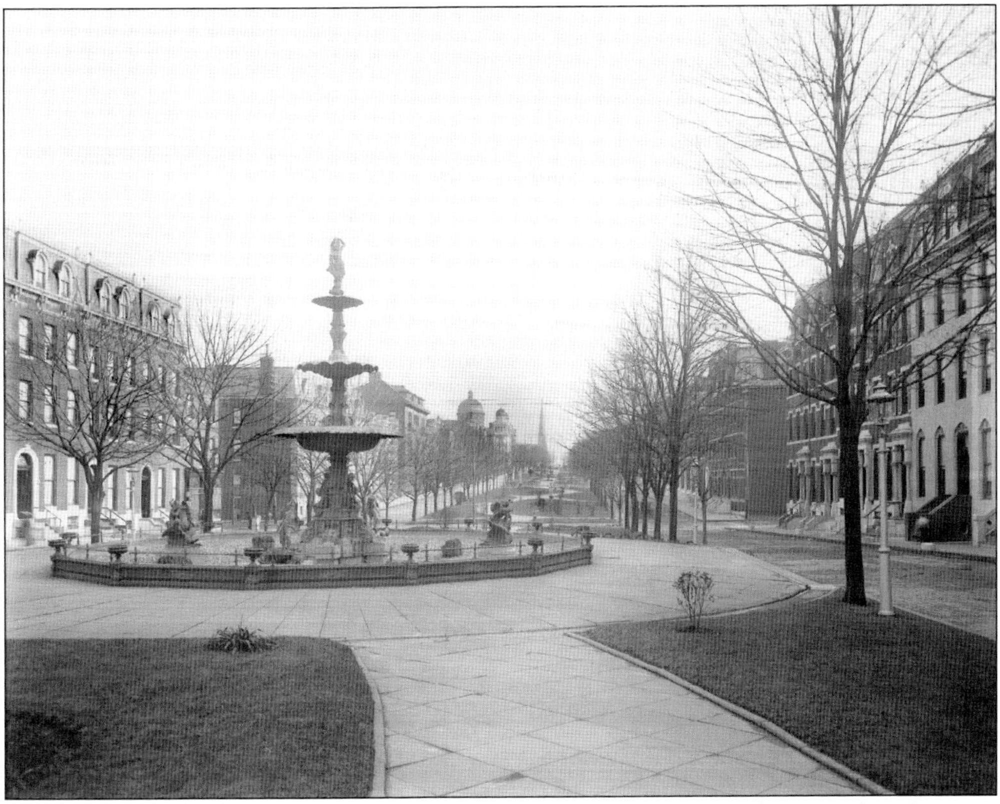

Eutaw Place was the first urban boulevard with a park in the center to be created in America. The park area was always full of kids sledding in the winter and was a showplace every year during the spring with remarkable landscaping. In the 1960s, the park was planned to become a parking lot but luckily was saved. It comes closer to its original grandeur with each year. (Library of Congress.)

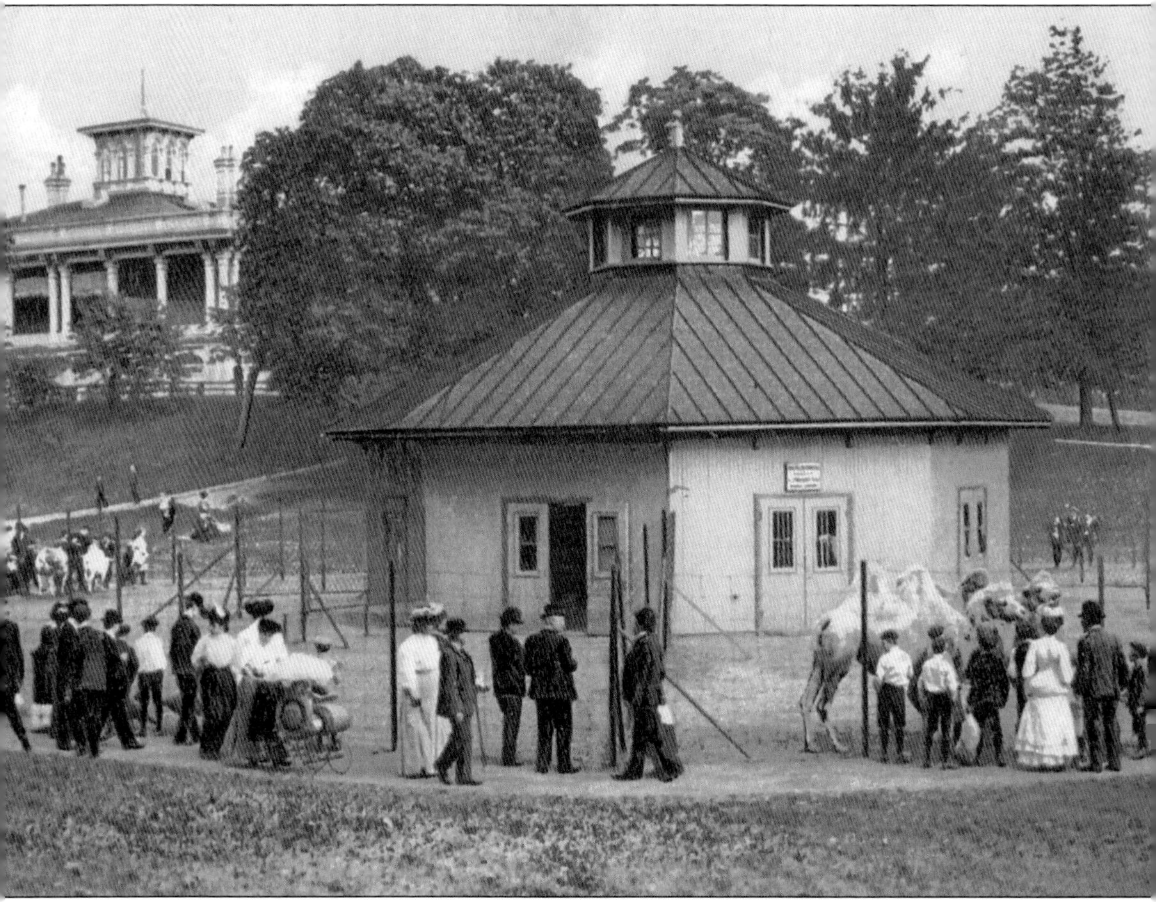

The Maryland Zoo in Baltimore (formerly the Baltimore Zoo) is located in Druid Hill Park next to Reservoir Hill. Home to more than 2,000 animals, the zoo is generally considered to be the third-oldest zoological park in the United States, having opened in 1876. The Maryland Zoo has gone through many changes throughout the years; most notable was erecting a fence to enclose the zoo in the early 1970s. Prior to the 1970s, one could walk or drive at leisure through the zoo as it was not considered a separate entity within Druid Hill Park. (Susan Adler.)

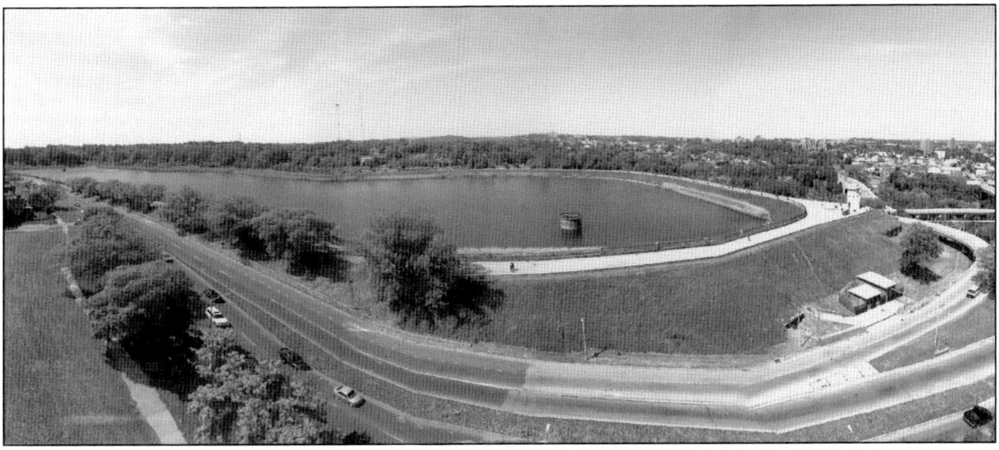

Unlike Boat Lake in Druid Hill Park, Druid Lake, the biggest lake in the park, was built to be used for the city's waterworks. When completed in 1871, it was considered the largest earthen dam in the United States at 119 feet tall. It holds 429 million gallons of water with an average depth of 30 feet. Druid Lake continues to serve as a part of the city water system today. In an effort to comply with federal Environmental Protection Agency code, Druid Lake will discontinue as a source for drinking water in the late 2010s but then will be turned into a recreational lake. Above is an aerial view of present day Druid Lake; below is a view of Druid Lake in the late 1800s and the adjacent William Wallace statue. (Above, Richard May; below, Susan Adler.)

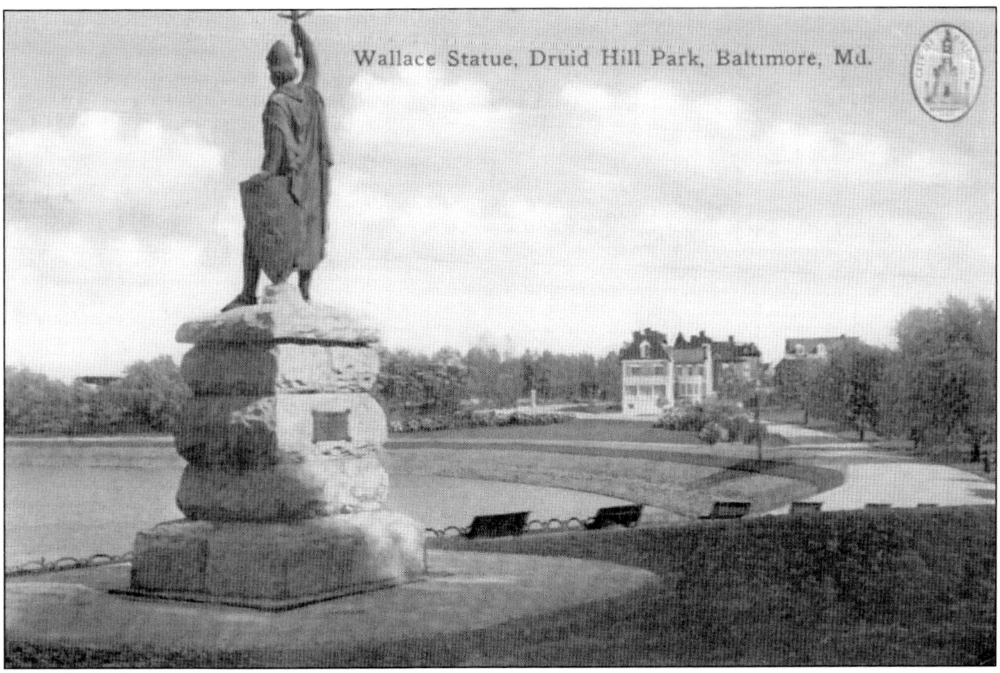

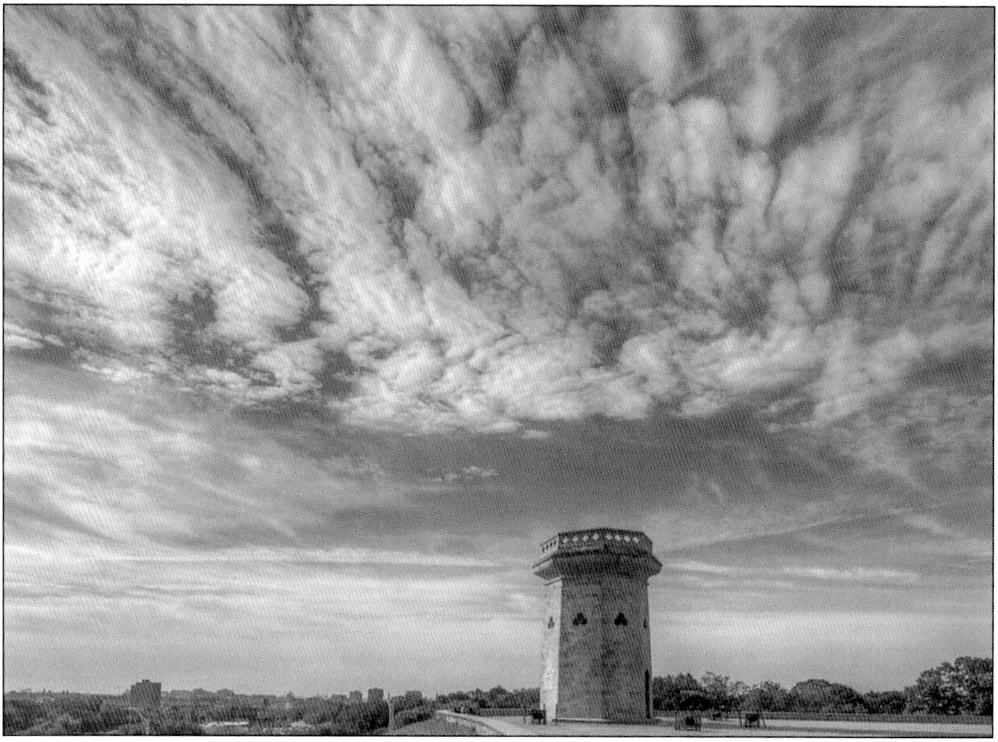

The Baltimore Tower, or the Moorish Tower, is located at the top of the earthen dam of Druid Lake, which is one of the highest points in the city. Designed by George Frederick, it was made of white marble and erected around 1870. Attempts to tear down the tower were thwarted in past decades because it was too costly. It is now considered a historic landmark. (Baltimore Foto.)

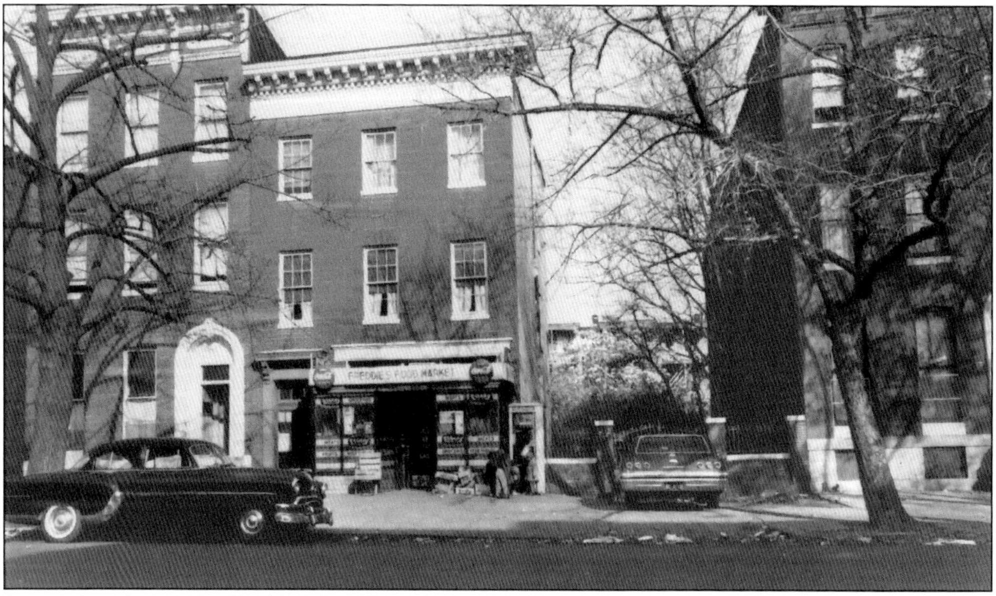

Opened in the 1960s, Freddie's Food Market was located at 2501 Madison Avenue. Prior to that, it was a pharmacy. While Freddie's has been closed for many years, the future is bright at 2501 Madison Avenue as the Druid Café is planning to open in 2012. (CHAP.)

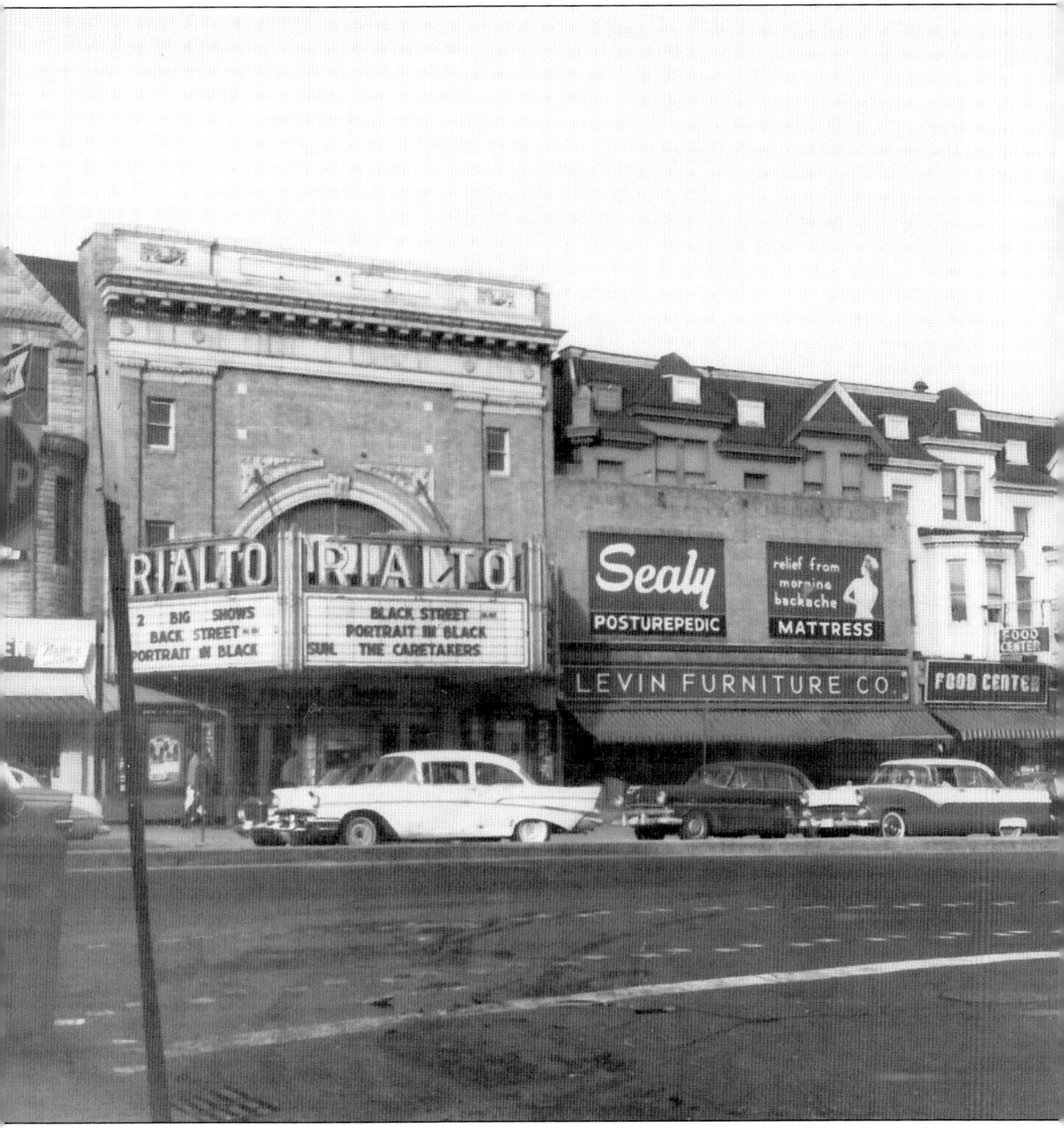

North Avenue, originally called Boundary Avenue, was alive with activity from the early 1900s to the 1960s. Banks, drugstores, candy shops, delis, and even theaters were along the North Avenue. At the corner of North and Linden Avenues was a stand that had every major newspaper one could want. This particular area shown is North Avenue just east of the intersection of Linden Avenue heading toward Bolton Street. The building shown on the far left was Nates and Leons, a famous delicatessen. In the middle is the Rialto Theater, which was the larger of the theaters located in the Reservoir Hill area. On the right is Levin Furniture Company, which left North Avenue in the 1960s but stayed open in other locations in Baltimore until 1992. Note that on the far right is a small food center, one of many in the area. There were no large grocery stores in the city until later years. (Jewish Museum of Maryland.)

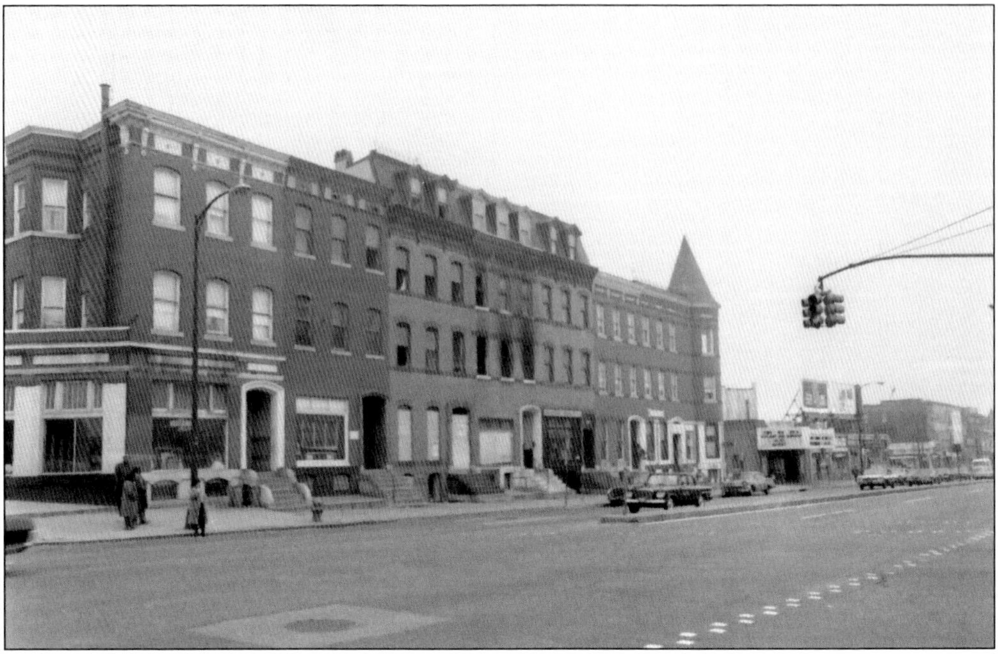

Pictured here is the North Avenue between Eutaw Place and Linden Avenue in the early 1960s. As seen, some of the structures had caught fire and burned. The architecture seen on this section of North Avenue is similar to that still seen today inside the neighborhood. A majority of these buildings have been demolished for a single-story health care facility. (CHAP.)

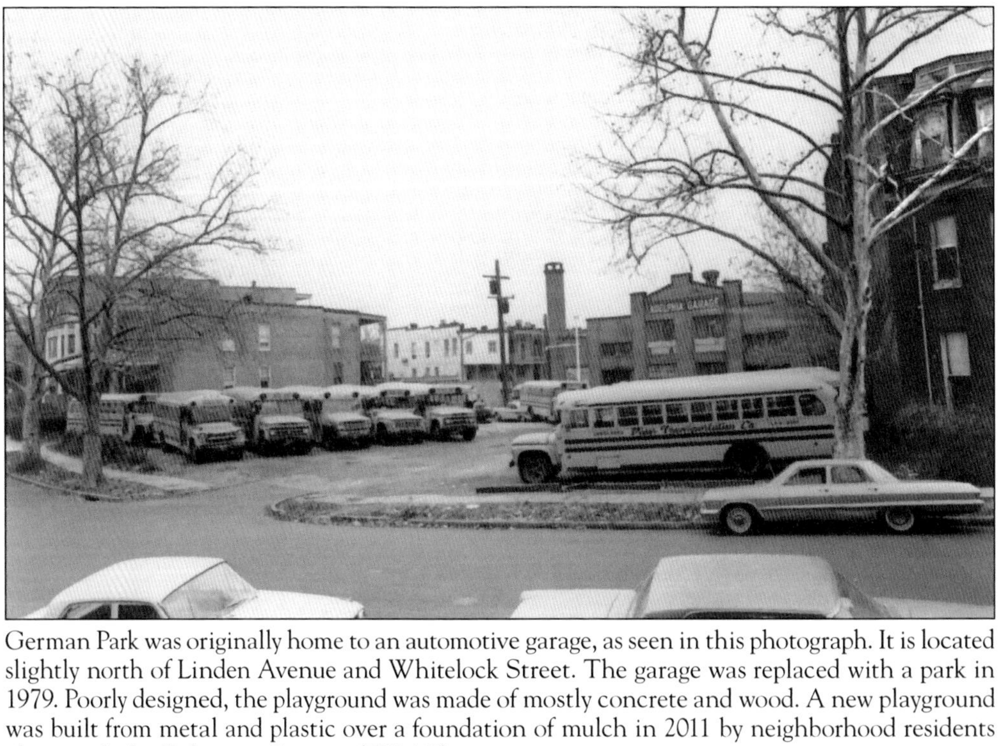

German Park was originally home to an automotive garage, as seen in this photograph. It is located slightly north of Linden Avenue and Whitelock Street. The garage was replaced with a park in 1979. Poorly designed, the playground was made of mostly concrete and wood. A new playground was built from metal and plastic over a foundation of mulch in 2011 by neighborhood residents along with the Baltimore Ravens. (CHAP.)

The White Coffee Pot was located at the corner of Linden and North Avenues until the late 1960s. The White Coffee Pot was a restaurant chain started in Baltimore that spread throughout the state to more than 30 locations in the 1960s. Everywhere they were located, they would become neighborhood-gathering spots. The last White Coffee Pot closed in 1993 in Randallstown, Maryland. (Baltimore Museum of Industry, BGE Collection.)

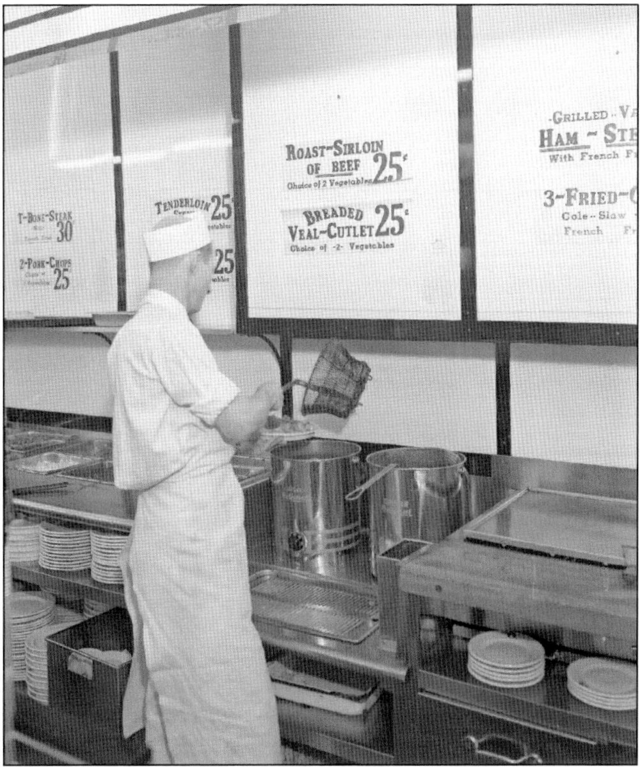

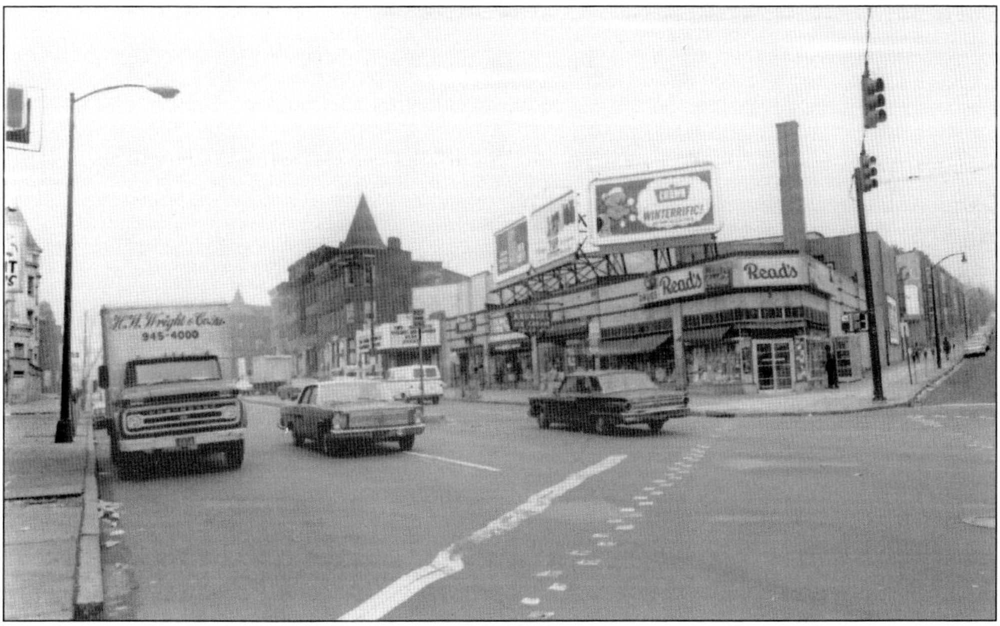

Read's Drugstore was a locally based chain that had 97 locations in the area at its peak. It is famous for a sit-in at the lunch counter of the original downtown location. Its slogan was "Run into Reads." Read's Drugstore was sold to Rite Aid in 1977, which still operates in many of the former Read's locations. Pictured is Read's drugstore at the intersection of North and Linden Avenues. (CHAP.)

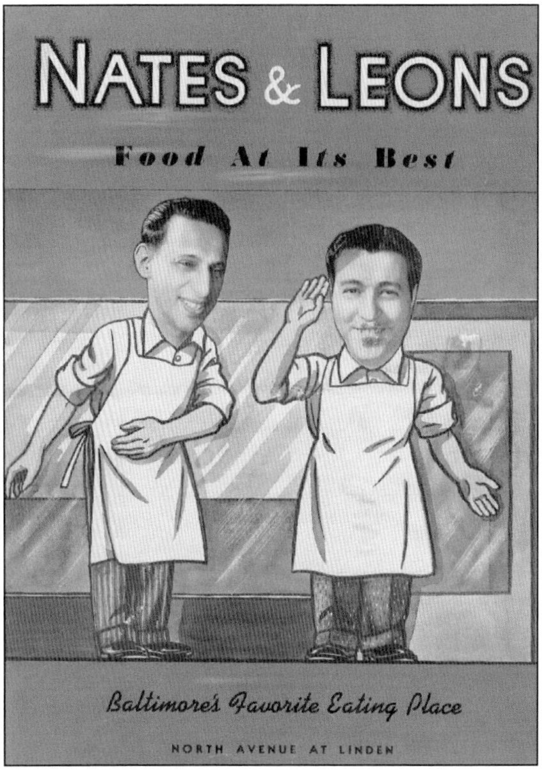

Well known throughout the city, Nates and Leons was a delicatessen restaurant at North and Linden Avenues. It drew show people, politicians, and many influential Baltimore citizens. Later, another location opened near the Pimlico Racing Course, home of the annual Preakness Stakes. Nates and Leons closed its North Avenue location in the late 1960s to make way for urban renewal. (Jewish Museum of Maryland.)

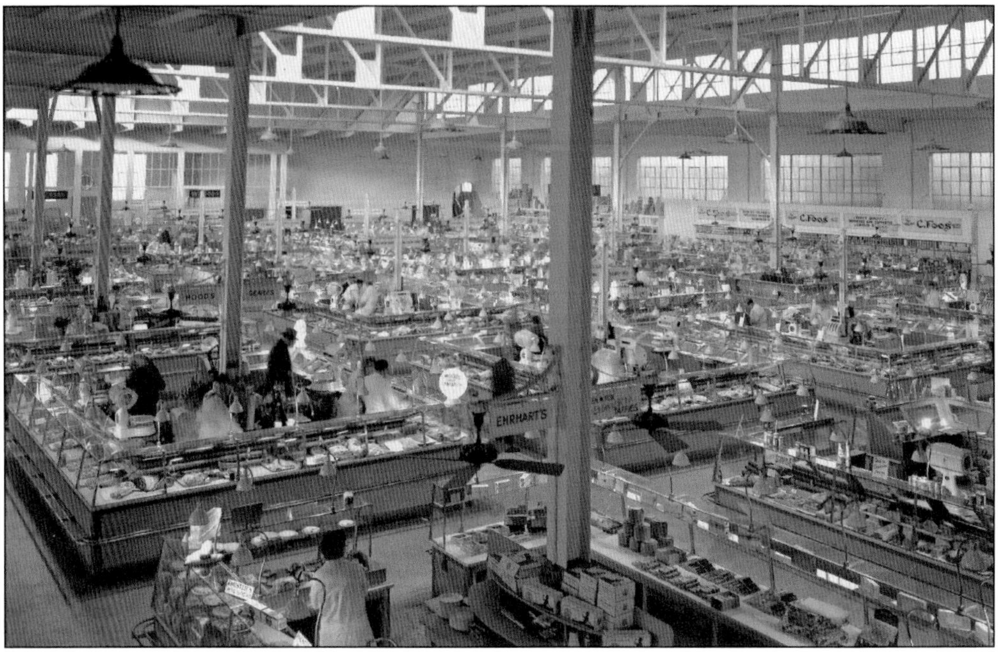

The North Avenue Market was the closest large market to Reservoir Hill, located at the intersection of North and Maryland Avenues. It was large with 240 stands, 24 stores, and a fish market. It opened in 1928 as the "most sanitary and most modern market in the country" at a cost of almost $2 million. (Baltimore Museum of Industry, BGE Collection.)

John Eager Howard Elementary School is the only school in Reservoir Hill. Once called School No. 61, it has been on the same site, but it was rebuilt once in the 1960s. The school's name, John Eager Howard, was chosen to commemorate Howard, who was a Maryland governor and US senator. One of 127 elementary schools in Baltimore, it serves approximately 300 students every year. The present day school building, seen at right, also includes a recreational center that is used for neighborhood meetings and other important community functions. Below, the picture catches a glimpse of the original school building in the top-left corner looking from Lennox Street. (Right, author's collection; below, CHAP.)

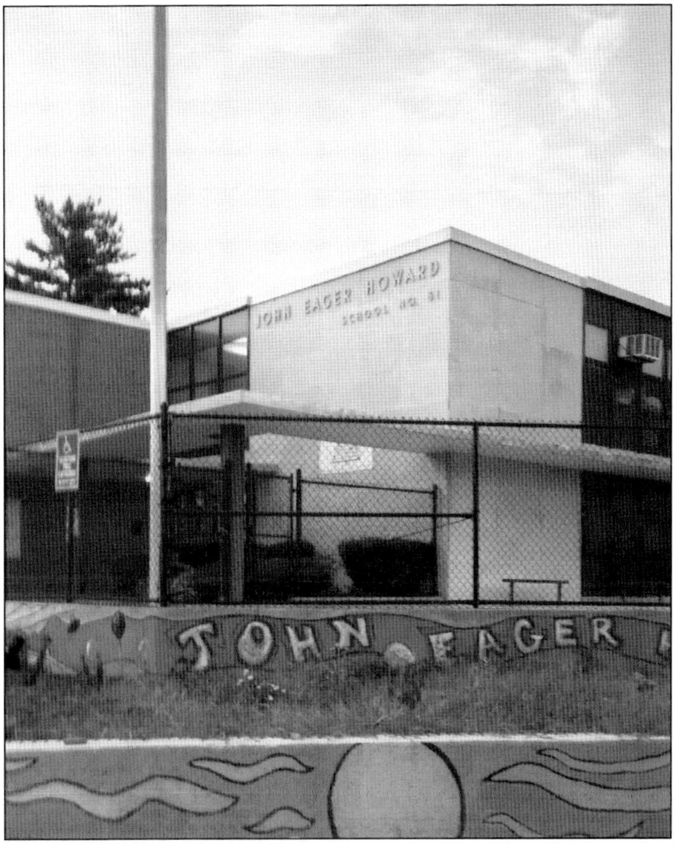

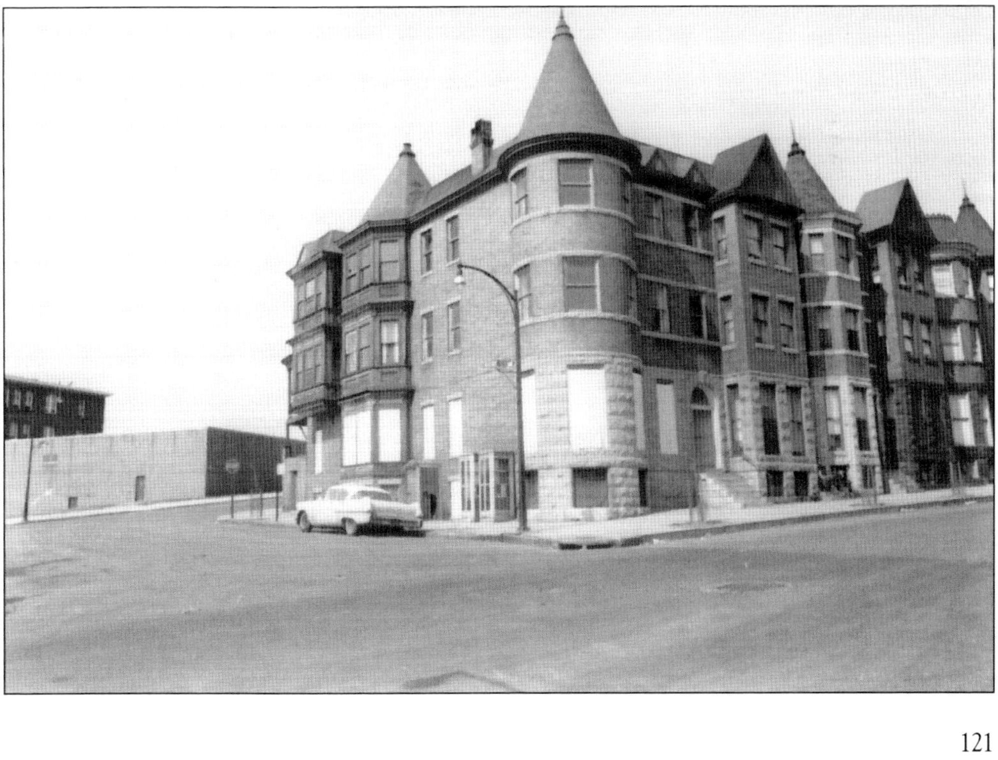

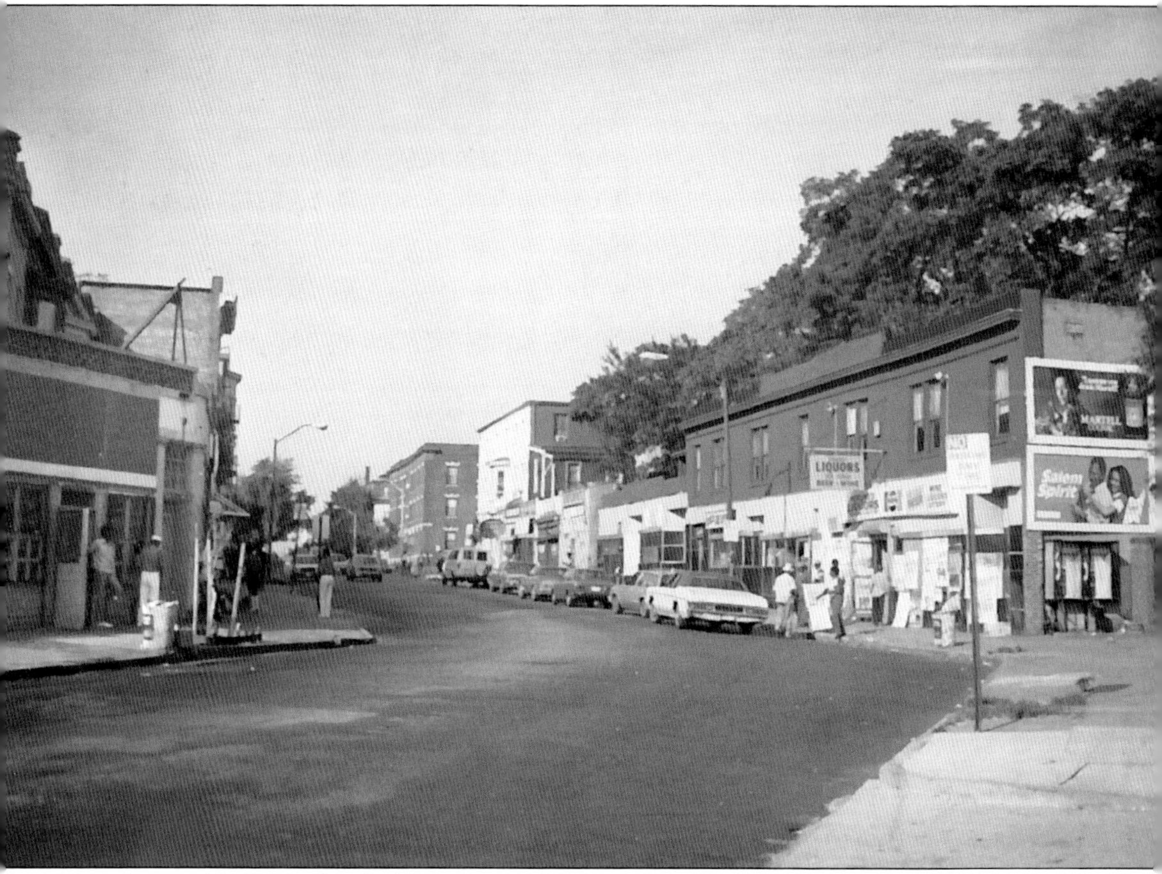

The 900 block of Whitelock Street was the main shopping area for daily needs, such as small grocery stores and delis, with other related stores. It was an important part of the neighborhood initially—built in the early 1900s—but it went through a steady decline starting in the 1950s. The Whitelock Street commercial area was demolished in 1994 and is now the site of the Whitelock Community Farm. After the race riots of 1968, Whitelock Street became known for its drugs and violence, which were ultimately the cause of its destruction. Also relocated from the demolition was St. Francis Neighborhood Center to its current location on Linden Avenue. St. Francis, an active part of Reservoir Hill since 1963, is committed to breaking the cycles of poverty. Above is a photograph of Whitelock Street in the early 1960s. (CHAP.)

Eight

Today's Reservoir Hill

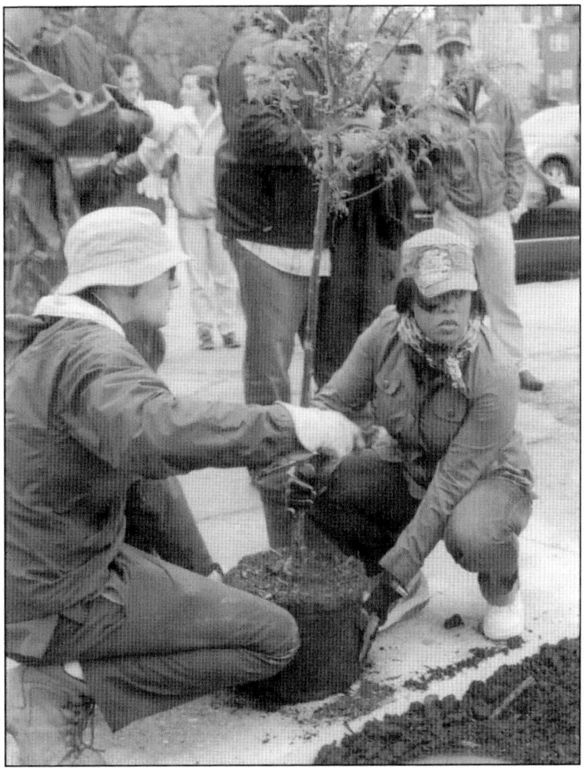

Whitelock Community Farm is a resident-supported urban farming effort located in the old Whitelock commercial area. The farm has helped revitalize the neighborhood through greening and positive community activity. Pictured are Mayor Stephanie Rawlings-Blake and resident Thor Nelson planting a tree. The farm provides fresh produce at one neighborhood food market. A new park across from Whitelock Farm is slated to open in 2013. (Howard P. Fink.)

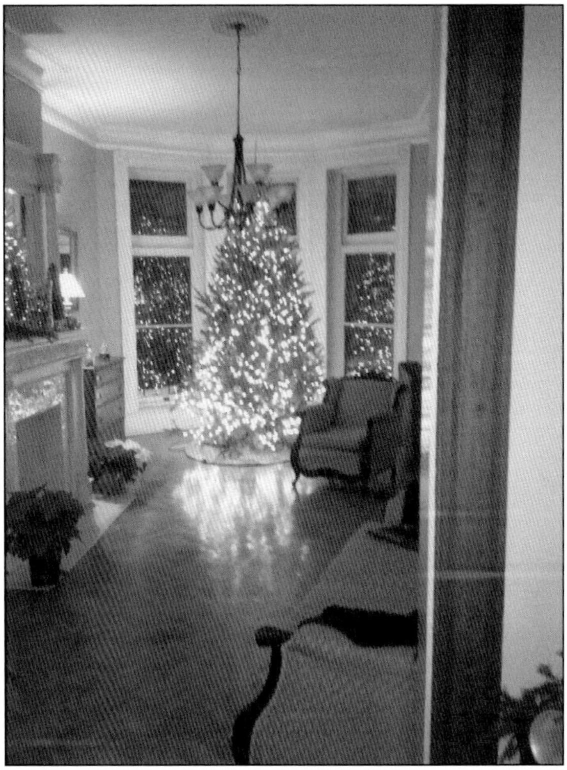

The Poinsettia Tour showcases homes on Eutaw Place and Madison Avenue at the beginning of each December. It started in 1988 and continues to grow and improve each year. The Poinsettia Tour also features Beth Am Synagogue on Eutaw Place and has some years shown the Emersonian and Esplanade apartment buildings. Seen here is the interior of a home on Eutaw Place. (Author's collection.)

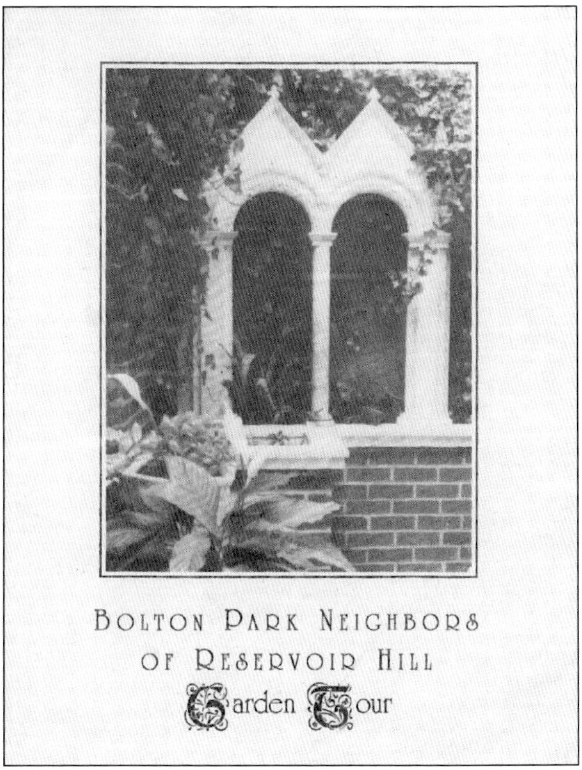

The Reservoir Hill Home and Garden Tour takes place every June. The Home and Garden Tour started in 1995 and now showcases over 30 gardens and homes in the southeastern portion of the neighborhood. Garden tours have been taking place in the Reservoir Hill area for over a century in one form or another. Pictured at right is a program for the home and garden tour from the late 1990s. (Teddy Krolik.)

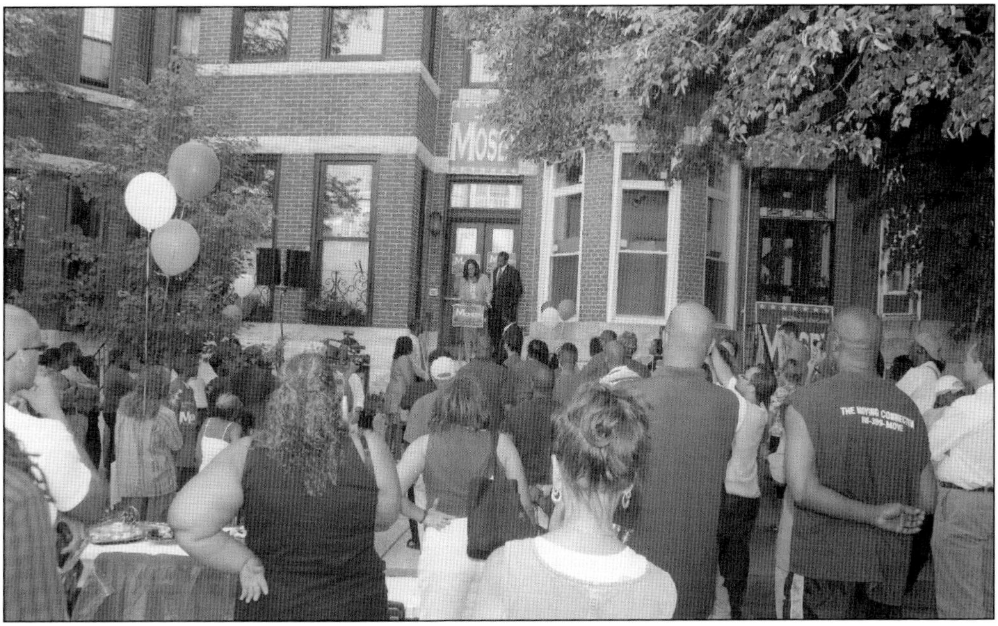

Councilman Nick Mosby represents the 7th district of Baltimore City, which includes the Reservoir Hill neighborhood. He was born and raised in Baltimore graduating from Baltimore Polytechnic Institute, followed by an electric engineering degree from Tuskegee University in Alabama. Councilman Mosby, the only councilman in Baltimore to beat an incumbent in 2011, has already made a lasting impact on Reservoir Hill. His leadership has brought forth results on major city and resident initiatives, including a plan for the largest renovation of Druid Hill Park since its inception. Above is Councilman Mosby speaking in front of his home in Reservoir Hill. Below is Councilman Mosby speaking at an event at John Eager Howard Recreation Center. (Both, Eli Lopatin.)

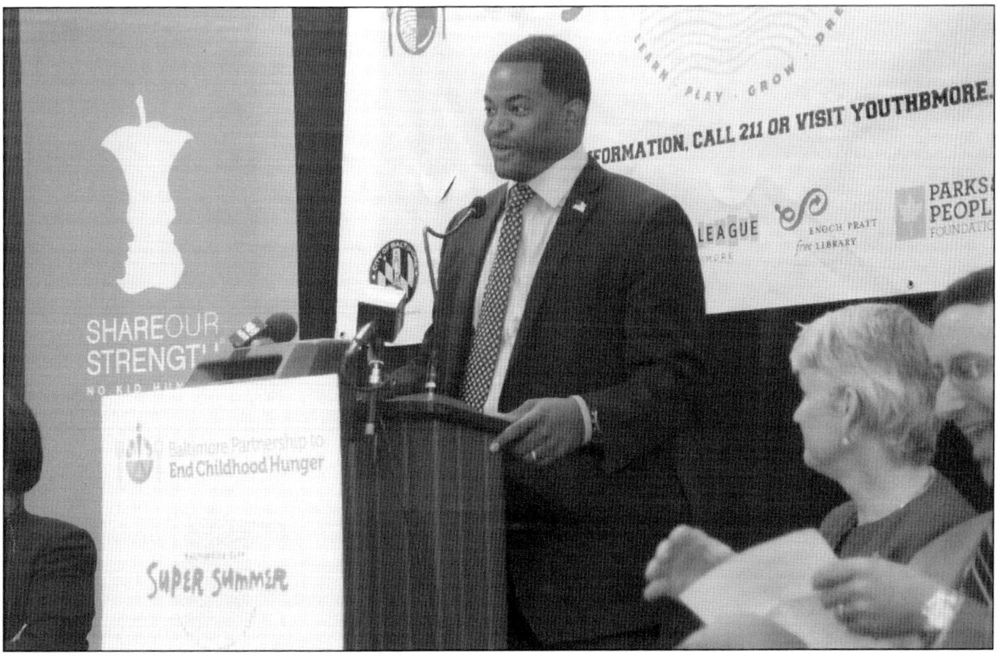

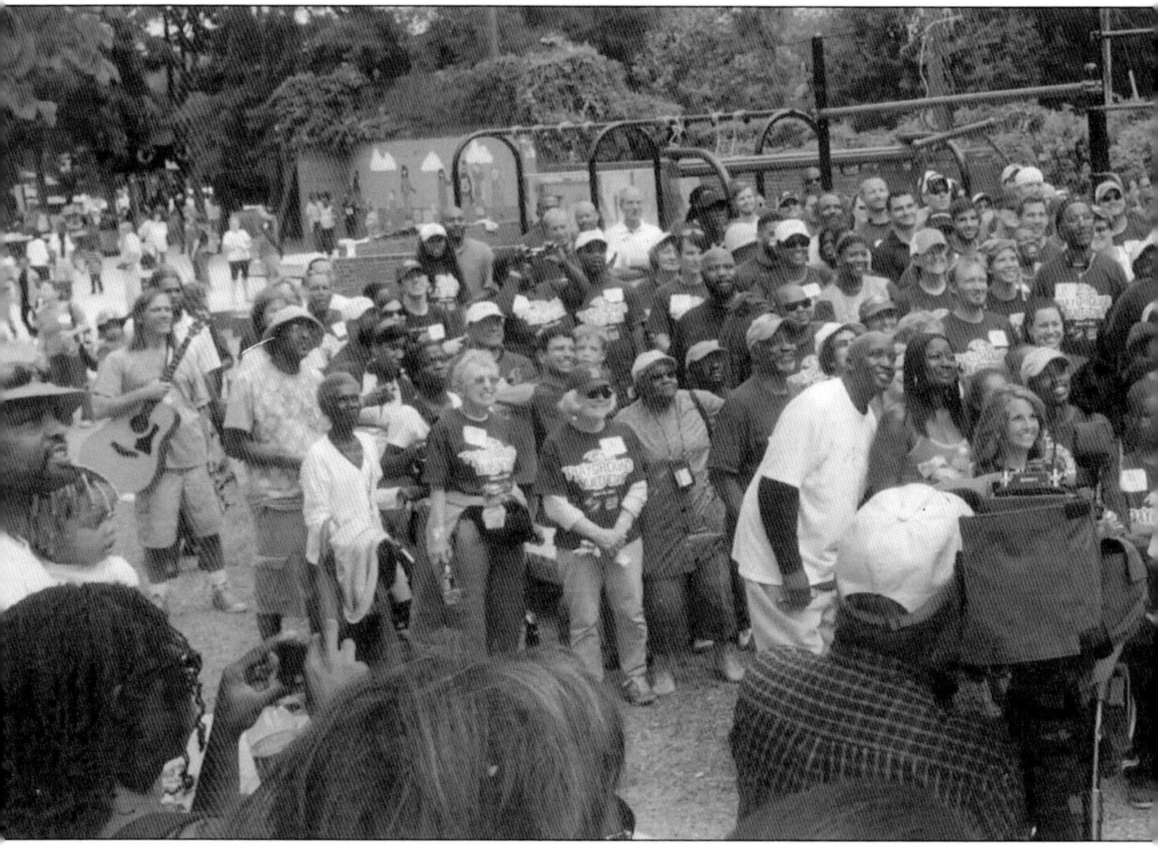

Today, Reservoir Hill, as well as the entire Mount Royal area of Baltimore, is a vibrant and diverse community. It is a microcosm of urban life in the 21st-century United States. Former and current residents led by Bolton Street resident Councilman Nick Mosby of the 7th district are providing a vision to make Reservoir Hill a premiere destination for Baltimore and other major cities, showing

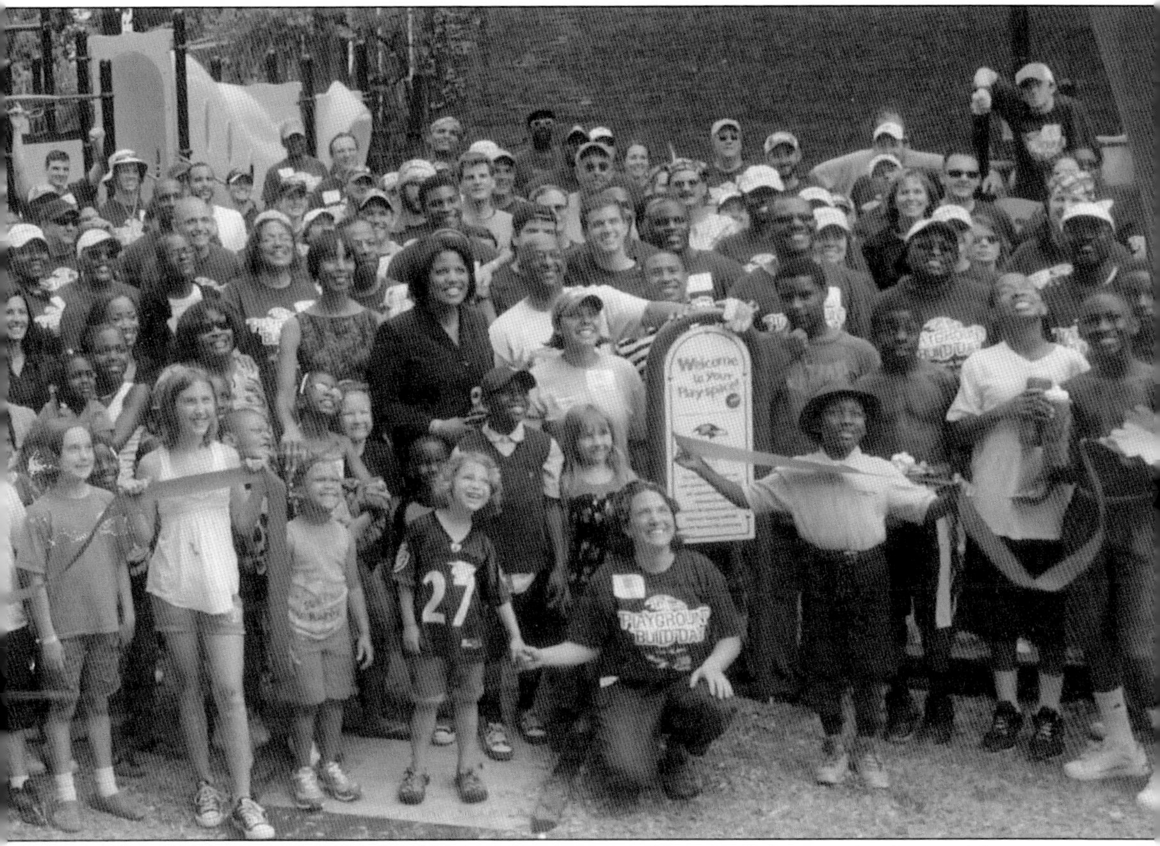

that the intersection of economic development and social responsibility are the future. Above is Mayor Stephanie Rawlings-Blake with community residents and supporters for the completion of German Park on Linden Avenue in 2011. (Howard P. Fink.)